THE
HISTORY OF
UKRAINE

THE HISTORY OF UKRAINE

Paul Kubicek

The Greenwood Histories of the Modern Nations
Frank W. Thackeray and John E. Findling, Series Editors

Greenwood Press
Westport, Connecticut • London

Library of Congress Cataloging-in-Publication Data

Kubicek, Paul.

The history of Ukraine / Paul Kubicek.

  p. cm. — (The Greenwood histories of the modern nations, ISSN 1096–2095)

Includes bibliographical references and index.

ISBN 978–0–313–34920–1 (alk. paper)

1. Ukraine—History. I. Title.

DK508.51.K825   2008

947.7—dc22   2008026717

British Library Cataloguing in Publication Data is available.

Library of Congress Catalog Card Number: 2008026717

ISBN: 978–0–313–34920–1

ISSN: 1096–2905

First published in 2008

Greenwood Press, 88 Post Road West, Westport, CT 06881

An imprint of Greenwood Publishing Group, Inc.

www.greenwood.com

Printed in the United States of America

The paper used in this book complies with the
Permanent Paper Standard issued by the National
Information Standards Organization (Z39.48–1984).

10 9 8 7 6 5 4 3 2 1

Every reasonable effort has been made to trace the owners of copyright materials in this
book, but in some instances this has proven impossible. The author and publisher will be
glad to receive information leading to a more complete acknowledgments in subsequent
printings of the book and in the meantime extend their apologies for any omissions.

Contents

Series Foreword

The *Greenwood Histories of the Modern Nations* series is intended to provide students and interested laypeople with up-to-date, concise, and analytical histories of many of the nations of the contemporary world. Not since the 1960s has there been a systematic attempt to publish a series of national histories and as series advisors, we believe that this series will be a valuable contribution to our understanding of other countries in our increasingly interdependent world.

Some 40 years ago, at the end of the 1960s, the cold war was an accepted reality of global politics. The process of decolonization was still in progress, the idea of a unified Europe with a single currency was unheard of, the United States was mired in a war in Vietnam, and the economic boom in Asia was still years in the future. Richard Nixon was president of the United States, Mao Tse-tung (not yet Mao Zedong) ruled China, Leonid Brezhnev guided the Soviet Union, and Harold Wilson was prime minister of the United Kingdom. Authoritarian dictators still controlled most of Latin America, the Middle East was reeling in the wake of the Six-Day War, and Shah Mohammad Reza Pahlavi was at the height of his power in Iran.

Since then, the cold war has ended, the Soviet Union has vanished, leaving 15 independent republics in its stead, the advent of the computer age has radically transformed global communications, the rising demand for oil makes the Middle East still a dangerous flashpoint, and the rise of new economic powers like the People's Republic of China and India threatens to bring about a new world order. All of these developments have had a dramatic impact on the recent history of every nation of the world.

For this series, which was launched in 1998, we first selected nations whose political, economic, and sociocultural affairs marked them as among the most important of our time. For each nation, we found an author who was recognized as a specialist in the history of that nation. These authors worked cooperatively with us and with Greenwood Press to produce volumes that reflect current research on their nations and that are interesting and informative to their readers. In the first decade of the series, more than 40 volumes were published and, as of 2008, some are moving into second editions.

The success of the series has encouraged us to broaden our scope to include additional nations whose histories have had significant effects on their regions, if not on the entire world. In addition, geopolitical changes have elevated other nations into positions of greater importance in world affairs, so we have chosen to include them in this series as well. The importance of a series such as this cannot be underestimated. As a superpower whose influence is felt all over the world, the United States can claim a "special" relationship with almost every other nation. Yet many Americans know very little about the histories of nations with which the United States relates. How did they get to be the way they are? What kind of political systems have evolved there? What kind of influence do they have on their own regions? What are the dominant political, religious, and cultural forces that move their leaders? These and many other questions are answered in the volumes of this series.

The authors who contribute to this series write comprehensive histories of their nations, dating back, in some instances, to prehistoric times. Each of them, however, has devoted a significant portion of their book to events of the past 40 years because the modern era has contributed the most to contemporary issues that have an impact on U.S. policy. Authors make every effort to be as up-to-date as possible so that readers can benefit from discussion and analysis of recent events.

In addition to the historical narrative, each volume contains an introductory chapter that provides an overview of the country's geography, political institutions, economic structure, and cultural attributes. This approach is meant to give readers a snapshot of the nation as it exists in the contemporary world. Each history also includes supplementary information following the narrative, which may include a timeline that represents a succinct chronology of the nation's historical evolution, biographical sketches of the nation's most important historical figures, and a glossary of important terms or concepts that are usually expressed in a foreign language. Finally, each author has prepared a comprehensive bibliography for readers who wish to pursue the subject further.

Readers of these volumes will find them fascinating and well written. More important, they will come away with a better understanding of the contemporary world and the nations that compose it. As series advisors, we hope that this series will contribute to a heightened sense of global understanding as we move through the early years of the twenty-first century.

Frank W. Thackeray and John E. Findling

Preface

Ukraine (*Ukraïna* in Ukrainian) means "on the edge" or "borderland," and for most of its history Ukraine has served as a sort of middle ground, divided between Russia and Poland (later Austria-Hungary) and occupying the far western edge of the vast Eurasian steppe, centered between Europe and Asia, West and East. During most of twentieth century, it was part of the Soviet Union, but it gained independence in 1991 when the Soviet Union disintegrated into 15 different countries. In terms of population, it is the second largest (after Russia) of the post-Soviet states, and, among all European countries, it is the second largest (again, after Russia) in territorial size. Although a new country, it has a long and complicated history, and the importance of this history is manifested today in various ways: the regional divisions between western and eastern parts of the country; its inexperience with both capitalism and democracy that has arguably made the post-Soviet transition more difficult; its lack of previous statehood that has complicated notions of Ukrainian identity; and, perhaps above all else, its relations with neighboring states, especially Russia, which ruled, either as the Russian Empire under the tsars or as the Soviet Union under the Communist Party, over most of Ukraine for centuries. Coming to grips with aspects of its history and charting its own course have been challenges for the new Ukrainian state.

This book details the main contours of Ukrainian history, focusing in particular on the Soviet period and the more recent post-Soviet experience. It draws on a variety of secondary sources, both those of a more general nature and more narrowly focused scholarly monographs. Part of this book, particularly the chapters on Ukraine's drive toward independence and the subsequent post-Soviet period, draws on my own research on Ukraine, which dates back to 1992–1993, when I was a lecturer with the Civic Education Project at Lviv State University. Although life in Ukraine during that time was without question difficult, I gained great appreciation for Ukrainian history and culture. I learned much from my students and academic colleagues and returned to Ukraine several times on various research projects. It was easy—too easy—to be pessimistic about Ukraine's development in the 1990s, and the Orange Revolution of 2004 gave a much needed shot of hope both to observers of Ukrainian politics and society and, more important, to the Ukrainian people. It is my sincere wish that a land that has seen so much strife and misery in its past, which is documented throughout this work, will experience a much brighter future.

A word on transliteration from Ukrainian and other languages. I am fully aware that there are differences between Ukrainian and Russian for names of places (e.g., Kyiv or Kiev, Odesa or Odessa) and people (e.g., Mykola Hohol or Nikolai Gogol). I use a modified version of the standard Library of Congress system, dropping, for simplification, indication of a soft sign (thus Lviv instead of L'viv) and the extra i or j at the end of last names and using i for the Ukrainian ï. Thus I refer to Hrushevsky instead of Hrushevskyi or Hrushevskyj. As for people or place names, if there is a well-established English form (e.g., Kiev, Odessa, Crimea, Dnieper, Gogol), I use it instead of the Ukrainian. In other cases (e.g., Lviv, Kharkiv, Zaporizhzhe) I favor the contemporary Ukrainian term. Last of all, one needs to recognize that the very terms *Ukraine* and *Ukrainians* became commonly used only in the 1800s. Before then Ukrainians were known as Rus, Ruthenians, Rusyns, and "Little Russians," and there was no territory called "Ukraine." Recognizing this, I frequently refer to "Ukrainian lands" and use terms such as "Rus" and "Ruthenians" to refer to early inhabitants of these lands.

Timeline of Historical Events

1596	Greek Catholic (Uniate) Church established by Union of Brest
1632–1647	Petro Mohyla serves as metropolitan of Kiev
1648	Beginning of Great Cossack Revolt under Bohdan Khmelnytsky
1654	Treaty of Pereiaslav brings Cossacks under protection of Russian tsar
1667	Treaty of Andrusovo gives Russia control over East Bank of Dnieper and Kiev
1687–1709	Ivan Mazepa serves as Hetman of the Cossacks
1709	Battle of Poltava, Tsar Peter I defeats Mazepa
1772–1774	Hapsburg Austria occupies Galicia and Bukovyna
1775	Russians destroy the Zaporizhian Sich
1783	Russia occupies Crimea
1785	Abolition of Hetmanate
1793–1795	Russia occupies Right Bank of Dnieper River and Volhynia
1840	Shevchenko's *The Kobza Player* appears
1845	Brotherhood of Saints Cyril and Methodius formed in Kiev
1848	Supreme Ruthenian Council established in Lviv
1876	Literature in Ukrainian banned in the Russian Empire
1890	First Ukrainian political party (Radicals) established in Lviv
1898	Mikhaylo Hrushevsky publishes *History of Ukraine-Rus*
1900	First Ukrainian political party in the Russian Empire
1914	Outbreak of World War I
1914–1915	Russian occupation of Galicia
February 1917	Tsar overthrown
March 1917	Ukrainian Central Rada (Council) established

November 1917	Bolshevik Revolution; Rada declares creation of the Ukrainian People's Republic
December 1917	First Soviet Ukrainian government formed in Kharkiv
January 1918	Ukrainian People's Republic declares independence
April 1918	Skoropadsky's Hetmanate established with German assistance
December 1918	Hetmanate overthrown; creation of the Directorate under Simon Petliura
1919	Bukovyna awarded to Romania, Transcarpathia to Czechoslovakia
1921	Ukrainian Socialist Soviet Republic (Uk SSR) established
1921	Treaty of Riga grants Poland control over Galicia and western Volhynia
1922	Uk SSR becomes part of Union of Soviet Socialist Republics (USSR)
1929	Formation of Organization of Ukrainian Nationalists (OUN)
1932–1933	Soviet authorities create famine in Ukraine
1933–1938	Stalinist Purges and Reign of Terror
1939	Soviet occupation of western Ukraine
1941	German invasion of USSR, OUN declares Ukrainian independence
1944	German army expelled from Ukraine; Ukrainian nationalists fight Soviet Red Army; Crimean Tatars deported to central Asia
1945	Western Ukraine annexed into USSR
1954	Crimea transferred from Russian Federation to Ukraine
1963–1972	Petro Shelest serves as Communist Party leader in Ukraine
1960s–1970s	Ukrainian dissidents campaign for human and national rights
1972–1989	Volodymyr Shcherbytsky serves as Communist Party leader in Ukraine

April 1986	Accident at Chernnobyl nuclear power plant
September 1989	First Congress of Rukh, the Ukrainian Popular Front
July 16, 1990	Ukrainian Declaration of Sovereignty
August 24, 1991	Ukrainian Declaration of Independence
December 1, 1991	Ukrainian independence affirmed by popular vote; Leonid Kravchuk elected president
July 1994	Leonid Kuchma elected president
1996	New Constitution adopted; new currency (*hryvna*) is introduced
1999	Vyacheslav Chornovil, leader of Rukh, killed; Kuchma reelected
2000	First year of positive economic growth in post-Soviet Ukraine
November 2000	Journalist Georgii Gongadze found dead; audiotapes implicate President Kuchma
2001	Former Prime Minister Viktor Yushchenko forms "Our Ukraine" opposition party
December 2004	Yushchenko elected president after mass protests of "Orange Revolution"
2006	"Orange Coalition" collapses; Viktor Yanukovych becomes prime minister
2007	New parliamentary elections; Yulia Tymoshenko becomes prime minister again

1

Introduction

GEOGRAPHY AND CLIMATE

Ukraine is located in Eastern Europe, bordered to the north and east by Russia and Belarus, to the west by Poland, Slovakia, Hungary, Romania, and Moldova, and to the south by the Black Sea and Sea of Azov (see Map 1.1). It extends approximately 800 miles (1,300 kilometers) from west to east and about 550 miles (900 kilometers) from north to south and has a coastline of approximately 1,700 miles (2,780 kilometers). Its total land area is about 233,000 square miles (603,700 square kilometers), making it slightly smaller than the state of Texas. Most of its land is open steppe, a treeless, flat expanse that is much like a prairie. Its only mountains are a bit of the Carpathian Mountains that extend into the far western part of the country and those along the Black Sea on the Crimean Peninsula, which is connected to the rest of Ukraine by a narrow strip of land. Lacking natural defenses, Ukraine has thus been the site of numerous battles, migrations, and cultural influences. The fertile black earth soil of its steppe regions, however, has helped earn it a reputation as a "breadbasket" for its agricultural production and has made agriculture a hallmark of Ukrainian life and culture.

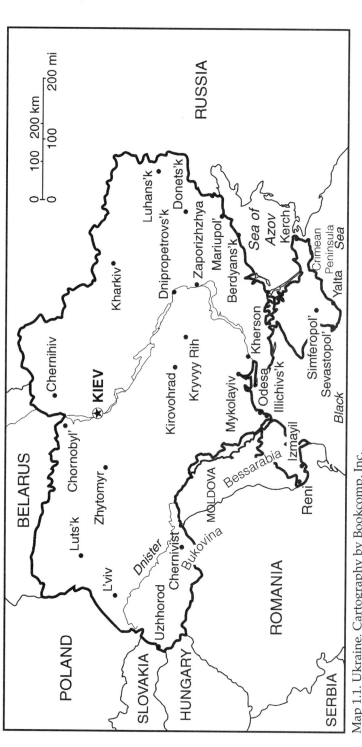

Map 1.1. Ukraine. Cartography by Bookcomp, Inc.

Ukraine is bisected by the Dnieper (Dnipro in Ukrainian) River, which flows north to south and into the Black Sea. Historically, this was an important trade route, and many of the first major settlements in Ukraine, including its capital city, Kiev (Kyïv in Ukrainian), were established on the banks of the Dnieper. The Dnieper also constituted a border between Russian and Polish-Lithuanian-controlled areas of Ukraine, and one still frequently encounters references to Left Bank (eastern) and Right Bank (western) Ukraine. The southern Buh and Dnister Rivers, which also flow into the Black Sea and are located in the western part of the country, were also once important trade routes and remain important sources of water.

Ukraine's climate is usually described as "continental," which means that it has cold, occasionally very cold (lows of –20° F or –30° C) winters. Average temperatures in January range from 26° F (–3° C) in the southwest to 18° F (–8° C) in the northeast. Its climate is far milder than in Russia, however, which, together with its soil, has made Ukraine more suitable for agriculture. Summers tend to be relatively mild, with average temperatures between 73° F (23° C) in the southwest and 66° F (19° C) in the northeast, although daily highs of over 90° F (32° C) are rather common in much of the country. Crimea, however, has more of a Mediterranean climate, with warmer and moister weather.

POPULATION

According to the 2001 census,[1] Ukraine has a population of 48.4 million people. This is down significantly (6%) from the figure from the 1989 census (when Ukraine was part of the Soviet Union) of 51.8 million people. According to estimates from 2007,[2] Ukraine has only 46.3 million people, with a rate of population decline of –.675% per year. Part of this decline is due to emigration, as poor economic conditions have driven many Ukrainians to leave Ukraine and work elsewhere, particularly in Russia, Poland, Germany, Hungary, Israel, Turkey, Canada, and Portugal. Fertility rates (1.24 births per woman) are also extremely low. Women also significantly outnumber men (54% to 46%), largely because they outlive them (74 years life expectancy for women compared with 62 years for men). Both declining birth rates and low life expectancy for men are considered major demographic problems.

According to the census data, most Ukrainians (67.2%) live in cities. The largest metropolitan areas in Ukraine are Kiev (3.2 million), Kharkiv (1.7 million), Donetsk (1.7 million), Dnipropetrovsk (1.5 million), and Odessa (1.1 million). The average population density for the entire country is 208 persons per square mile (80 persons per square kilometer), but there is much variation across the country. In general, the more industrialized regions of eastern Ukraine are much more densely populated than the western part of the country. For example, population density in the eastern Donetsk region is 183 people per square kilometer, whereas in the west in regions such as Volyn (53 people per square kilometer) and Zhitomir (46 people per square kilometer) it is much lower. Notably, on both a percentage and total basis, the most significant population declines have been in the eastern regions and in Crimea.

Ukraine is home to more than 100 different national or ethnic groups. By far the largest groups, however, are ethnic Ukrainians (78% in 2001) and ethnic Russians (17% in 2001), both of which are Slavic peoples that claim a common heritage. Ethnic Russians, who came to Ukraine in large numbers in the late nineteenth and early twentieth centuries to work in mines and factories, are a larger percentage of the population in the eastern and southern regions. Notably, the 2001 census saw a 5% increase in the number of people who identify themselves as Ukrainians and a similar drop for those who identified as Russians compared with figures from the last Soviet census in 1989, most likely a reflection that Ukraine is now a separate country and Ukrainian nationality has more prestige. The census, however, does not ask about people with a mixed ethnic background, which is relatively common given intermarriages between Ukrainians and Russians. The remaining ethnic or national groups in Ukraine, such as Belorussians, Crimean Tatars (a Turkic-Muslim people), Poles, Romanians, Greeks, and Jews, each totaled less than 1% of the population.

LANGUAGE

The state language of Ukraine is Ukrainian, an east Slavic language that uses the Cyrillic alphabet, a script composed of a mixture of Latin, Greek, and uniquely "Slavic" letters. Ukrainian is derived from the eastern Slavic language used more than a millennium ago during the time of Kievan Rus. Both Russian and Belarussian claim a similar heritage, and, not surprisingly, Ukrainian is closely related to both of these other modern east Slavic languages. Each, however, uses a slightly different version of the Cyrillic alphabet (e.g., in Ukrainian one finds the letters I and Ï but not the Russian or Belarussian Э or Ы), and there are differences in pronunciation. Some speakers of Russian might claim otherwise, but Russian and Ukrainian, although similar in many respects, are not mutually intelligible. In addition, because of Ukraine's close relationship with Poland, Ukrainian shares many words (e.g., *tak* for "yes," *robity* for "to do") with Polish, considered a western Slavic language.

It was only in the mid-1800s, thanks to the efforts of poets such as Taras Shevchenko (1814–1861), that Ukrainian developed into a literary language and achieved some degree of standardization. Ukrainian, however, has several regional dialects, the main distinctions being among "Left Bank" and "Right Bank" Ukrainian and the Ukrainian spoken by members of the Ukrainian diaspora that immigrated to countries such as Canada, the United States, and

Australia in the early twentieth century. Some people in western Ukraine claim to speak a separate Slavic language, Rusyn or Ruthenian, although some insist this is simply yet another dialect of Ukrainian. Traditionally many Ukrainians were illiterate peasants who did not attend school, but today 99.9% of adult Ukrainians can read and write.

Promotion of the Ukrainian language has been a major issue in post-Soviet Ukraine, as many Ukrainian speakers complained that under Soviet rule, Ukrainian was marginalized and that Ukrainians were therefore in danger of losing an important aspect of their culture. Indeed, Russian was the main language of administration, commerce, and education, and many Russians considered Ukrainian to be a peasant dialect of Russian. Many Ukrainians have worked hard to change this attitude, as Ukrainian language has been mandatory in schools and is the language for all government business. On the streets of many Ukrainian cities, particularly in the more Russified east, one still hears a lot of Russian, and most Ukrainians do know Russian. At times, one hears conversations in which one person speaks Russian and one Ukrainian, each perfectly understanding the other but speaking the language with which they are more comfortable. More problematic for some has been the rise of *surzhyk*, taken from a term for a flour made from mixed grains, which is a mish-mash of both Russian and Ukrainian.

According to the 2001 census, 67.5% of the population list Ukrainian as their native language and 29.6% claim Russian. This constitutes a 3% increase in the use of Ukrainian and a similar decline for Russian compared with 1989. Russian speakers, unhappy with what they feel is unfair "Ukrainianization" by the state, have lobbied for Russian to be given official status at the national, or at least a regional, level. This has been an important issue in post-Soviet Ukrainian elections, with those favoring Ukrainian believing that the Ukrainian language is a key part of Ukrainian identity and those favoring Russian arguing that Ukraine should officially recognize the rights of a sizable number of native Russian speakers and become, like Canada, officially bilingual.

RELIGION

Although religious practice was discouraged and even repressed under the Soviet Union, religion is an important part of Ukrainian society and culture today. According to surveys conducted in 2003 by the Razumkov Center, a Ukrainian social science research institute, 75% of Ukrainians claim to believe in God and 37% attend church regularly.[3] They have many from which to choose. According to official statistics, as of 2006 there were more than 30,000 registered religious organizations and church parishes in Ukraine. Of these, the vast majority represent Orthodox Christianity, which became the official religion of medieval Kievan Rus (see Chapter 2) in 988. Orthodoxy claims that it is the true church of Jesus Christ, having split with the Roman Catholic Church in 1054. Nonetheless, it shares many of the same beliefs with Protestants and Catholics (e.g., the Holy Trinity, Christ's resurrection, an afterlife, use of the Old and New Testament). Orthodox churches are distinctive because of their rounded cupolas, icons (simple paintings on wood of holy figures that are often kissed by worshippers), and iconostasis (walls of icons separating the nave from the sanctuary). Their services feature standing worshippers (there are no seats), much singing, and generous use of incense. Most Orthodox churches still use the older Julian calendar, meaning that the dates of many of their Church holidays differ from those of other Christian faiths (e.g., Orthodox Christmas is January 7).

Today, however, there is no single Orthodox Church in Ukraine; rather, there are three: the Ukrainian Orthodox Church (Moscow Patriarchate) [UOC-MP], the Ukrainian Orthodox Church (Kiev Patriarchate) [UOC-KP], and the Ukrainian Autocephalous Orthodox Church [UAOC]. The UOC-MP is the successor to the Ukrainian branch of the Russian Orthodox Church, and it was the only Christian church allowed under Soviet times. Although it was renamed in 1990, its heads still answer to the Patriarch, head of the Church, in Moscow. Its services are conducted in Russian, and it is far more prevalent in the eastern, Russian-speaking regions of Ukraine. It retains the largest number of parish churches in Ukraine today, although rival churches have laid claim to many of the UOC-MP's parishes.[4]

The UOC-KP was founded in 1992 in an effort to bestow on Ukraine its own national church that would be independent from Moscow. Its establishment was highly controversial for several reasons: (1) many looked with disfavor on the idea of a "national" church; (2) it engaged in property disputes with the UOC-MP; and (3) its leader, Patriarch Filaret, who assumed office in 1995, is a particularly controversial figure, as he served in the past as leader of the Russian Orthodox Church in Ukraine and has been linked with efforts under Soviet times to suppress other churches. Unlike the UOC-MP, it is not recognized by the Eastern Orthodox Communion as a legitimate national church, but it continues to fight for status both within Ukraine and internationally. It conducts its services in Ukrainian and most of its parishioners reside in western Ukraine.

The UAOC was founded in western Ukraine in 1919 at a time when many in that region sought an independent Ukraine. It is autocephalous, meaning that although it retains the same rites as other Orthodox churches, its head bishop does not report to a higher-ranking bishop. Therefore it fashioned itself as a more independent, Ukrainian church, and for this reason it was banned by Soviet authorities in 1930. It continued to exist among diaspora Ukrainians, and it has built new churches or restored older ones away from the UOC-MP. The vast majority of its parishioners reside in western Ukraine.

The other major Ukrainian church is the Ukrainian Greek Catholic Church, sometimes called the Ukrainian Catholic Church or the Uniate Church. This church was created by the Union of Brest in 1596 when most of western Ukraine was ruled by the Grand Duchy of Poland-Lithuania (discussed more in Chapter 3). The goal of the Union of Brest was to create a hybrid Catholic-Orthodox Church so that the Orthodox population of late sixteenth century-Ukrainian lands would identify more with Catholic Poland-Lithuania and not be under the religious authority of the Patriarch in Moscow. This church adheres to Orthodox rites and allows its priests to marry, but it recognizes the authority of the Pope. It was repressed when Ukraine was under tsarist Russian rule, and, owing to its associations with Ukrainian nationalism, it was banned by the Soviets in 1946. Like the UAOC, it retained sizable support among diaspora communities. Although it moved its headquarters from the western Ukrainian city of Lviv to Kiev in 2005, most of its parishioners live in western Ukraine.

Surveys by the aforementioned Razumkov Center in 2003 revealed that just over half (50.4%) of Ukrainian churchgoers associate themselves with the UOC-KP, 26.1% belong to the UOC-MP, 8% claim to be Greek Catholics, and 7.2% attend UAOC services.

There are other religious communities in Ukraine as well. Just over 2% of believers, mainly ethnic Poles in western Ukraine, claim to be Roman Catholic. A similar number claim to be Protestants, and there are more than 4,000 Protestant communities (e.g., Baptists, Mormons, Seventh-Day Adventists) in Ukraine. Ukraine used to be the home of vibrant Jewish communities, especially in Odessa and Lviv. Hasidic Judaism was founded in Ukraine in 1740, and by 1800 Ukrainian lands included nearly 3 million Jews. Most of Ukraine's Jews, however, perished in the Holocaust, killed by both Germans and, it should be said, some of their Ukrainian neighbors. Many of those that survived emigrated to Israel or the United States, and today fewer than 1% of Ukrainians, according to the Razkumov Survey, claim to practice Judaism. The largest Muslim group in Ukraine are the Crimean Tatars, who were exiled en masse to central Asia in 1944 during World War II. Since 1991, many have returned to their homeland, and more than 250,000 live in Ukraine today.

REGIONALISM

As eluded to in the discussions on ethnicity, language, and religion, Ukraine possesses significant regional divisions. The main regional divide in Ukraine is between west and east. It is a reflection of different paths of historical development. Eastern Ukraine has been subjected to Russian (later Soviet) rule since the middle of the 1600s; western parts of Ukraine were ruled by Poland-Lithuania, Austria, and (later) Poland and Romania; it was not incorporated into the Soviet Union until 1944. For this reason, eastern Ukraine contains more ethnic Russians and has been subjected to more Russification. For example, in the Donetsk and Luhansk regions in the far southeastern part of the country, 38% of the population is ethnically Russian and more than half of the ethnic Ukrainians in these regions claim Russian as their native language.[5] In contrast, Ukrainian citizens in western Ukraine are far more likely to identify themselves as ethnically Ukrainian, remained more Ukrainian-speaking,[6] and were able to retain cultural institutions such as the Ukrainian Greek Catholic Church. Ukrainians in tsarist Russia and the Soviet Union lived under a repressive political system. Those under Polish or Austrian rule lived in a more liberal, tolerant political environment, making them freer to develop their own political and social institutions. Eastern Ukraine, under tsars and then under the Soviets, became quite urbanized and industrialized. Most of Ukraine's biggest cities, and, indeed, most of its population, lives in eastern Ukraine. Western Ukraine, in contrast, was far more rural, comprising the least economically developed part of both Poland and the Austro-Hungarian Empire.[7]

This east-west divide has manifested itself in various ways in contemporary Ukraine and has been a major subject of study and concern. Those in eastern Ukraine tend to favor closer ties with Russia, vote for more left-wing political parties (e.g., the Communist Party or the Socialist Party), and want to preserve the status of the Russian language. Those in western Ukraine favor closer ties to the European Union, NATO, and the United States; vote for more "national-democratic" parties such as Rukh and Our Ukraine; and tend to favor promotion of the Ukrainian language. In elections throughout the post-Soviet period, there is a marked contrast in both public opinion on key issues (e.g., economic reform, foreign policy) and in voting patterns between these two regions of the country.[8] During the "Orange Revolution" of 2004–2005 (see Chapter 10), the "Orange" forces of Viktor Yushchenko predominated in the West, Kiev, and in some "border" regions along the Dnieper River, whereas the "Blue" Party of Regions were centered in eastern Ukraine, particularly Donetsk and Luhansk. Some fear that acute regional divisions grounded in language, political culture, and economics could tear Ukraine apart, although there were some signs throughout the 1990s that a "Ukrainian" identity is growing.[9]

Some posit that one should look beyond a simple east-west dichotomy in Ukraine. Crimea, which has a special autonomous status within Ukraine, is geographically, demographically, and historically unique. It was under the control of the Tatars until the late 1700s and is the only region in Ukraine with an ethnic Russian majority (59% in 2001). It is part of Ukraine only because it was transferred in 1954, when Ukraine was part of the Soviet Union, from Russian jurisdiction to Ukrainian jurisdiction as a celebration of 300 years of Russian-Ukrainian friendship dating from the Treaty of Pereiaslav (see

Chapter 3). This event, which seemed like a technicality at the time—after all, both Russia and Ukraine were part of the Soviet Union—took on great significance once Ukraine became independent and many people in both Russia and Crimea wanted Crimea to rejoin Russia. Although the threat of Crimean separatism did seem serious in the 1990s, it was defused. Some who live in Odessa and its surroundings, which were also heavily Russified and never a core part of Ukrainian lands, invoke the eighteenth-century tsarist name for their region, "New Russia" (*Novorossiia*) and claim that they are not really part of Ukraine. Many residents of the far western and mountainous region (*oblast*) of Transcarpathia claim that they are Rusyns,[10] not Ukrainians, and therefore deserve some sort of special status or protection.

GOVERNMENT

Until 1991, with one brief exception (1918–1921), Ukrainians have not had a state of their own in modern times. Consequently, Ukraine lacks traditions of statehood, let alone democracy or representative government. Under the Soviet Union, Ukraine was 1 of 15 republics (akin to states in the United States or provinces in Canada) and had its own branches of government in Kiev, the republican capital. The Soviet Union, however, was ruled from Moscow and by the Communist Party, which outlawed any other political parties, controlled the media and the economy, and prohibited expressions of Ukrainian nationalism.

Ukraine gained its independence in 1991, the culmination of many events that are described in Chapter 8. Many hoped that when Ukraine gained its freedom from Soviet rule, its people would be able to enjoy the benefits of democratic government. Establishing a vibrant and effective democracy, however, has proved difficult.[11] As discussed more in Chapter 9, under both President Leonid Kravchuk (1991–1994) and President Leonid Kuchma (1994–2004), Ukraine's democratic progress was rather limited. Major problems included political corruption, governmental control over the media, weak civic associations and political opposition, rigged elections, and incessant bickering among rival political groups. After acrimonious debate, Ukraine developed a new constitution in 1996 that gave much power to the president. By the late 1990s, the state became more openly nondemocratic, and in 2000 President Kuchma was caught on audiotape apparently ordering the murder of an opposition journalist. This event led to large public protests that were forcibly put down by the government.

In the 2004 elections, Kuchma's designated successor, Viktor Yanukovych, attempted to steal the election with falsified voting results. The opposition, led by former Prime Minister Viktor Yushchenko, however, anticipated such shenanigans, and launched public protests that drew millions of Ukrainians into the streets. This was the "Orange Revolution," named after the colors of Yushchenko's party. Eventually, thanks to the protests, intervention by Ukrainian courts, and international mediation, a new round of elections was held and Yushchenko, who had also been mysteriously poisoned during the election campaign, became president. Although this event ushered in a new round of hope for many Ukrainians, the country remains dogged by intense political feuds and divisions, with Viktor Yanukovych, in a development that surprised many, becoming prime minister in 2006. Not surprisingly, cooperation between President Yushchenko and Prime Minister Yanukovych, who are bitter rivals, has been difficult and has generated several political crises.

As a result of constitutional changes that occurred during the "Orange Revolution," Ukraine has a parliamentary-presidential system. The head of state is the president, elected every five years by popular vote. The president must obtain a majority of the vote; if no candidate receives a majority, there is a run-off election between the top two vote-getters. Whereas under Kuchma the president had a wide range of powers, at present most of the Ukrainian president's powers are in the area of foreign and military policy.

The Ukrainian legislature is called the *Verkhovna Rada* (Supreme Council). It is normally elected every five years, although, as in 2007, early elections can be held under special circumstances. The *Verkhovna Rada* has 450 seats that are distributed by proportional representation from a party list system. This means that voters choose a political party, and the number of seats a party receives is proportionate to the percentage of its vote. For example, if a party gets 20% of the vote, it would win 90 seats (20% of 450), enabling the top 90 names on that party's list to become members of the *Verkhovna Rada*. To win seats, a party must receive at least 3% of the vote. The *Verkhovna Rada,* in turn, selects the prime minister, who in turn names all other government ministers (members of the cabinet), except the foreign and defense ministers, who are chosen by the president. The prime minister is the head of government and has the primary policy-making role. Laws are passed by the *Verkhovna Rada.* The President may veto legislation, but the *Verkhovna Rada* can override a presidential veto with a two-thirds vote. It may also amend the Constitution with a two-thirds vote.

Ukraine has a Constitutional Court, which was created in 1996 and is the only body with the jurisdiction to rule on constitutional matters. It is composed of 18 judges, appointed in equal measure by the president, the *Vekhovna Rada,* and the Congress of Judges. Judges serve nine-year terms. The general court system is topped by the Supreme Court, whose judges are appointed by parliament. There is no fixed number of judges (as of 2007 there were 85). The Supreme Court consists of several judicial chambers (e.g., court for civil cases, court for criminal cases). Beneath the Supreme Court are local courts and appeals courts. The prosecutor general, responsible for prosecuting cases on behalf of the state, is appointed by the president. Reform of the judiciary, which has been subject to corruption, has been a much-discussed, if not implemented, project in post-Soviet Ukraine.

Ukraine is a unitary, not a federal, state, meaning that power is not shared between the national government and regional or subnational governments. Ukraine is divided into 24 regions (*oblasts*), each of which has its own administration and is in turn subdivided into districts and cities. Crimea has a special status as an autonomous republic, having its own parliament that can pass laws that apply exclusively to Crimea but that cannot go against the Ukrainian Constitution or national-level laws. Kiev and Sevastopol (the main port and military base in Crimea) rank as cities with a special status, not subject to any *oblast* level authority.

Ukraine has dozens of political parties, and its party system is very fluid. Many of those that formed in the immediate aftermath of independence have disappeared or merged to form new parties. Few Ukrainians belong to political parties, and many political parties are dominated by just a few individuals. In the 2007 parliamentary elections, 20 parties and blocs nominated candidates. Five made it past the 3% threshold: the Party of Regions (34.4%); the Bloc of Yulia Tymoshenko (BYuT) (30.7%); Our Ukraine (14.2%); the Communist Party (5.4%); and the Lytvyn Bloc (4%).

ECONOMY

The Ukrainian economy was traditionally dominated by agriculture, and Ukrainians themselves were primarily peasants or small farmers, residing in the countryside while other nationalities (e.g., Russians, Poles, Germans, Jews) resided in the cities and were merchants, artisans, and civil servants. Over time, Ukrainians have become more urbanized, but even as industrialization occurred in the late nineteenth and twentieth centuries, agriculture remained an important source of income for many. When Ukraine was part of the Soviet Union, it accounted for a quarter of Soviet agricultural production despite accounting for only 3% of the country's land area. Main crops were sugar beets, potatoes, corn, wheat, barley, and other grains, and meat and dairy production were also important industries. According to the World Bank, agriculture in 2005 accounted for 11% of Ukraine's Gross National Product (GNP), and nearly a fifth of the population is employed in agriculture and food processing.[12]

Ukraine has a significant industrial sector, largely built during Soviet times. Much of the "heavy industry" (e.g., chemical and steel plants, mining, production of industrial equipment, auto industries, arms manufacturing) is in eastern Ukraine. Although many of the factories are dilapidated because of a lack of recent investment and pose major environmental problems, industrial products, especially steel, are some of Ukraine's leading exports. Ukraine, however, does not have significant oil or gas reserves and is dependent on Russia for its energy needs. This situation has occasionally led to political crises, as Russia has raised prices for fuel and/or threatened to cut off fuel supplies because Ukraine has not paid for previous fuel imports.

As part of the Soviet Union, Ukraine had a communist economic system. This meant that there was no private property and that much of the economy (e.g., prices for goods, production targets) was determined by the state. Factories and farms were owned by the state or were collective property, which, in effect, meant that it was controlled by the state. Although state planning and investment did contribute to the growth of industries in Ukraine, by the 1980s it was clear that communism was not efficient or innovative. The economic failure of communism is one of the primary reasons for its collapse.

Upon independence, economic reform appeared to be an obvious need. Many Ukrainians wanted to move away from communism and adopt a more free market system. Others, however, were reluctant to embrace capitalism, as the communist system guaranteed jobs, and welfare provisions and state funding of economic enterprises were crucial to their survival. In particular, many in eastern Ukraine feared that capitalism would mean bankruptcy for large industrial enterprises and massive unemployment.

Throughout the 1990s, Ukraine, unlike Poland, Hungary, and the Czech Republic, which adopted market-oriented policies, moved very slowly with economic reform. Prices were freed, although the state continued to support many industries. Many firms were privatized, but the process was often corrupt and the new owners lacked the ability or the money necessary to make their enterprises profitable. As a result, Ukraine experienced severe economic problems in the 1990s: inflation reached 4,735% in 1993 and the economy declined, on average, by 14% *each year* from 1991 to 1995.[13] A few, usually those with political connections, did very well in corrupt business deals, but many companies claimed they could not pay their workers, and living standards plummeted as many people fell into poverty. The verb "to Ukrainianize" acquired the meaning "to bring to ruin."

Since 2000, when reforms were accelerated, the Ukrainian economy has rebounded. Ukraine has attracted more foreign investment ($7.8 billion by 2005) and experienced sustained growth, averaging 8% from 2001–2006. The currency, the *hryvnia,* which was introduced in 1996, has remained fairly steady, with inflation running only about 8% a year from 2001–2006. Unemployment figures are harder to come by, as many people are working "off the books" to avoid taxation, but the International Labor Organization estimates that unemployment is approximately 7%.[14]

This is not to say that all is fine. Poverty, particularly among elderly citizens who receive small pensions, remains acute. Average wages are still only about

$200 a month. The World Bank reports that the average income per person as of 2005 was only $1,520, compared with $4,460 for Russia, $7,160 for Poland, and $43,560 for the United States.[15] Corruption and corporate governance are major concerns. Inequality is also a problem, reflected not only in the emergence of super-rich "oligarchs" but also because rural incomes lag far behind those in major cities such as Kiev, Kharkiv, and Donetsk, which have more developed industrial and service sectors. As noted, many Ukrainians are leaving to look for better opportunities elsewhere.

FOREIGN RELATIONS

Post-Soviet Ukraine's international orientation has been a major area of interest. Under the Soviet Union, Ukraine did not have an independent foreign policy, although, because of a compromise engineered in 1945 when the United Nations was founded, it, together with Belarus, gained a seat in the UN's General Assembly. Since gaining independence, Ukraine has had to develop its own foreign policy.

Recognizing its geopolitical position between Europe and Russia, Ukraine pursued a "multi-vector foreign policy" throughout the 1990s; that is, it was interested in cultivating good relations with a number of foreign actors. Obviously relations with Russia were important. Because of ties developed both before and during the Soviet Union, Russia was Ukraine's main trade partner, and much of the Ukrainian economy was integrated with that of Russia. Ukraine joined the Commonwealth of Independent States (CIS) in 1991, which was designed to promote a peaceful breakup of the Soviet Union and preserve many of the economic, political, and security ties among the former Soviet republics. Leonid Kuchma was elected president in 1994 on a platform that called for closer ties to Russia with the slogan "Fewer Walls, More Bridges."

Many Ukrainians, however, do not want a close relationship with Russia, fearing that Russia would want to play an imperial role over Ukraine or seek to somehow incorporate Ukraine back into Russia. In the 1990s, Ukraine and Russia had significant disputes over the fate of Soviet-era nuclear weapons on Ukrainian territory and division of the Soviet Black Sea fleet, which was based in Crimea. Eventually, both of these issues were settled peacefully—Ukraine surrendered the weapons and the fleet was divided—and Ukraine and Russia concluded a Treaty of Friendship and Cooperation in 1998. Nonetheless, there are still problems in Russian-Ukrainian relations. These include a territorial dispute over the Kerch Straits in the Sea of Azov in 2003, Russian support for the clearly fraudulent elections during the Orange Revolution, and Russian attempts to raise the price of gas that it sells to Ukraine. Energy dependency on Russia is a source of concern to many Ukrainians, as it gives Russia the potential to exert coercion on Ukraine. Concerns about Russia led Ukraine to join the so-called GUAM (Georgia-Ukraine-Azerbaijan-Moldova) group, which is focused on developing new oil and gas pipelines from the Caspian Sea that would bypass Russia.

Ukraine, however, has also eagerly courted good relations with the European Union and the United States. Indeed, successive post-Soviet Ukrainian governments have emphasized that they give priority to Euro-Atlantic integration. Ukraine has cooperated with the North Atlantic Treaty Organization (NATO), joining NATO's Partnership for Peace initiative in 1994. Ukraine has sent peacekeepers to support NATO operations in Bosnia and Kosovo. It has also sought closer relations with the European Union (EU). In 1998, a Partnership and Cooperation Agreement between the EU and Ukraine went into force and was later supplemented in 1999 with the development of the EU's Common Strategy for Ukraine. Ukraine has received several billion dollars in assistance from the EU and from the United States for economic reform, cleanup from the Chernobyl nuclear power plant accident, and democratization. Because of political corruption, lack of progress toward democracy, and allegations of Ukrainian arms sales to Saddam Hussein's Iraq, however, Ukraine's relations with both Europe and the United States soured in the later years of the Kuchma administration.

Since the Orange Revolution, President Yushchenko has attempted to orient Ukraine more clearly toward the West. He has made it clear that he wants Ukraine to join the EU, and EU membership is generally supported by most Ukrainians. The EU, however, has offered Ukraine only the prospect of enhanced cooperation through its European Neighborhood Program. Poland has become Ukraine's primary advocate within the EU, demonstrating that Ukraine and Poland may be putting centuries of an at times acrimonious relationship behind them. Yushchenko has also advocated Ukrainian NATO membership, but this is a very controversial subject within Ukraine, as many Ukrainians do not want their country to join an alliance that they perceive as directed toward Russia. This last point reflects the fact that Ukraine's foreign orientation remains tied up with geography, the country's history, and its own regional divisions.

NOTES

1. All-Ukrainian Population Census of 2001, available in English at www.ukrcensus.gov.ua/eng/, accessed August 14, 2007.

2. CIA World Factbook 2007, available at https://www.cia.gov/library/publications/the-world-factbook/geos/up.html, accessed August 15, 2007.

3. This, and other data in this section, comes from "Religion in Ukraine," accessible at en.wikipedia.org/wiki/Religion_in_Ukraine, accessed August 14, 2007.

4. A good source for disputes among churches is Andrew Wilson, *The Ukrainians: Unexpected Nation* (New Haven, CT: Yale University Press, 2000), pp. 234–252.

5. See All-Ukrainian Population Census of 2001.

6. For example, according to the 2001 census, the population of the western regions of Lviv (95%) and Ivano-Frankivsk (98%) are overwhelmingly ethnic Ukrainian. Fewer than 1% of ethnic Ukrainians in these regions claim Russian as their native language.

7. According to the 2001 census, the eastern regions of Donetsk (90%), Luhansk (86%), Dnieperpetrovsk (83%), and Zaporizhzhia (76%) over overwhelmingly urban. In contrast, those regions with an urban population of less than 50% (Transcarpathia, Vinnytsia, Ivano-Frankivsk, Chernivtsi, Rivne, and Ternopil) are all in western Ukraine.

8. Paul Kubicek, "Regional Polarisation in Ukraine: Public Opinion, Voting, and Legislative Behaviour," *Europe-Asia Studies* 52, no. 2 (2000): pp. 273–294.

9. Taras Kuzio, *Ukraine: State and Nation Building* (London: Routledge, 1998).

10. Those interested in the Rusyns (or Ruthenians) should consult Paul R. Magosci and Ivan Pop, eds., *Encyclopedia of Rusyn History of Culture* (Toronto: University of Toronto Press, 2002).

11. Good sources include Kuzio, 1998, and Paul D'Anieri, *Understanding Ukrainian Politics: Power, Politics, and Institutional Design* (Armonk, NY: M. E. Sharpe, 2006).

12. Data from www.worldbank.org, accessed August 15, 2007. Unless otherwise cited, all data in this section come from the World Bank.

13. World Bank, *World Development Report 1996: From Plan to Market* (New York: Oxford University Press, 1996), pp. 173–174.

14. CIA World Factbook 2007.

15. Taking into account purchasing power parity (the prices of products on the Ukrainian market), the CIA World Factbook estimates income per person to be $7,800.

2

Kievan Rus: The Foundation of Ukrainian Culture

Even though Ukraine is a newly independent state, it has a long history. Although various peoples can claim the mantle as the "first Ukrainians," most accounts date the beginnings of Ukraine to the mid-to-late 800s with the founding of the kingdom of Rus, whose capital was Kiev. Not only was Rus identifiable as a Slavic kingdom (although the origins of its founders are disputed), but it also adopted Christianity as its official religion. Its heritage—in terms of language, religion, art, architectural monuments, in a word, culture— are still discernible in Ukraine today. Although Russians also claim descent from Kievan Rus, Ukrainians often point with pride to the accomplishments of Kievan Rus and attempt to use its history both to ground their own identity and to separate themselves from their more populous and traditionally more powerful eastern neighbor.

PRE-SLAVIC UKRAINE

The earliest traces of human habitation in present-day Ukraine date back approximately 150,000 years, and materials from prehistoric peoples (e.g., flint weapons, primitive tools, graves) have been found across the country. By 5000– 4000 B.C.E., the first agricultural peoples settled southwestern Ukraine. Little is known about these early agrarian peoples—the so-called Trypillian culture—who lived in large villages and, by 2700 B.C.E., had expanded eastward to form settlements along the Dnieper River near Kiev. Some Ukrainians, seeking to anchor their identity in a more prestigious past, have claimed that the Trypillians invented the wheel, writing, and agriculture; helped found Sumerian and Hittite civilizations; built Stonehenge; and were ancestors to Christ, Buddha, and Zarathustra. No evidence has ever emerged for what one scholar calls such "outlandish claims."[1] In any event, it would be difficult to call such people Ukrainians—they did not speak Ukrainian, had no conception of "Ukraine," and obviously were not Christians. Archaeological evidence suggests that the Trypillians disappeared by 2000 B.C.E., replaced by various nomadic tribes who found the climate and soils of Ukraine suitable for raising their herds.

The first mention in literature of any inhabitants of Ukraine comes from Homer's *Odyssey*, which refers to the "land of the Cimmerians" on the northern shore of the Black Sea. Homer, however, tells us no more about the Cimmerians, although scholars have pieced together evidence that the Cimmerians were skilled horsemen and introduced the Iron Age to Ukraine.

Much more is known about the Scythians, who settled in what is now southern Ukraine (in Crimea and along the Black Sea coast) in the seventh century B.C.E. Some claim that the prophet Jeremiah refers to them as a "cruel and pitiless" people from a northern land that will "devour your harvest and bread" and "devour your sons and daughters."[2] In the fifth century B.C.E., Herodotus, the Greek father of history, visited Scythia and described them as fierce, nomadic tribal people who ritually drank human blood, spoke a Persian language, and were ruled by a type of military aristocracy. In addition to war plunder, they traded with Greek colonies along the Black Sea coast. By the fourth century B.C.E., the Scythians had pushed westward toward the Danube, but Philip of Macedon, the father of Alexander the Great, defeated them in 339 B.C.E.[3] Some claim that the Scythians, supposedly descended from Noah's son Japheth, are the ancestors of the Slavs, and the Russian writer Alexander Blok famously suggested in his poem *Scythians* (1918) "Yes, we are Scythians! Yes, we are Asians/with slanted and greedy eyes." As with the Trypillians, some Ukrainians make grand claims from the Scythians, among them that Scythians are responsible for the Golden Age of Greece.[4] Today one can view large burial mounds of Scythian chiefs (according to Herodotus, members of a chief's tribe, his servants, and one of his wives were sacrificed as part of his funeral and buried with him[5]) throughout southern Ukraine, and the names of many of the region's rivers (e.g., Dnieper, Dniester, Donets, Danube) may derive from the Persian/Scythian language.

After the decline of the Scythians, the Sarmatians, another Persian-speaking tribe from the east, were the major presence in southern Ukraine, although there were still remnants of the Scythians as well as Greek colonies along the

Black Sea coast. Like the Scythians, the Sarmatians were fierce warriors, although they also had trading relationships with peoples as far away as China. Also like the Scythians, some Ukrainians (and Poles as well) sought to claim Sarmatian lineage, with Bohdan Khmelnytsky, the seventeenth-century Cossack leader, declaring himself "prince of the Sarmatians."[6] Their rule over the region, however, was repeatedly challenged by other nomadic peoples heading westward from the Eurasian steppes. By the time of the third century C.E., they were overrun by a combination of Huns from the east, Germanic Goths from the north, and Romans from the west.

THE EARLIEST EASTERN SLAVS

None of the peoples thus far mentioned were Slavic and, to the extent that we define Ukrainians today as a Slavic people, their connections to this ancient past are tenuous at best. The roots of what might be called Ukrainian civilization or a Ukrainian nation therefore are to be found in the origins of the Slavic peoples or, more precisely, the eastern Slavs.

Most scholars adhere to the view that the Slavs, composed of various tribes, originally inhabited lands near the Carpathian Mountains in modern-day Poland and western Ukraine. From there, particularly in the seventh century C.E., they spread out in all directions, moving into new lands (e.g., the Balkans, modern Russia) as colonists. As they migrated, their language evolved into three subgroups: western Slavic (from which Polish and Czech developed); south Slavic (a precursor to languages such as Serbian and Bulgarian), and east Slavic (the root of Ukrainian, Belorussian, and Russian).

In the case of Ukraine, the history of the earliest Slavic peoples is obscure, as there are few written records about them. According to some accounts, including that of the *Russian Primary Chronicle* (sometimes rendered as the *Tale of the Bygone Years*), compiled in the early twelfth century, the Slavs (like the aforementioned Scythians) are descendents of Noah's third son Japheth, who received the northern and western sectors of the earth after the flood. Less mythic is the more archaeological-based contention that the Antes tribal federation was the first eastern Slavic culture. Controversies continue, however, about whether the Antes were native to the region or immigrants, whether they are truly Slavic (i.e., some suggest they were more Gothic or Germanic), and the time period of their emergence, which is dated in some accounts as early as the second century C.E.[7] One of the largest of the Antes tribes was the Polianians, who, according to a legend in the *Russian Primary Chronicle,* in 482 C.E. founded the city of Kiev (Kyïv in Ukrainian), which allegedly took its name from Kyi, a Polianian prince. Some believe that the Polianians had a literate culture, a sort of pre-Cyrillic alphabet that predated the codification of the Cyrillic alphabet by Saints Cyril and Methodius in 863. There is no direct evidence for this contention, but there is more solid basis to claim that the Polianians had contact with the Greek Byzantine Empire centered in Constantinople (now Istanbul) and were familiar with Christianity.[8]

The decentralized Antes federation was defeated in 602 by the Avars, a Turkic tribe that would rule over much of East-Central Europe. Eastern Slavic culture and identity, such as it was, survived, however, and the Avar Empire fell in the early 800s. Eventually, several of the eastern Slavic tribes in more southerly regions fell under the control of the Khazars, a Turkic people. Farther to the north, the Varangians,[9] a Scandinavian people, held sway over numerous tribes of eastern Slavs. Dominated by outsiders, the Slavic lands in present-day Ukraine were, in the middle of the ninth century, "an economic, cultural, and political backwater."[10]

FOUNDATION OF RUS

By the early eleventh century, however, Kiev was the capital of a powerful principality that was rapidly becoming one of the most developed societies in all of Europe: Rus. Ukrainians today eagerly claim the glories of Rus, still preserved in a few sites in Kiev and elsewhere in the country, as their own. The rise of Kievan Rus, however, is an issue shrouded by controversy.

The central question is this: Who were the founders of Kievan Rus? One version, the so-called Scandinavian or Viking theory, is found in the *Russian Primary Chronicle*. It relates:

> 860–862: The tributaries of the Varangians drove them back beyond the sea and, refusing them further tribute, set out to govern themselves. There was no law among them, but tribe rose against tribe. Discord thus ensued among them, and they began to war one against the other. They said to themselves, "Let us seek a prince who may rule over us, and judge us according to the law." They accordingly went overseas to the Varangian Russes: these particular Varangians were known as Russes, just as some are called Swedes, and others Normans, English, and Gotlanders . . . [They] then said to the people of Rus, "Our whole land is great and rich, and there is no order in it. Come to rule and reign over us." They thus selected three brothers, with their kinsfolk, who took with them all the Russes and migrated.[11]

The remainder of the tale informs us that Riurik, the oldest brother, ruled in Novgorod, a settlement in what is now northwestern Russia that became known as "land of the Rus." After the death of his two brothers, he became the sole ruler among the Rus and dispatched colonists to other towns inhabited by Slavs. Askold and Dir, members of the Novgorod nobility, (*boyars*) obtained permission from Riurik to sail down the Dnieper, where they became rulers over the Polianians in Kiev. They prospered, even launching a major military assault on Constantinople. Allegedly, they also converted to Christianity, although they did not demand the same of all their subjects. Their rule was cut short, however. Riurik died in 879 and Oleh (Helgi in Scandinavian), a pagan who served as regent for Riurik's young son Ihor (Ingvar in Scandinavian), attacked Kiev, killed Askold and Dir in 882, and set himself up as prince of Kiev, establishing it as the new capital for the Rus and declaring that it should be, according to the *Chronicle*, the "mother of all Russian cities."[12]

The reasons why this tale is controversial are not hard to discern. It suggests that the unruly Slavs could not govern themselves and *invited* Scandinavians to come and rule them. Most historians do not take this rendering at face value and argue that the Scandinavians pushed into Slavic lands not because of an invitation but because they were after resources (e.g., furs and precious metals) and sought control over trade routes leading south to Constantinople and the Middle East via rivers such as the Dnieper (which flowed into the Black Sea) and the Volga (which flowed into the Caspian Sea). Noting that the *Russian Primary Chronicle* was compiled centuries after these events, some believe it may have been based on earlier self-serving Scandinavian legends and is full of contradictions and inaccuracies, and thus are apt to dismiss this story all together. For example, while acknowledging the presence of many Scandinavians in and around Kiev in the ninth century, Mikhaylo Hrushevsky (1866–1934), Ukraine's best known historian, claims that "the early history of Ukraine remains obscure," grounded in "legends and scanty descriptions by foreigners."[13] A pointed source of argument is the derivation of the term *Rus*. Hrushevsky maintains that it derives from the local Slavic people living around Kiev, whereas others note that it likely comes from the western Finnic word for Swedes, *Ruotsi*.[14] Even if the earliest rulers of Kievan Rus were not Slavs, however, there is little question that, as the *Chronicle* notes, they *became* Slavs (e.g., note how they acquire Slavic names).

Figure 2.1 provides a basic genealogy of the early rulers of Kievan Rus. Oleh, the first historically verifiable ruler of Kievan Rus, reigned until 912 and established what is known as the Riurikid Dynasty (after Riurik of Novgorod). Oleh extended his authority over more of the Slavic tribes in the region. Kievan Rus grew as both a trading empire and a military power, with Oleh's armies attacking Constantinople and gaining a favorable trade treaty from the Greek rulers of that city in 911. Ihor (912–945) was less successful in his military campaigns against Constantinople and also had to contend with rebellions among the Slavic tribes who did not want to pay tribute to the rulers in Kiev. Olha (Helga in Scandinavian), his wife, served as regent (945–962) for their son, Sviatoslav. She is favorably portrayed in the old chronicles, perhaps because of her conversion to Christianity, but also because she reestablished control over the

Figure 2.1. The Early Riurikid Rulers of Kievan Rus

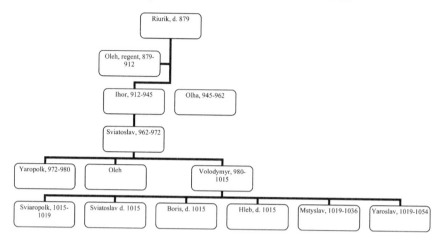

various tribes and put the realm's financial standing in good order. Sviatoslav (962–972) was an outstanding warrior who defeated competing Slavic tribes, Volga Bulgars, and Khazars and extended his realm to the Volga River, the Caspian Sea, and the northern Caucasus Mountains. In 968, he formed an alliance with Constantinople and captured rich cities to the west, along the Danube River in modern-day Romania and Bulgaria. He even wanted to move his capital to Bulgaria. His success, however, turned Constantinople against him, and the Greeks forced Sviatoslav to withdraw back to Kiev. During his retreat, he was defeated and killed by the nomadic Pechenegs, who allegedly made a chalice out of his skull. His death in turn would set off a veritable civil war among his three sons. Yaropolk, the oldest, established his rule (972–980) only after killing off the middle brother, Oleh. Volodymyr (Vladimir in Russian), fearing a similar fate, fled to Scandinavia.

THE GOLDEN AGE OF RUS

In 980, Volodymyr, assisted with military force from the Varangians, overthrew his brother Yaropolk and consolidated power in his hands. His rule (980–1015) would usher in a new epoch in the history of Rus. Internal conflict among the members of the Riurikid dynasty ended. Economic and cultural development took center stage and over time Rus expanded its borders to become, territorially, the largest state in Europe. It stretched from the Carpathian Mountains in the west northward and eastward to areas that included modern-day St. Petersburg and Moscow. It developed dynastic ties with states in Western Europe and even launched inconclusive attacks on Constantinople, the powerful capital of the Byzantine (Greek) Empire.

The most lasting achievement of Volodymyr to Kievan Rus and later to Ukrainian culture was his adoption of Orthodox Christianity in 988. Before this event, there were Christians among the Rus, including Olha, Volodymyr's grandmother; and legends even claimed that St. Andrew, brother of St. Peter, came on a mission to the Scythians in 55 c.e.; however, there had been no wholesale effort to convert the Slavic tribes en masse to Christianity. Volodymyr himself came to power as a pagan, promoting worship of Perun, the thunder god modeled on Scandinavian deities such as Thor. Early in his reign he was known for his cruelty as well as his collection of hundreds of concubines. The story of Volodymyr's (and subsequently Rus's) conversion is told in the *Russian Primary Chronicle.* According to this account, Volodymyr decided that he needed to modernize his new empire, which, among other things, meant the adoption of a new religion. He considered several options. Islam was rejected because it meant circumcision and abstinence from pork and alcohol. "Drinking," he allegedly said, "is the joy of the Russes and we cannot exist without that pleasure." Judaism, the religion of a stateless people, lacked sufficient prestige. Catholic ceremonies were too austere, and, besides, becoming Catholic would mean he would have to pledge fealty to the Pope. Finally, Orthodox Christianity, as practiced by the Byzantine (Greek) Empire, proved to be most impressive, both for the splendor of its churches (particularly Hagia Sophia in Constantinople) and the wonders of their services. Observers from Rus reported that on entering the Greek churches they "knew not whether we were in heaven or earth. For on earth there is no such splendour or beauty, and we are at a loss of how to describe it. We only know that God dwells there among men, and their service is fairer than the ceremonies of other nations."[15] Volodymyr was duly baptized and soon thereafter by Volodymyr's orders the residents of Kiev were herded into a tributary of the Dnieper and baptized while idols of the pagan gods were thrown into the water. Over the next few years, all of Rus was converted to Orthodox Christianity.

The true motivation behind this epochal event, however, may be more prosaic. In 987, Volodymyr helped the Byzantine emperors put down an internal revolt. In return, he demanded to marry Anna, their sister. They reluctantly agreed, although they in turn demanded that Volodymyr convert to Christianity. Eager to forge a dynastic alliance with the powerful Byzantines, who were considered to be the successors of Rome, he agreed. When the Byzantines tried to put the marriage off, Volodymyr seized Greek cities in Crimea and threatened to march on Constantinople. Volodymyr and Anna were then wed, thereby tying not only Volodymyr but also Rus to Byzantium.

This event had great consequences. By choosing Christianity instead of Islam, Volodymyr linked Rus (and, consequently, its successors) to Europe, not the Middle East. By choosing Orthodoxy over Catholicism (the two formally split in 1054), however, he separated the eastern Slavic peoples from their western Catholic neighbors such as the Poles. Orthodoxy, however, helped give Rus a sense of common identity and provided the basis for much of eastern Slavic culture. To later generations, Volodymyr would be known as Volodymyr the Great.

In his time, Volodymyr profited from his decision. He brought in Greek priests and craftsmen to build and administer churches. The Greeks brought with them new skills and helped create an economic and cultural awakening. The doctrines of the Orthodox faith also supported the monarch's right to rule, thus giving Volodymyr a new source of legitimacy. As a Christian ruler, he had better contacts with many other European leaders, enhancing both his own prestige and trade opportunities for his realm.

After Volodymyr's death, Kievan Rus experienced another round of political instability, as Sviatopolk, his eldest son, murdered three of his brothers in an effort to consolidate his rule. Yaroslav, another of Volodymyr's sons, called on the Varangians for assistance and defeated Sviatopolk in 1019. Yaroslav, who was based in the northern city of Novgorod, divided Rus with his brother Mstyslav, who ruled in Chernihiv. When Mstyslav died in 1036, Yaroslav became the sole ruler of Rus and moved to Kiev to assume the throne.

Yaroslav's reign as prince of Kiev (1036–1054) is usually considered the high point in the history of Kievan Rus, earning him the moniker Yaroslav the Wise. Like his father, he successfully fought off foreign enemies and expanded the borders of the realm from the Baltic to the Black Sea. He ordered the construction of churches and monasteries, the latter becoming important centers of learning. Among the 400 churches built in the city of Kiev during his reign, the most famous is St. Sophia's, which was constructed from 1037–1044. Its original exterior design, as well as its wondrous interior frescos and mosaics, were modeled after Hagia Sophia in Constantinople. Given a baroque makeover, it still stands today as a place of both spiritual and political significance, the clearest reminder of Kiev's ancient glory. Kiev's other famous religious institution, the Kiev *Pechersk Lavra,* also known as the Kiev Monastery of the Caves, was founded in 1051, the same year that Yaroslav named Ilarion as the first non-Greek metropolitan (bishop) of Rus. Works in Greek were translated into Church Slavonic, the liturgical language, which became the religious and literary language of the Rus. Most people, however, were illiterate and for them, icon painting, the two-dimensional representations of holy figures on wood, became a widespread art form and an important means for them to connect to their religion.

Economically, Kievan Rus was relatively prosperous. An envoy from France reported that "This land [Rus] is more unified, happier, stronger, and more civilized than France herself."[16] Estimates of its total population vary widely from 3 to 12 million people, but there is little doubt that its wealth brought both growth and social differentiation. Although most of the Rus were peasants, there was a sizable craftsman and merchant class, and products such as agricultural produce, furs, honey, and wax, as well as slaves captured in battles went south to Constantinople and were exchanged for luxury goods.

Yaroslav is well known for developing a common legal code, the *Ruska pravda* (Rus Justice). This code is generally seen as progressive, protecting private property and replacing blood revenge with fines against offenders (although the fines varied depending on the victim's socioeconomic status). Although Yaroslav was a monarch and placed his sons as leaders in various cities in Rus, these municipalities had both a *boyar* (noble) council (known as a *duma*, the modern Russian term for parliament) and a town assembly, which provided input to the princes and discussed the various issues of the day. Significantly, when a new prince ascended the throne, the town assembly had the right to enter into an agreement with him in which the citizens accepted his rule in return for the prince agreeing not to overstep his traditional authority.[17]

Through arranged marriages, Yaroslav helped solidify Rus's ties to other European powers. He himself married the daughter of the King of Sweden. He married three of his daughters to the kings of Norway, Hungary, and France and his sons to princesses from Poland and Byzantium. He became known as the "father-in-law of Europe," a reflection of the power of Kievan Rus.

Unfortunately, the Golden Age of Kiev did not last much beyond Yaroslav's reign. He placed his sons in charge of the various principalities of Rus, and, according to *The Russian Primary Chronicle*, on his deathbed he exhorted them not to fight with each other, as he and his own brothers had done. The eldest son would rule in Kiev and, upon his death, the next oldest would take his place, meaning the brothers would rotate positions in turn. This worked for a time, but eventually the idea of rotation among brothers ran up against the idea of transmission from father to son, especially as the number of princes grew. Uncles would thus battle nephews over the right to rule a particular territory. In addition, the citizens of Kiev revolted against Prince Iziaslav (who enlisted aid from Poland to put down the rebellion), and attacks from the nomadic Polovtsian tribes from the eastern steppes became harder to defend. Town assemblies also contributed to political instability, as they became more assertive, demanding that certain princes step down and others take their place.

All was not entirely lost. Volodymyr Monomakh (1113–1125), a grandson of both Yaroslav the Wise and the Byzantine Emperor Constantine IX, restored some of Kiev's glory. Before assuming the throne, he defeated the Polovtsians in several campaigns and when his father died, he ascended the throne because his popularity would help prevent another bout of social unrest among the citizens of Kiev. He managed to unite most of the fragmented Rus lands and made legal reforms to expand the rights of the lower classes.

THE END OF KIEVAN RUS

After the death of Volodymyr Monomakh in 1125, Kievan Rus went into a significant decline, from which it could not recover. The chronic problem of political fragmentation returned, with various princes seeking autonomy for regions under their control. As a consequence, throughout the twelfth century, a number of regions (e.g., Halych [also called Galicia] and Volynia in the west, Chernihiv just to the north of Kiev, and Vladimir, Novgorod, and Smolensk farther to the north) gained de facto independence from Kiev. Kievan Rus became "an entity that had multiple centers related by language, common religiocultural bonds, and dynastic ties, but these centers were largely independent and often in competition with each other."[18] Control of Kiev, however, was still a prize, subject to political instability (24 princes ruled it from 1146 to 1246) and even military attacks from would-be princes.

In addition, Kievan Rus suffered from economic decline. The Dnieper trade route became less important thanks to the emergence of Italian merchants who opened and controlled new trade links and the Crusader raids on Constantinople. Moreover, attacks from nomadic tribes made it difficult for Rus to control its southern border toward the Black Sea. Various efforts to unite the principalities of Rus and defeat these enemies came to naught. *The Song of Ihor's Campaign,* a chronicle dating from 1187, records the campaigns of Prince Ihor of Chernihiv against the Polovtsians, who had previously been subdued by Monomakh. This time, however:

> Brother says to brother:
> "This is mine and that is mine too"
> and the princes have begun to say
> of what is small: "This is big"
> while against their own selves
> they forge discord
> while from all sides with victories
> pagans enter the Russian [Rus] land.[19]

The final blow came at the hands of the Mongols, who originated in central Asia and whose mobile and well-led armies conquered much of Asia, the Middle East, and Eastern Europe. In 1237, Batu, grandson of the notorious Mongol leader Genghis Khan, led an army that overran the cities in northeastern Rus such as Suzdal and Vladimir. In 1240, the Mongols attacked Kiev. Despite brave resistance by its citizens, Kiev fell. All but a few of its churches were burned and its city walls were razed to the ground. Kiev would not recover its glory, and, in a move rich in symbolic and practical importance, in 1299, its Metropolitan was transferred to Vladimir and then later to Moscow.

Danylo (1237–1264), the leader of Galicia-Volhynia, tried to recapture Kiev and push the Mongols back. He appealed to European powers such as Poland and Hungary for assistance, and even Pope Innocent IV blessed his efforts by granting him a royal crown in 1253. Unfortunately, however, military reinforcements were not forthcoming, and Danylo was forced to meet the Mongols' demands to raze his elaborate defensive fortifications as the price for avoiding near certain destruction. Despite this failure, Danylo and his successors ruled over Galicia-Volhynia until 1349. The kingdom was an important power in the region, actively involved in Polish affairs and gaining its own metropolitan from Constantinople. Danylo's grandson, Yurii, even declared himself "King of Rus." Some commentators have suggested that Galicia-Volhynia was the first true "national Ukrainian state,"[20] and its extensive ties to western (i.e., non-Russian) culture have made it a source of attraction and inspiration for the more European-oriented western Ukrainians today. In the 1340s, however, Galicia succumbed to Polish attacks and Volhynia came under Lithuanian rule, eradicating the last major political unit of Rus on Ukrainian territory.

WHO CAN CLAIM THE HERITAGE OF RUS?

Before moving on with the historical narrative, it is worth addressing perhaps the most important and controversial historiographical question regarding Kievan Rus: who can claim its mantle? Because Rus covered a large geographical area—most of today's Ukraine and Belarus and large parts of European Russia—Ukrainians, Belarussians, and Russians all claim that Kievan Rus was "their" first state. The critical question is whether Kievan Rus civilization eventually passed to the Russian Empire or remained, latent perhaps, in Ukraine itself.

Most Russian historical accounts treat Kievan Rus as part of Russian national history. After all, the very term *Russian* (*russky* in Russian language) comes from Rus, as does *Rossiia* (the Russian language term for Russia), taken from the Greek word for Rus. Kiev, capital of modern Ukraine, as noted, is deemed to be the "mother of Russian cities." Volodymyr the Great (Vladimir the Great in Russian) is the patron saint of Ukraine *and* Russia. Thus the idea that Kiev is now in a different country has been difficult for many Russians to swallow. Moreover, all of Russia's most ancient cities—Vladimir, Suzdal, Novgorod, Pskov, Rostov, and Moscow itself (first referred to in 1147)—were part of Kievan Rus. In this interpretation, after Kiev fell to the Mongols, people from Kiev immigrated to the north and Rus culture was preserved in those principalities that managed over time to gain some measure of autonomy from the Mongols. By the 1400s, Moscow emerged as the most powerful of these principalities and freed itself from Mongol control. Moscow became the capital of a new Slavic kingdom, which grew into the largest Slavic state, and after the fall of Constantinople to the Turks in 1453, assumed itself to be the "Third Rome," a center of the Orthodox faith. As there was no eastern Slavic state after the 1300s on what is today Ukrainian territory, Russians conclude that Russia is the only possible successor to Kievan Rus.

Many Ukrainians would dispute this account. Hrushevsky, for example, claimed a separate history for Rus-Ukraine grounded in ethnicity, not state-building. Central in his argument is that the people who lived around Kiev were ethnically distinct from those residing farther to the north, and that these Polianians/Kievan Rus, who according to him remained in central Ukraine, provide the ethnic stock for Ukrainians today. Such a view—that the peoples of the various regions of Kievan Rus were not really united into a single ethnic people—is supported by early accounts from the chronicles that point to differences between the more "civilized" Polianians and the more "bestial" tribes in the northern forests, as well as records that document conflicts among the princes and principalities of Kievan Rus.[21] Moreover, Hrushevsky and others have claimed that the more liberal and western-oriented political and cultural traditions of Kievan Rus were better carried on in "Ukrainian" territory under later Lithuanian and Polish rule than under the more despotic rulers of Moscow, who were arguably influenced by Mongol practices and lived in a harsher, less hospitable environment. In terms of religion, some Ukrainian scholars assert that the Orthodox faith of Kievan Rus was marked by independence, "tolerance," "Christian universalism," and "patriotism," as opposed to later manifestations of the faith in Moscow, which were marked by "irrationalism" and subservience to Byzantine traditions.[22] Some also point to the allegedly closer connection between the modern Ukrainian language and that spoken in Kievan Rus.[23] Residents in what is today Ukraine continued for centuries to refer to themselves as *Russes* or *Rusyny*, which is rendered into English as "Ruthenians."

The importance of this dispute is hard to overestimate, as it is central to notions of Ukrainian identity. If the Russian interpretation is correct, it is hard to conceive of a separate Ukrainian history or identity, making Ukrainians, as they were once known, "Little Russians." Conversely, those favoring the Rus-Ukraine not only press for a separation between Russians and Ukrainians but argue for both the longer lineage of the Ukrainian people (thereby making Russians, perhaps, "little Ukrainians") and the "superiority" of "Rus-Ukrainian" culture to that which emerged in Moscow.

How to resolve these claims? Rather than espouse the nationalistic claims on either side, there is a middle ground position that Kievan Rus gave birth to all the east Slavic nations. This means that Russians and Ukrainians (and, for that matter, Belarusians) can claim its heritage. The idea that the Rus were a single people is supported by frequent assertions in the chronicles of the Rus as a single entity and the fact that their common battles against rival tribes

shows that "internal differences could be subsumed and that the main line between 'us' and 'them' lay on the outside."[24] Orthodox Christianity was common throughout Rus and included a common liturgy and similar styles in
both church architecture and icon painting. There was a common legal system
throughout the country. Evidence also strongly suggests there was a common
language. Leaving aside his claims on ethnicity, Hrushevsky himself notes
that Rus had a uniform law, literature, culture, and "complex of customs"
and that despite some political disintegration, "there remained a deep internal
unity among all the lands of Rus."[25]

On balance, one can therefore argue that the Rus possessed substantial attributes of ethnic unity. They were not, in many ways, a modern, self-conscious
nation; at the same time, however, there was no Ukrainian or Russian identity
either. The differences among the Rus likely became more pronounced after
1240, and, as we shall see, by the 1400s there was no question that Russia—
centered around Moscow—and the territory of contemporary Ukraine—ruled
by the Grand Duchy of Lithuania and Poland—were on separate paths. This
theory, however, does not deny that Rus was simply that which existed before
the modern Ukrainian and Russian nations. Just as Saudi Arabia and Egypt
both claim to be Arabic, although the roots of Arab culture clearly lie in the Ara-
bian Peninsula, both Russia and Ukraine can share the heritage of Kievan Rus.

NOTES

1. Andrew Wilson, *The Ukrainians: Unexpected Nation* (New Haven, CT: Yale
University Press, 2000), p. 27.

2. Jeremiah 6: 22–23 and 5: 15–17, in *The New English Bible* (New York:
Oxford University Press, 1976), pp. 812–815.

3. Orest Subtelny, *Ukraine: A History*, 3rd edition (Toronto: University of
Toronto Press, 2000), pp. 9–11.

4. Wilson, 2000, p. 29.

5. Michael Hrushevsky, *A History of Ukraine*, ed. by O. J. Frederiksen (New
Haven, CT: Archon Books, 1970), p. 15.

6. Wilson, 2000, p. 31.

7. Compare accounts in Subtelny, 2000, p. 21; and Wilson, 2000, pp. 31–32.

8. Wilson, 2000, pp. 31–34.

9. The Varangians are also known as Vikings, Normans, or Norsemen and
conquered Iceland and parts of Great Britain, Ireland, and France in the ninth
and tenth centuries.

10. Subtelny, 2000, p. 22.

11. Samuel Cross and Olgerd Sherbowitz-Wetzor, eds. and trans., *The Russian Primary Chronicle* Laurentian Text (Cambridge: Mediaeval Academy of
America, 1953), p. 59.

12. Ibid, p. 61.

13. Hrushevsky, 1970, p. 42.

14. Ibid, pp. 42–43, and Simon Franklin and Jonathan Shepard, *The Emergence of Rus, 750–1200* (New York: Longman, 1996), p. 28.

15. Both quotes from *The Russian Primary Chronicle,* p. 97, 111.

16. Bishop Gautier Saveraux, sent by Henri I of France, quoted in Anna Reid, *Borderland: A Journey Through the History of Ukraine* (Boulder: Westview, 1997), p. 10.

17. Subtelny, 2000, p. 44.

18. Subtelny, 2000, p. 38.

19. *The Song of Igor's Campaign,* trans. Vladimir Nabokov (London: Weidenfeld and Nicolson, 1961), p. 45.

20. Stepan Tomashivskyi (1875–1930) quoted in Wilson, 2000, p. 17.

21. Important sources are M. Hrushevsky, *Istoria Ukrainy-Rusy* (History of Ukraine-Rus) (New York: Knyhospilka, 1954), and Hrushevsky, "The Traditional Scheme of 'Russian' History and the Problem of a Rational Organization of the History of the Eastern Slavs," *Annals of the Ukrainian Academy of Arts and Sciences in the United States* 2 (1952): pp. 355–364. One should note though that the Chronicles were compiled in Kiev, not in more northerly cities.

22. Wilson, 2000, p. 12. See also John Fennell, *A History of the Russian Church to 1448* (London: Longman, 1995).

23. Ivan Yushchuk, "Status rosiis'koi movy" (Status of the Russian language) *Slovo Prosvity* 2 (February 1998).

24. Wilson, 2000, p. 4.

25. Hrushevsky, 1970, p. 88.

3

The Polish-Lithuanian Period and the Rise of the Cossacks

Those who might be tempted to view Ukrainian history through the prism of Russian history should be reminded that for more than 400 years, from 1240 to the 1660s, Ukrainian lands were separated from Russia, which developed its own state under the leadership of the princes of Moscow. During this time, most of Ukraine was ruled by either Lithuania or Poland, which joined together in 1569 to form the Polish-Lithuanian Commonwealth. These states had both different political practices than Moscovite Russia and a more westward geopolitical orientation, and aspects of this heritage are important for many Ukrainians today who want to decouple Ukraine's destiny from that of Russia. Under the Polish-Lithuanian Commonwealth, parts of Ukraine became the dominion of the Cossacks, a group that many Ukrainians claim as heroes. Seeking more self-rule, the Cossacks revolted several times against Polish-Lithuanian rule. Their greatest rebellion, however, ended when the Cossack leadership appealed to the Russian tsar for help. That decision, enshrined in the 1654 Treaty of Pereiaslav, would help link much of Ukraine with Russia for nearly 350 years.

LITHUANIAN EXPANSION INTO UKRAINE

By the early 1300s, there was a severe power vacuum in the central Ukrainian lands. Kiev had been devastated by the Mongol invasion in 1240, and in 1299 its religious authorities moved to the city of Vladimir in the northeast and eventually settled in Moscow. For extended periods of time Kiev did not even have a resident prince. Most Ukrainian principalities were technically under the control of the Mongols, but internal disputes among different Mongol groups prevented them from exercising decisive or lasting control in Ukraine.

One of the first groups to take advantage of this situation was the Lithuanians, a pagan people who lived along the Baltic Sea. After having fended off attacks from the Germanic Teutonic Knights, they turned their attention to the east. In the early 1300s, they occupied what is today Belarus, and in the 1340s, they pushed into Ukraine. Grand Prince Algirdas declared, "All Rus must simply belong to the Lithuanians."[1]

In the 1350s, the Lithuanians gained control over several Left Bank settlements, and in 1362 they occupied Kiev. The next year they defeated the Mongols at the Battle of the Blue Waters, which allowed them to push farther to the south along the Dnieper. By the end of 1300s, their control extended as far as the Black Sea, making Lithuania, today a very small country, the largest political entity in Europe.

Although the Lithuanians did have some formidable military capability, this expansion should not be understood exclusively as a military conquest. The Lithuanians managed to gain control over the region because they were welcomed by local Slavic populations. They were deemed preferable to the Mongols, in part because they were less exploitative but also because they granted local nobles the right to participate in government. Many Ukrainian elites thus willingly joined up with the Lithuanians. In addition, the Lithuanians proved to be adaptable and tolerant. Many converted to Orthodoxy, and Ruthenian, the language of the Ukrainians and Belorussians, became the official language of government. Legal codes were also adapted from practices of Kievan Rus. The official name of the country itself was the Grand Principality of Lithuania, Rus, and Samogitia, and the rulers called themselves "Grand Princes of Lithuanians and Ruthenians," the latter being the designation for the local Slavic peoples. Noting that the nominally Lithuanian rulers over time looked, spoke, and acted much like their Kievan Rus predecessors, some Ukrainian historians see "Lithuania-Rus" as a reconstituted Rus state, not a foreign entity imposed on the local Slavic peoples.[2]

POLISH EXPANSION INTO UKRAINE

At roughly the same time that Lithuanians were moving into the central Ukrainian lands around Kiev, Poles occupied the Kingdom of Galicia, which, as noted in Chapter 2, was after the invasion of the Mongols the most powerful of the old principalities of Kievan Rus on Ukrainian territory. The Polish invasion occurred in 1340 under the rule of Casimir the Great (1310–1370). Polish rule was challenged, however, by both local nobles and the Lithuanians. In 1366, fighting between the Poles and the Lithuanians stopped, with the Poles gaining all of Galicia and part of Volhynia.

The Poles entrenched themselves further in the region thanks to the Union of Krevo in 1385, in which Jagwiga, the 11-year old queen of Poland, and Jagiello (also rendered as Iogaila), Grand Prince of Lithuania, agreed to marry and create a single monarchy. In return for becoming King of Poland, Jagiello had to agree that he and all Lithuanians would convert to Catholicism and attach "for all eternity" his Lithuanian and Ruthenian lands to Poland. Polish nobles found him a more attractive match for her girl queen than the more powerful Austrian Prince Wilhelm, to whom she had been previously engaged. Still, this did not prevent Jagwiga from secretly marrying Wilhelm, who was driven out of Poland by the local nobility. Jagwiga followed after him, but was compelled to return, annul her previous marriage, and marry Jagiello for the sake of Poland and of Catholicism.[3]

Polish rule, however, proved problematic. Intent to spread Catholicism and grant noble privileges only to those who would convert, the Poles were less tolerant of the Orthodox faith and rights of Ruthenians than the Lithuanians had been. For example, in Polish-ruled Galicia, Latin, not Ruthenian, was the official language, and Catholic nobles were given land grants in the region in return for supporting the Polish crown. Lithuanian and Ruthenian opposition to the Union of Krevo galvanized around Vytautas, Jagiello's cousin, who in 1392 forced Jagiello to recognize his de facto control over Lithuanian and Ruthenian lands. When Vytautas died in 1430, Jagiello's youngest brother, Svidrigaillo, was elected grand prince and declared a desire to limit or even break off ties with Poland. Polish forces invaded, precipitating a civil war in Lithuanian/Ruthenian lands that focused on their relationship with Poland and the status of the Orthodox population. Svidrigaillo was defeated and in ensuing years, Polish control over Ukrainian lands expanded. In 1471, Kiev and its surrounding territories were formally incorporated as a common province of the kingdom, ending any pretense of Ukrainian self-rule.

In addition to local resistance, the Poles also had to contend with outside powers that were interested in gaining dominion over Ukrainian territory. To the east, Moscow emerged as a powerful entity, ruling over older eastern Slavic cities such as Vladimir and Novgorod and decisively defeating the Mongols in 1480. When Constantinople was conquered by the Muslim Ottoman Turks in 1453, Moscow took upon itself the role of defender and center of the Orthodox faith, gradually carving out the idea that it was the "Third Rome." Some of the Ukrainian Orthodox population, feeling discriminating against by Polish pro-Catholic policies, turned to Moscow for support. In the

1490s, when Moscovite forces approached Chernihiv and other Left Bank cities under a military campaign against Lithuania, many locals welcomed them. In 1508, several Ukrainian nobles, supported by Moscow, rose up against Poland to defend the Orthodox faith. They failed, however, and were forced to flee to Moscow. To the south, the Crimean Khanate, ruled by the Tatars (a faction of the Mongols) and backed by the Ottomans, controlled the Black Sea coast and periodically launched raids into Ukrainian lands along the Dnieper in order to captures slaves and other treasure. In 1482, they destroyed much of Kiev, apparently in fulfillment of a request made by Tsar Ivan III of Moscow, who had declared himself "sovereign of all Rus."[4]

UKRAINE UNDER THE POLISH-LITHUANIAN COMMONWEALTH

By the 1500s, it was thus apparent that Lithuania was in decline. In 1522, it lost Chernihiv and Starodub, in what is now northeastern Ukraine, to Moscow. Raids from the Crimean Tatars continued. From 1562 to 1570, Lithuania was involved in another major war with Moscow. Facing the prospect of losing much of their territory, the Lithuanians turned to Poland for assistance. The Poles agreed, but only if Poland and Lithuania, which by the terms of the Union of Krevo had a common monarch but de facto preserved much Lithuanian autonomy, joined together as a single political entity. Despite misgivings, Lithuanian and Ruthenian leaders eventually agreed to Polish demands.

The result, created by the Union of Lublin in 1569, was the Polish-Lithuanian Commonwealth (*Rzeczpospolita*). It had a common, elected king; a common parliament (*Sejm*) elected by the nobility (*szlachta*), which was determined by heredity and/or military service; and a single currency and foreign policy. The powers of the king were limited: the *Sejm* was responsible for making laws, and taxes or armies could not be raised without its assent. To the extent that the Commonwealth had a constitutional government, an elected monarchy, and relatively broad political representation (approximately 10% of the population could vote for the *Sejm*), it was a rather progressive system.

The Commonwealth was a major force in European politics. It was the largest territorial state in Europe. It included virtually all of modern-day Ukraine, save for southern regions that were ruled by the Ottomans or their Crimean Tatar allies. The Poles defeated the Russians in a series of military campaigns from 1578–1582, and in 1610, the Poles even managed to have the son of Sigismund III, the Polish king, elected tsar of Moscow, although he was replaced after a nationalist rebellion led by Mikhail Romanov in 1613. The Commonwealth was also a multiethnic state, containing large numbers of Germans, Jews, and Armenians in addition to Poles, Lithuanians, and Ruthenians.

At a time when other states (e.g., France, England, Spain) in Europe were moving toward more centralization, the Polish-Lithuanian Commonwealth was remarkably decentralized. The nobility retained much political power, making it, in the words of Norman Davies, an eminent historian of Poland, a "nobleman's paradise" and a "noble democracy."[5] In addition to electing the king, nobles enjoyed wide privileges in local government, including control of local councils (*sejmiki*) and courts. Many were able to acquire vast landholdings, forming little "kinglets," ignoring rulings made in Krakow, the royal capital, and quarreling among themselves.[6] Eventually, powerful local nobles, enjoying the right of individual vetoes over legislative activity, were able to paralyze the work of the *Sejm.*

The Commonwealth became a classic feudal state, and the rising power of the landed nobility came at the expense of the crown, towns, and peasants. Viewing urban residents as commercial rivals, the nobles stripped them of voting rights in the *Sejm* and forbade native merchants from traveling abroad for goods. The pace of urbanization slowed as townsmen and craftsmen moved to the countryside. As for the peasants, after 1505, the *Sejm* forbade them from leaving their villages without the local lord's permission. They became serfs, little better than a slave, as the landlords restricted their rights and imposed more arduous labor requirements on them. These developments had a pronounced impact on largely agricultural Ukraine. One observer noted that Ukrainian peasants were placed in a "very miserable state," with local lords having "absolute power not only over their possessions, but also their lives, so great is the liberty of Polish nobles."[7] Despite the impoverishment of the peasants, Ukrainian lands, organized into feudal estates, became a major supplier of grain to feed the growing populations of Western Europe.

As for the local Ruthenian nobility, it was under great pressure to convert to Catholicism and Polonize itself. Non-Catholics could not belong to the *szlachta*, and Orthodox institutions of higher learning were closed. Polish authorities even limited the number of Ruthenian families that could live in urban settlements and imposed punitive taxes on them. Polish elites also cultivated a myth that they were descended from the ancient Sarmatians (see Chapter 2), and local Ruthenian nobles bought into this insofar as it offered them the possibility of forming a common bond with their Polish counterparts. One Ruthenian, writing in the early 1600s, complained:

And so, step by step, by their learning they [Poles] enticed all the Rus lords into the Roman faith so that the descendents of the Rus princes were rebaptised from the Orthodox faith into the Roman one, and changed their family names and their Christian names as if they had never been descendents of their pious forebears. As a result, Greek Orthodoxy lost its fervour and was scorned or neglected, because people obtaining superior status in life, despising their own Orthodoxy, stopped seeking ecclesiastical offices, and installed mediocrities in these offices just to satisfy the needs of those who were of low birth.[8]

For example, the Ruthenian Vyshnevetskys became the [Polonized] Wisniowieckis, one of the largest landholders in the Commonwealth and supplier of many of the forces that served the Polish king against Cossack attacks. The importance of these developments can hardly be overstated. Stripped of much of their cultural and economic elite, the Ruthenians became a "leaderless people," a "non-historic nation."[9] "Ruthenian" became synonymous with "peasant," and the Ruthenian language—the precursor to today's Ukrainian and Belorussian—would not evolve into a literary language until the nineteenth century.

THE UNION OF BREST AND
THE POLITICS OF RELIGION

Wholesale conversion of all Ruthenians to Catholicism was both politically and practically impossible. Faced with the prospect, however, that the Orthodox Ruthenians, which constituted upwards of a quarter of the Commonwealth's population, might harbor loyalty toward their Orthodox brethren in Moscow and become a source of political instability, the Polish nobles offered a compromise solution: a new church that would preserve the Orthodox rites and liturgy but pledge its loyalty to the Pope.

This synthesis was put forward by the Union of Brest in 1596, which created the Greek Catholic [sometimes called the Ukrainian Catholic or Uniate] Church. Some leaders of the Orthodox Church eagerly embraced it, as it offered them a means of courting favor of the ruling class and the prospect of gaining admission to the upper house of the *Sejm*. Less cynically, perhaps, one could also suggest that the idea of a Greek Catholic Church offered an opportunity to restore the spirituality and intellectual credibility of the Orthodox faith by borrowing from the Latin West, as well as raising the status of all Ruthenians throughout the Commonwealth.[10] Others, however, rejected it as theologically, culturally, and politically unsound. Two of the four new Greek Catholic bishops, fearing uproar from the Orthodox faithful, immediately reverted back to Orthodoxy. Orthodox Church officials throughout Ukraine deemed it a betrayal. Disputes arose over Church property. Some Orthodox nobles, after having their complaints to the king ignored, threatened rebellion, and the Cossacks took up arms in defense of Orthodoxy. The Polish crown took sides in this dispute, deeming those who rejected the new church as *dysunici* (disuniates) and denying any recognition to the Orthodox Church.[11]

Many responded to the creation of the Greek Catholic Church with polemical debates, rebellion, or emigration; but its emergence also spurred, paradoxically, a religious revival. Brotherhood societies, which were attached to churches in many cities, were a key part in preserving Orthodox culture through educational activities and publishing. Their work helped produce a cohort of young teachers who were more willing to defend their own religious traditions and less likely to succumb to the temptation of converting to Catholicism. The brotherhoods also helped lay the groundwork for the ecclesiastical and educational reforms of Petro Mohyla (1596–1647). Mohyla, an ethnic Moldovan who had been educated in Paris and had previously maintained good relations with Polish authorities, helped broker the compromise in 1632 by which the Polish king agreed to recognize Orthodoxy. Mohyla became metropolitan of Kiev and launched a series of reforms: standardization and updating of the Orthodox liturgy, imposition of obligations of pastoral care on a previously passive and corrupt clergy, and modernization of education that included borrowing from the Catholic Jesuit model and the study of Latin. He founded the Mohyla Collegium, which in effect was the first university in the eastern Slavic world.[12] Although some criticized him as an agent for Latinization, in retrospect his project is understood as one to create or reanimate distinct Ruthenian or Ukrainian traditions, thereby giving Ukrainians their own sense of religious identity, separate from both Rome and Moscow.[13]

In the end, Orthodoxy survived in the Commonwealth. Not only did Mohyla's reforms—which, to be sure, remained controversial—help spur an intellectual revival, but Greek Catholicism lost some of its attraction. Despite earlier promises to the contrary, its bishops were not admitted to the Polish parliament. Its members continued to be treated as second-class citizens, not Catholic enough to those Poles committed to the Counter Reformation. Although the Greek Catholic Church would remain a significant presence in western Ukraine, the Orthodox Church would retain the loyalties of most Ukrainians. Contrary to the spirit of Mohyla's reforms, however, the Ukrainian Orthodox Church never achieved independence; and, as we shall see later, in the 1660s it, along with Kiev and East Bank Ukraine, fell under the control of Moscow.

THE EMERGENCE OF THE COSSACKS

The feudal estate system of the Polish-Lithuanian Commonwealth did not extend to its farthest corners. Along the lower reaches of the Dnieper River, in the so-called Wild Field (*dyke pole*) along the periphery of Poland-Lithuania, Moscovy, and the Crimean Khanate, a new group of people emerged: the Cossacks. Derived from the Turkic word *qazaq*, Cossacks were free men, a collection of runaway serfs, religious refugees, disaffected noblemen, and common

criminals that were beyond the effective control of any governmental authority. First mentioned in 1492 in a complaint by the Crimean *khan* (king) about
an attack on a Tatar ship, the Cossacks took advantage of the richness and
remoteness of the land (also called *Ukraina,* meaning "on the border") to become fishermen, farmers, trappers, and, perhaps above all else, bandits. Often
supported by Polish and Russian authorities, they launched raids to the south
against the Tatars and Turks to win plunder and stave off Tatar raids that
had previously decimated much of central Ukraine. Largely left to administer
themselves for several decades, the Cossacks along the Dnieper formed their
own *sichs* (forts), and by the 1550s, the main *Sich* (open to entry to any Christian male, barred to any woman) was located on an island in the Dnieper River
in Zaporizhzhia (literally, "beyond the rapids"). This *Sich* had its own assembly (called a *rada,* the modern Ukrainian term for parliament) and elected its
own rulers, or *hetmans.*

Cossacks are celebrated today as Ukrainian freedom fighters, acquiring a
mythic status equivalent to that of the American cowboy. Mikhaylo Hrushevsky noted that their actions provided the "initiative for a strong national
movement" and that their courage in attacking the menacing Tatars "gave
new hope to the downtrodden Ukrainian people."[14] It would be inaccurate,
however, to designate them as Ukrainians in the modern sense. First, other
Cossack bands resided in Russia, particularly along the Don River, making the
Cossack phenomenon not unique to Ukrainian lands. Second, the Cossacks
were not an ethnic community. Although primarily Slavic and Orthodox—
indeed, defending Orthodoxy against the Catholic Poles, Muslim Tatars, and
Jewish merchants became one of their primary causes—the Cossacks included
renegade Poles, Moldovans, Greeks, and even a few Jews and Muslim Tatars.
Third, not all Ukrainians were Cossacks. Indeed, few Ukrainians from Galicia, the most populous Ukrainian province, joined the Cossacks. In short, the
Cossack "nation" was "not the same as 'Ruthenia,' either geographically or
socially."[15] As for the idea, popular among many Ukrainians, that they had
created the first Ukrainian "state," their political organization was not similar
to a modern state in many fundamental ways: it had no defined borders, no
written laws, no common currency, no division between the army and administration, and no permanent capital. Although the popular Ukrainian mythology portrays the Cossacks as freedom-loving, if unruly, democrats, other
observers choose to focus on their flamboyant clothing, violence, and drinking. According to one seventeenth-century envoy from Venice, "This Republic
[the Cossack *Sich*] could be compared to the Spartan, if the Cossacks respected
sobriety as highly as did the Spartans."[16]

Without question, however, the Cossacks became a potent military force.
Cossacks served with Polish forces in campaigns along the Baltic and against
Moscow in the early 1600s. Cossack forces launched major naval raids along

the Black Sea between 1600 and 1620, taking several Ottoman strongholds and even managing to burn the suburbs of Istanbul (formerly Constantinople) in 1615 and in 1620. In 1621, the Cossacks rescued the Poles from certain defeat by the Turks at the Battle of Khotyn. Although the Cossacks had bemoaned the capture and enslavement of Slavic peoples by the Tatars and Turks, they proved at least the equals of their enemies in this respect, allowing Paul of Aleppo (Syria) to write in the mid-1600s that "Every gentlemen of fortune owns seventy or eighty Tatar males, and every rich matron fifty or sixty women or girls." They were praised throughout Europe as heroic Crusaders. "The horrible Turk opened his mouth," one Polish writer noted, "but the brave Rus thrust his arm within."[17]

This was all well and good from the perspective of the Polish crown. The problem, however, was that despite efforts to register the Cossacks as, in effect, a branch of the Polish army, they could not be easily controlled and were wont to complain and turn their arms against Polish authority. Significant Cossack rebellions occurred in 1591, 1594–1596, 1625, 1635, and 1637. These uprisings, portrayed by some as an effort to promote "Ukrainian" rights, were spurred by several, at times inconsistent, reasons: Polish hostility to Orthodoxy and the Cossacks's perception that they were the true defenders of Orthodoxy; the desire of the Cossacks to achieve the rights of the Polish gentry; disputes over ownership of land; inconsistent treatment of the Cossacks by the Poles, who, in peacetime, often failed to make good on their wartime promises; and desire for more political autonomy. Although never successful in a purely military sense, Cossack rebellions were a factor in the decision to recognize Orthodoxy in 1632. After a major Polish victory over rebellious Cossacks in 1637, however, the Poles proved less willing to compromise, stripping registered Cossacks of the right of self-administration, abolishing the office of *hetman*, making serfs out of thousands of Cossacks by legally tying them to lands that were given to the Polish gentry, and launching a reign of terror. One Polish noble opined, "The Cossacks are the fingernails of our body politic. They tend to grow too long and need frequent clipping."[18]

THE GREAT REVOLT OF BOHDAN KHMELNYTSKY

The Cossacks, however, were not easily subdued. In 1648, they launched their greatest revolt under the leadership of Hetman Bohdan Khmelnytsky (1595–1657), who ranks as one of the leading and most mythologized figures in Ukrainian history. Born to members of Ruthenian nobility, Khmelnytsky attended Jesuit schools and served in the Polish Army. In the 1620s and 1630s, he managed his family's estate in central Ukraine, avoiding involvement in Cossack rebellions and climbing up the ranks of loyal, registered Cossacks. He seemed an unlikely figure to lead a major rebellion. In 1646, however, a

Polish neighbor raided his estate, beat to death his young son, and kidnapped the woman he planned to marry. Failing to find justice in local courts or the Senate in Warsaw, Khmelnytsky fled to the *Sich,* where he was elected Hetman and persuaded the Cossacks to rise once again under his leadership. Receiving assistance from their erstwhile enemies, the Tatars, the Cossacks marched north to meet Polish forces.

Khmelnytsky and the Cossacks initially had great success. They smashed a Polish force at the Battle of Yellow Waters in April 1648, and throughout 1648, Cossacks prevailed over Polish forces as they marched toward Warsaw. They won much support throughout the Ukrainian countryside, and many peasants took advantage of the rebellion to attack both their Polish landlords and Jews, who were both a cultural and an economic target. According to one account:

> Wherever they found the *szlachta,* royal officials, or Jews, they killed them all, sparing neither women nor children. They pillaged the estates of the Jews and nobles, burned churches and killed their priests, leaving nothing whole. It was a rare individual in those days who had not soaked his hands in blood.[19]

The Orthodox Church sought to turn Khmelnytsky's rebellion into a holy Crusade, with Sylvestr Kotiv, Mohyla's successor as metropolitan of Kiev, declaring Khmelnytsky "the new Moses" and "gift from God" (the literal Ukrainian meaning of *Boh-dan*).[20] By 1649, Khmelytsky had taken control of most of central Ukraine, which was dubbed "the Hetmanate," with Kiev as its capital.

It was unclear, however, what Khmelnytsky's aims truly were. Throughout 1648, he wrote letters to the Polish king listing his grievances but signed them "Hetman of His Gracious Majesty's Zaporizhzhian Host." He failed to press his advantage and drive into Galicia when it seemed ripe for the taking in late 1648. Whereas many in Ukraine today refer to 1648 as a war of national liberation, it is significant that many Ruthenian nobles—both those who were Polonized and others who remained Orthodox—fought against Khmelnytsky. In 1650, Khmelnytsky even turned his forces away from Ukrainian lands and launched raids into Moldova, where he hoped to implant his son Tymish as ruler. Moreover, there were significant divisions among the Cossacks themselves, especially over the question of whether or not serfdom should be abolished (Khmelnytsky, as a landowner, favored retaining it). The Cossack elite, like the Poles, increasingly justified their position by claiming descent from the Sarmatians (as the Poles had also done), making them more of a class than a representative of all the incipient Ukrainian nation.[21] As a price for Tatar support during his campaigns, Khmelnytsky allowed them to march whole villages of Ruthenians/Ukrainians to Crimean slave markets for auction.[22]

Later Soviet historians, admittedly eager to deny any "Ukrainian" content to this rebellion, tended to argue that it was a peasant uprising, grounded more in socioeconomic grievances than nascent nationalist aspirations.

Whatever his aims, Khmelnytsky did not succeed. In 1649, the Tatar khan withdrew his support during a major battle, compelling Khmelnytsky to reach a temporary settlement with the Poles. This agreement banned the Polish army and Jews from most of the territories of the Hetmanate, but required peasants to return to servitude. In 1651, another round of fighting with the Poles began. In a major confrontation—northeast of Lviv near the town of Berestechko, in which both the Polish army and a combined Cossack-Tatar army placed 150,000 men on the field, the Cossacks were defeated, in large part (again) because of the Tatars, who defected during the battle and abducted Khmelnytsky himself. After signing another peace agreement, Khmelnytsky returned to battle in 1652, defeating a Polish force in the Battle of Batih. It was apparent, however, that Khmelnytsky would not be able to administer a decisive blow to the Polish kingdom.

At this point Khmelnytsky turned to a new source of outside support: Moscow. Russia had clear interests in Ukraine: a desire to expand its own influence to the west, weaken its rival Poland, and defend the rights of the Orthodox population. In January 1654, at Pereiaslav, a small settlement near Kiev, Khmelnytsky agreed to accept the Russian tsar's overlordship of Ukraine. Khmelnytsky had hoped that the Russians would commit to confirm the rights of the Cossacks on their lands, but they refused to do so. Instead, Khmelnytsky made a unilateral oath of obedience to the tsar, who now became "autocrat of all Great and Little Russia [Ukraine]." With the Treaty of Pereiaslav, Russia, previously isolated to the farthest reaches of Europe, took a major step toward becoming a great power, soon becoming the dominant force in eastern Europe. Although Khmelnytsky would later be criticized for this move, various interpretations of the Treaty of Pereiaslav have tried to defend Khmelnytsky by arguing that he sought merely a military alliance, some sort of vassalage relationship (whereby the tsar would protect the Cossacks but not interfere in their internal affairs), or perhaps a personal union with a common monarch but separate governments.[23]

In any event, after concluding this treaty, Russia invaded Polish lands. Sweden, which had fought with Poland in the early 1600s, also intervened, seizing Warsaw in September 1655. The Swedes, the Cossacks, and the Transylvanian kingdom (part of present-day Romania) launched a joint campaign to partition Poland. The Swedes, however, also attacked the Russians, creating tensions between the Cossacks and the Russians. Without consulting the Cossacks, the Russians concluded a peace with Poland in 1656, and the Swedish-Cossack-Transylvanian force was defeated. Khmelnytsky, facing internal rebellion among the Cossacks, died in 1657.

KHMELNYTSKY'S LEGACY

Khmelnytsky's death did not end the fighting in the region. It raged off and on for another 30 years, a catastrophic period known in Ukraine as "the Ruin." Fearful of Russia's growing power, Ivan Vyhovsky, Khmelnytsky's successor as Hetman, tried to reach an understanding with the Poles. In 1658, the Cossacks and Poles concluded the Treaty of Hadiach, under which the provinces of Kiev, Chernihiv, and Bratslav would become a separate principality and the third and equal partner in the Commonwealth. This principality would have far-reaching autonomy, able to choose its hetman and have its own courts, currency, and army. Traditional Cossack rights were to be guaranteed, and a quota of Cossacks would be accepted each year into the nobility. The Union of Brest was to be abolished and henceforth Catholics and Orthodox would have equality.

Had this treaty been implemented, most Ukrainian lands would have been free from Russian influence, and Ukraine could have evolved into an independent state. Indeed, its terms did more to provide self-government on Ukrainian lands than any previous arrangement under Polish or Lithuanian rule; however, the treaty never came into force. Even before it was signed, a large Russian army invaded Ukraine. Vyhovsky managed to defeat it, but, accused by some Cossacks of selling out to the Poles, he faced rebellion and resigned and went to Poland in 1659. Khmelnytsky's 18-year old son Yurii became Hetman, and he was bullied by the Russians into signing a new treaty that gave the Russians control over Cossack foreign relations and the right to station troops in all major Hetmanate cities. Fighting between Poland and Russia over Ukrainian lands broke out in 1660. Ukraine was divided, a status that was affirmed by the Treaty of Andrusovo in 1667, by which Russia received the Left Bank and Poland retained control over the Right Bank. The Russians were also supposed to return Kiev to Polish rule by 1669, but this did not occur. Fighting among Poles, Russians, Cossacks, and Tatars continued across Ukrainian lands until 1686, when the so-called Eternal Peace between Poland and Russia essentially affirmed the division of the Treaty of Andrusovo and, in a great humiliation to the Poles, gave the Russians the right to intervene to protect the Orthodox faithful who still resided in the Commonwealth. The net effect of Khmelnytsky's rebellion, ostensibly designed to promote Ukrainian autonomy and unity, ended up dividing Ukraine in two and delivering part of it to Russia.

Given this result, how are we to assess Khmelnytsky's legacy? As noted, Ukrainians are apt to praise him as a hero, a man who sought to unite Ukraine and fight for its independence. This, arguably, contains much mythology, as it is unclear precisely for whom (all Ukrainians? all Cossacks? the Cossack elite?) Khmelnytsky was fighting. We do know that he failed in whatever aim he had, and his decision in 1654 to submit to the rule of the Russian tsar ushered in a new, mostly repressive period in Ukrainian history. Taras Shevchenko, the great nineteenth-century Ukrainian poet, wrote:

> You boast that we once
> Brought Poland to its ruin.
> You were right: Poland fell,
> But you were crushed by her fall as well.[24]

Tsarist Russia erected a statue to Khmelnytsky, which still stands today across from Saint Sophia Cathedral in Kiev. He is pointing his mace to the northeast, toward Moscow, a gesture that symbolizes, for Russian purposes, the great bonds between the Russian and Ukrainian peoples and the fact that, to quote a Soviet-era document, he understood that "the salvation of the Ukrainian people lay only in unity with the great Russian people."[25] Perhaps, however, this design of the statue is better than the original plan, which called for Khmelnytsky and his horse to be trampling a Polish nobleman, a Catholic priest, and a Jew. Indeed, considering that his rebellions led to the brutal deaths of tens of thousands of Jews, Khmelnytsky, a national hero to many in today's Ukraine, is best known among Jews for the Khmelnytsky massacres that bear his name.

NOTES

1. Quoted in Orest Subtelny, *Ukraine: A History*, 3rd ed. (Toronto: University of Toronto Press, 2000), p. 70.

2. Subtelny, 2000, p. 72.

3. Michael Hrushevsky, *A History of Ukraine*, ed. by O. J. Frederiksen (New Haven, CT: Archon Books, 1970), pp. 129–130.

4. Jaroslaw Pelenski, *The Contest for the Legacy of Kievan Rus* (Boulder: East European Mongraphs, 1998), pp. 103–132.

5. Norman Davies, *God's Playground: A History of Poland*, Volume 1 (New York: Columbia University Press, 1982), pp. 201, 321.

6. Anna Reid, *Borderland: A Journey Through the History of Ukraine* (Boulder: Westview, 1997), p. 27.

7. Gillaume le Vasseur de Beauplan, *A Description of Ukraine* (Cambridge, MA: Harvard University Press 1993), p. 14.

8. Ihor Shevchenko, *Ukraine Between East and West* (Edmonton: Canadian Institute of Ukrainian Studies, 1996), p. 118.

9. Reid, 1997, p. 30.

10. Jerzy Lukowski and Hubert Zawadzki, *A Concise History of Poland* (Cambridge: Cambridge University Press, 2001), p. 69.

11. Davies, 1982, p. 174.

12. Converted into a seminary in 1817, the Kiev-Mohyla Academy reopened in 1991 and is Ukraine's leading independent university.

13. Good treatment of Mohyla can be found in Andrew Wilson, *The Ukrainians: Unexpected Nation* (New Haven, CT: Yale University Press, 2000), pp. 54–55 and Subtelny, 2000, pp. 120–121.

14. Hrushevsky, 1970, p. 149 and p. 161.

15. Wilson, 2000, p. 60.

16. Alberto Vimina, quoted in Reid, 1997, p. 31.

17. Both from Reid, 1997, p. 32.

18. Subtelny, 2000, p. 118.

19. Subtelny, 2000, 127.

20. Wilson, 2000, p. 61.

21. Wilson, 2000, p. 63.

22. Reid, 1997, p. 37.

23. Subtelny, 2000, p. 135.

24. From Taras Shevchenko, "To the Dead, the Living, and the Yet Unborn, My Countrymen, All Who Live in and outside Ukraine," translated by the author.

25. Subtelny, 2000, p. 135.

4

Ukraine under the
Russian Empire

After the unsuccessful Cossack revolts of the mid-seventeenth century, most Ukrainian lands fell under Russian control. For a time, the Cossacks enjoyed autonomy, but their last great revolt under Hetman Ivan Mazepa (1687–1709) resulted in a crushing defeat, and Russian tsars gradually strengthened their control over Ukrainian lands and pushed their dominion farther west and south. Because Ukrainians were culturally and linguistically closely related to Russians, Russian tsars tended to view Ukraine as Russian land and Ukrainians were dubbed "Little Russians." The political authorities discouraged the rise of a distinct Ukrainian identity. Whereas some segments of Ukrainian society were well integrated into the Russian Empire, Ukrainian writers and cultural figures such as Taras Shevchenko (1814–1861) also emerged to articulate a vision of Ukrainian culture distinct from that of Russia. Although political conditions under Russian rule were not auspicious for the development of a separate Ukrainian political entity, by the early twentieth century after centuries of Russian rule there was, ironically, a stronger sense of Ukrainian nationhood than there had been in the 1600s.

THE COSSACK HETMANATE

After the chaos created by Khmelnytsky's revolt (1648–1654) and the subsequent period of the Ruin subsided, Ukrainian lands were divided in two. In 1686, Poles and Russians affirmed the terms of the Treaty of Andrusovo (1667), whereby Poland gained most of Right Bank (western) Ukraine and Russia had dominion over Left Bank (eastern) Ukraine and Kiev. The Russian tsar held formal sovereignty over Left Bank Ukraine, but the Cossacks did retain some form of self-government. There were actually three self-governing Cossack territories: the Hetmanate, the Zaporizhian Sich, and the Sloboda ("Free") Ukraine, all pictured on Map 4.1. Of the three, the Hetmanate was the largest and most politically significant.

As a result of the reassertion of control of the Right Bank by Poland and the autonomy still enjoyed by the Zaporizhian Sich, the Cossack Hetmanate of the late 1600s occupied only about one-third of the territory once controlled by Khmelnytsky. Its administrative capital was the town of Baturyn, located to the northeast of Kiev. The Hetmanate, called *Malorossiia* (Little Russia) by the Russian tsars, bordered Russia to the north and east and was more densely populated than the lands to the south. Some of its residents referred to it as "Ukraine" (literally, on the border) the first time such a designation was formally used for this territory. It included 11 major cities and more than 1,800 villages, with a total population in 1700 of approximately 1.2 million people.[1]

The Hetmanate's basic political structure did not markedly change from the time of Khmelnytsky. It was run by the Cossack military and land-owning elite, the *starshyna*. This elite expanded its power by appropriating office-related lands held by the Hetmanate, depriving the Cossack government of income. In return for military service to the tsar, the *starshyna* were exempt from taxation, were given rights to engage in trade, and could distill alcoholic beverages, not an insignificant privilege.

Most residents of the Hetmanate were poor peasants. Data suggest that less than 1% of the population controlled over half the land, leaving little for the bulk of the population. Moreover, the average peasant suffered because he was expected to be both a farmer and a soldier, a problem when military conflicts, such as Peter I's Great Northern War (1700–1721), dragged on interminably. Many Cossacks fell into debt and had to sell their meager holdings to their *starshyna* creditors. Landlords also gradually increased labor demands on their tenants, and the average peasant also lost rights to elect military officers and participate in decision-making councils. Tensions between the *starshyna* and the "rabble" (*chern*) were exploited on multiple occasions by Russian authorities, and many peasants from the Hetmanate fled to the south.[2] In 1692, a disgruntled official from the Hetmanate fled to the Zaporizhian Sich and organized a revolt against the "blood-sucking" *starshyna* in order to "tear away

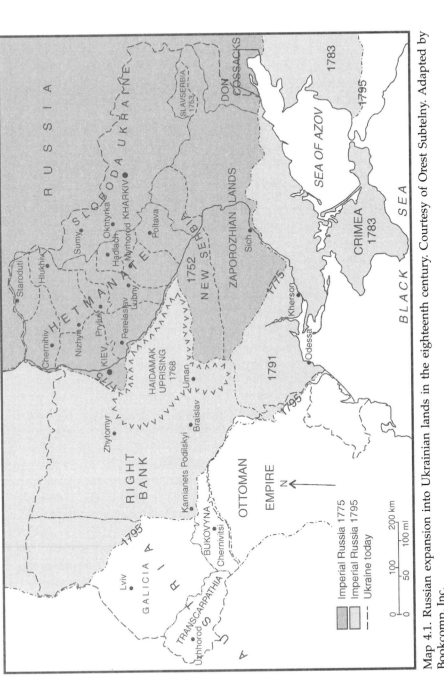

Map 4.1. Russian expansion into Ukrainian lands in the eighteenth century. Courtesy of Orest Subtelny. Adapted by Bookcomp, Inc.

our fatherland Ukraine from Muscovite rule." The Tatars, employed on behalf of the rebellion, turned on the Cossack population instead, however, and this revolt petered out.[3]

MAZEPA'S REVOLT AND THE END OF COSSACK AUTONOMY

The most significant Cossack rebellion in the post-Khmelnytsky period was directed by the Hetmanate against Russian rule. The leader of this revolt was Ivan Mazepa, who was born into a Right Bank Ukrainian noble family in 1639 and had been educated in both Kiev and Warsaw. He served as an emissary from the Polish king to Cossack Ukraine in the 1660s. He was captured by the Zaporizhian Cossacks but managed to win their confidence and, in the 1680s, established good relations with the Russians. With their support, he was elected Hetman in 1687.

There was little to suspect that Mazepa would rise up against his benefactors. For most of his two-decade rule as Hetman, he pursued the policies of his predecessors, issuing more land grants to the *starshyna* and cultivating good ties with Russian tsars, which allowed him to augment his own land holdings to become one of the wealthiest men in Europe. He was a patron of the arts, building Orthodox churches in the Cossack or "Ruthenian" Baroque throughout the Hetmanate. These included St. Nicholas, the grandest church in Kiev (destroyed by the communists in 1934) and a Baroque makeover of the venerable St. Sophia's. He put down the aforementioned peasant-based revolt in 1692 and lent his support to the campaigns of Tsar Peter I (1682–1725, often referred to as "Peter the Great") against the Ottomans and Tatars. He became a close advisor of Peter, leading Cossack officers to quip, "The tsar would sooner disbelieve an angel than Mazepa" and Russian officials to declare, "There has never been a hetman so helpful and beneficial to the tsar as Ivan Stepanovych Mazepa."[4] In 1703, during a Cossack revolt in Polish-controlled Ukraine, Mazepa won Peter's approval to send in his own forces to occupy the Right Bank. Mazepa was thus able to unify many of the Ukrainian lands.

Mazepa's alliance with Peter, however, began to show signs of strain. The Great Northern War, whose main antagonists were Russia and Sweden, began in 1700; and, after a series of defeats, Peter launched reforms to centralize his authority. Much of the autonomy promised to the Cossacks was placed in jeopardy. Cossacks, who traditionally fought on the southern front against Tatars, Ottomans, and Poles, were sent north to fight against the Swedes. Given the superior military technology of the Swedes, the results were often disastrous for the Cossacks. Morale worsened in 1705 when Peter decided to assign Russian and German officers to Cossack regiments. Contemptuous of the "backward" Cossacks, these officers often used them as cannon fodder.

Although both the *starshyna* and average peasants felt the burdens of war, Mazepa himself felt insecure amid rumors that the tsar intended to replace him with a Russian or foreign general.

The final blow came in 1708 when Peter I refused to defend Ukraine against invasion from the Polish allies of Sweden. Defense against the Poles had, after all, been the basis for the Treaty of Pereiaslav. When Charles XII of Sweden diverted his forces from Moscow and entered Ukraine, Mazepa allied with him in the hope that this would spare Ukraine from devastation. In an agreement concluded in the spring of 1709, Charles XII agreed to protect Ukraine and refrain from making peace with the tsar until Ukraine was free of Russian control.

Peter labeled Mazepa the "new Judas." His commanders attacked the Hetmanate's capital at Baturyn and massacred its inhabitants. A Russian reign of terror descended on Ukrainian lands. Fearful of Russian retributions and unsure about an alliance with the Protestant Swedes, many Ukrainians refused to join Mazepa, who had at his command only 4,000 Cossack troops. In May 1709, the Russians destroyed the Zaporizhian Sich (which had sided with Mazepa), and in June of that year the Russians defeated the Swedes and Cossacks at the Battle of Poltava, one of the most important battles in European history, as it ended Sweden's quest to become the dominant power in northern Europe and allowed the Russians to expand westward along the Baltic coast. For Ukraine, the battle was the end of their hopes to break away from Russia. Pursued by the Russians, Charles XII and Mazepa fled to Ottoman-controlled Moldavia. Mazepa died there on September 21, 1709.

After the failure of Mazepa's revolt, the Hetmanate was absorbed into the Russian Empire. Russian troops were stationed on the lands of the Hetmanate, and a Russian became the Cossack's army top commander. In 1722, the tsar set up a Little Russian Collegium, made up of Russian officers based in Ukraine, to share power with the hetman. Meanwhile, Cossack forces were sent to the north to help build Peter's new capital, St. Petersburg. For the first time, Russians were allowed to acquire large landholdings in Ukraine, and Prince Aleksandr Menshikov, a favorite of Peter, became the Hetmanate's largest landowner. Publishing was supervised lest Ukrainian books promote ideas contrary to those found in Russian publications. In 1721, Peter subordinated the Orthodox Church to the state and abolished the Kiev Patriarchate. The Ukrainian economy, particularly export of grain, came under control of the Russian state. Russian authorities supervised the election of new hetmans, working to ensure that the choice would be subservient to Russian desires. From 1734–1750, Russia set up a new body, the Governing Council of the Hetman's Office, a committee headed by a Russian prince, to rule in lieu of elections for a single hetman.

The Hetmanate's incorporation into Russia, however, was a drawn-out process. Although the powers of the Hetmanate were increasingly restricted, the Hetmanate itself was not abolished until 1785. Part of the Russian calculation was to not unduly antagonize the "Little Russians" because Russia needed their support for wars with the Ottomans. Russian-Turkish conflicts throughout the 1700s, however, were devastating for Ukrainians, who were conscripted to fight and expected to provide material support to Russian forces on Ukrainian lands. Whereas Russians rejected appeals that would increase the political power of the hetman and the Cossack *starshyna* (i.e., a proposal in 1763 to create parliament of nobles and make the position of hetman hereditary), Russian authorities did win favor by expanding the economic rights of the *starshyna*, including allowing more labor obligations on the peasantry and, in 1783, introducing serfdom in Ukrainian lands, thereby preventing peasants from moving and tying them to the land and, consequently, to a particular landlord.

Catherine II finished the work of Peter, not only in defeating Ottoman forces in the south but also in ending the final vestiges of Ukrainian autonomy. Like Peter, she was a centralizer, who desired to rid Russia of "feudal relics" such as a special status for the Hetmanate. "These provinces," she declared, "should be Russified . . . That task will be easy if wise men are chosen as governors. When the hetmans are gone from Little Russia, every effort should be made to eradicate them and their age from memory." The Cossack elite were offered a carrot and stick: manifestations of the "disease of self-willfulness and independence" would be punished, but those loyal to the Russian state would be eligible for posts in the Russian imperial government and enjoy the same rights as the Russian nobility.[5] Conflicts with the Ottomans over southern Ukraine and Crimea provided the pretext to abolish separate Ukrainian Cossack military units. Revolt, however, was not feasible, and, given the introduction of serfdom and reforms that exempted the Cossack nobility from military service, the leadership of the former Hetmanate accepted formal incorporation into the Russian Empire with barely a complaint.

What are we to make of the Hetmanate, in particular, of Mazepa? Without question, the Hetmanate period, like Khmelnytsky's revolt, provided inspiration for future Ukrainian thinkers and writers. Taras Shevchenko would write:

Once there was a Hetmanate
But it will not return.
Once it was, we ruled ourselves
But no more shall do so.
Yet we will never forget
The glory of the Cossacks.[6]

Mazepa inspired three operas, a poem by Liszt, a tribute by Victor Hugo, and these fine lines from Lord Byron:

Can less have said or more have done
Than thee, Mazeppa [*sic*]! On the earth
So fit a pair had never birth,
Since Alexander's days til now,
As thy Bucephalus and thou,
All Scythia's fame to thine should yield
For pricking on o'er flood and field.[7]

For many in Ukraine, Mazepa is a romantic hero, and his rebellion and the Cossack Hetmanate an example of Ukrainians' desire for freedom. Others, however, note that the Hetmanate served the interest of a narrow elite and that Mazepa was only a self-interested opportunist, whose revolt could not marshal the support of the majority of Cossacks. Certainly, Mazepa's actions were a failure, and, short term at least, led to the destruction of their autonomy. Longer term, however, the Hetmanate provided more material for the Ukrainian national idea, and a white-washed version of freedom-loving Cossacks would be resurrected by later generations to distinguish themselves from Russians and inspire demands for Ukrainian independence.

RUSSIAN TERRITORIAL EXPANSION

Concomitant with liquidation of the Hetmanate was Russian territorial expansion to other "Ukrainian lands." By adding lands to the west of the Dnieper River and finally wresting the Black Sea coastline from Ottoman control, by the end of the 1700s the Russian tsar ruled over most of the lands that make up contemporary Ukraine.

In 1775, the Russian army destroyed the Zaporizhian Sich, which for more than a century had served as base for the region's Cossacks and a haven for runaway peasants. The Zaporizhians had also offered support to Emil Pugachev, a Russian Cossack who launched a rebellion in southern Russia in 1772. From 1768–1775, however, many of the Zaporizhians served in Catherine II's army, fighting the Tatars and Ottoman Turks. Once these long-time enemies of Russia were defeated, however, the Crown had less use for the Zaporozhians. On June 4, 1775, when most of the Zaporizhian forces were still at the front, the Russian army razed the Sich to the ground. The Cossack leadership was exiled to Siberia, and what is now southern Ukraine became part of the Russian Empire. The Zaporizhian lands were divided among Russian nobility and German and Serbian colonists, and Russian authorities attempted to liquidate the Zaporizhian Cossacks from popular memory.

Meanwhile, the Russians advanced farther south as well, finally realizing their long-held goal of conquering the Tatar-controlled Crimean peninsula. By the terms of the Treaty of Kuchuk Kainarji of 1774, the Ottomans, which had been patrons of the Tatars, renounced their claims of sovereignty over the region. In 1783, Catherine II announced the absorption of Crimea into the Russian Empire. Ethnic Tatars remained in Crimea, but the region was now open to Russian settlement, and the Russians established important military bases in Crimea. This victory over the Turks and Tatars removed a major source of conflict on the Empire's southern borders, making settlement of southern Ukraine possible. It also marked Europe's final victory over the last remnant of the Mongols who had invaded Europe five centuries previously.

Farther to the west, along the Black Sea coast, the Russians also began settling what would be called *Novorossiia* (New Russia). This area had received a sprinkling of settlers throughout the 1700s, but it was sort of a "no man's land," bordered by the Zaporizhian Sich, Poland-Lithuania, the Ottomans, and the Russians. With its victories over the Zaporizhians and the Turks and the weakening of the Polish-Lithuanian Commonwealth, it came under Russian control. Catherine II gave attractive inducements of 4,000 acres of land for Russians (mostly nobles and army officers) who settled there, and they in turn offered a relatively liberal labor regime (two days a week of labor obligations) to recruit a mixture of Ukrainian and Russian peasants to work the land. Along the lower Dnieper River and Black Sea coast, new port cities sprang up, often on the sites of old Greek cities or Turkish fortresses. These included Kherson, Yekaterinoslav (present-day Dnieprpetrovsk), Oleksandrivsk (today known as Zaporizhzhe), and, most famously, Odessa, which became a booming cosmopolitan center composed of Russians, Jews, Ukrainians, Greeks, French, Italians, and Armenians. Grain was the main commodity shipped through these ports, and trade from the Black Sea region increased astronomically in the late 1700s. Landowners, mainly ethnic Russians, who once produced for domestic consumption, now took advantage of Ukraine's rich "black earth" soil and began producing for international markets. Ukraine, once a frontier land, was on its way to becoming a granary not only for Russia but for the rest of Europe as well.

The final area to fall under Russian control was Right Bank Ukraine, which had been part of the Polish-Lithuanian Commonwealth. The Commonwealth, however, had a weak central government, which was preyed upon both by its own nobility and by neighboring foreign powers. Its Ukrainian lands remained unstable throughout the 1700s, where there were periodic rebellions of peasants (largely Ukrainian or "Ruthenian" in origin) against their Polish landlords. Russia, which claimed to be the protector of those of Orthodox faith that lived in the Commonwealth, was particularly effective in applying pressure to undermine efforts to revitalize the Commonwealth. Finally, the three neighboring powers moved in, partitioning Poland-Lithuania in 1772, 1775, and 1795. As a result, Poland-Lithuania disappeared from the map. Russia received most (62%) of its territory and the largest share (45%) of its population.

By 1795, all of Right Bank Ukraine and the region of Volhynia fell under Russian control, with Austria (see Chapter 5) gaining Galicia and Bukovyna. As seen in Table 4.1, by the end of the 1700s roughly 90% of Ukrainian-inhabited territory was under Russian control.

RUSSIFICATION OF THE "LITTLE RUSSIANS"

Russian rule on Ukrainian lands was, for most Ukrainians, repressive. Whatever limited democratic institutions Ukrainians might have enjoyed under Cossack or Polish-Lithuanian rule were destroyed, replaced by an autocratic government in which there was no constitution, no political rights, no elected assembly, and no separation of powers. The Russian tsar was the supreme authority, dominating both secular governmental institutions and exercising control over the Russian Orthodox Church. Local courts were controlled by the landlords, and the police—both regular forces and, after 1826, a secret police—were harsh. Military conscription, introduced in Ukraine in 1797, entailed a commitment of 25 years, which, given Russia's frequent military campaigns and the harsh conditions within the Russian military, often meant a

Table 4.1. Ukrainian Lands at the End of the Eighteenth Century

Territory	Land Area (sq km)	Population
Left-Bank Hetmanate (Russian Empire)	92,000	2,300,000
Sloboda Ukraine (Russian Empire)	70,000	1,000,000
Southern Ukraine (Russian Empire)	185,000	1,000,000
Right Bank Ukraine (Russian Empire)	170,000	3,400,000
Eastern Galicia (Habsburg Empire)	55,000	1,800,000
Transcarpathia (Habsburg Empire)	13,000	250,000
Bukovyna (Habsburg Empire)	5,000	150,000
Total	585,000	10,000,000

Source: Orest Subtelny, *Ukraine: A History,* 3rd ed. (Toronto: University of Toronto Press, 2000), p. 189.

death sentence. Most Ukrainians (this term would gain currency only later, as the Russian authorities preferred to call them "Little Russians") were enserfed peasants, tied to the land and to the labor demands imposed on them by land-lords. Whereas many landlords grew rich on the grain trade, most peasants lived in squalid conditions. Illiteracy rates were high; health provisions were minimal.

Russian rule, however, also had an important cultural component. Because the "Little Russians" were linguistically and culturally similar to the "Great Russians," the government viewed Ukraine as essentially Russian land, al-though Russia did not take advantage of temporary occupation of parts of eastern Galicia during the Napoleonic Wars to try to unify all the "Little Rus-sians" into the Empire. A medal struck in 1793 in honor of Catherine II read, "I have recovered what was torn away,"[8] an indication that Ukrainian lands—from the Right Bank to Crimea—were deemed as historically "Russian," even though they had never been ruled by Moscow. Rather, such an attitude was a clear indication that Russia was appropriating the patrimony of Kievan Rus; and, to the extent that the population on these now Russian lands spoke a lan-guage different from proper Russian,[9] were not Orthodox, or, heaven forbid, conceived of themselves as something other than Russian, they would have to be "Russified."

Russification took on various forms. The most obvious indicator that some of the "Little Russians" were not properly Russian was that they attended non-Orthodox churches. This was especially true in Right Bank Ukraine, which had been under Polish-Lithuanian rule, where many Ukrainians had con-verted to Catholicism (many of these had become fully Polonized) and, more commonly, were adherents to the Greek Catholic (Uniate) faith. Initially, the Russians displayed some tolerance toward the Greek Catholic Church, but, after a Polish revolt in 1830–31 that had some support by the Greek Catholic hierarchy, the Russian authorities took a dimmer view on its activities. In 1839, at the Synod of Polotsk (in today's Belarus), the Greek Catholic Church was banned on Russian territory, and its parishes were transferred to the Russian Orthodox Church.

Russian authorities, however, did not force all inhabitants to profess Chris-tian Orthodoxy. Large numbers of Jews lived in what is today European Russia, Ukraine, Belarus, and Poland. Because of their exclusion from govern-ment service, Jews were overrepresented in commercial enterprises and were a sizable presence in urban centers such as Kiev and Odessa and, later in the 1800s, in the rapidly growing cities of eastern Ukraine. When Russia gained control of the Right Bank, however, it did not want its large population of Jews to move elsewhere in the Empire, so it restricted their residence to the so-called Pale of Settlement in Russia's western provinces, which included much of Ukraine. The number of Jews on the Right Bank grew from just over 100,000 in the late 1700s to over a million by 1880.[10] Although many Jews were very Russified, Jewish settlements (*shtetls*) were able to preserve their own traditions, including use of the Yiddish language. Anti-Semitism, however, was widespread in Russia and Ukraine, and large *pogroms* (violent attacks on Jews) occurred in 1881–1883 and 1903–1905.

Education provided another means for Russian authorities to "Russify" the population. The first university in modern Ukraine was established in Kharkiv (Kharkov in Russian) in 1805 and a university was established in Kiev in 1834. Both were Russian-language institutions. Primary education was also in Russian, which meant that Polish-language schools on Right Bank Ukraine were closed. This hurt Ukrainians because they could not afford to educate their children at home instead. As a consequence, literacy rates under Russian rule actually fell.[11]

Nevertheless, there was no comprehensive program to remake the Ukrainian peasant masses into Russians. Rather, because they were "Little Russians," the assumption seemed to be that they would naturally, through a sort of osmosis, eventually embrace "Great Russian" culture. There was, at least until an explicit crackdown on works in the Ukrainian language in the 1860s and 1870s, no coherent "Ukrainian" policy, let alone a conscious policy to define a modern Russian identity. Thus "rather than trying to assimilate the peasant masses, the authorities concerned themselves with preventing nationalists and radicals [who emerged in the later half of the 19th century] from reaching out to the villages."[12]

As for the elite, including vestiges of the Cossack nobility, they were able to acquire lands and enter governmental service, but the expectation—largely realized—was that they would abandon the "peasant culture" of "Little Russians" and, by necessity, assimilate into the broader Russian culture. Thus although it is true that individual Ukrainians—landowners, bureaucrats, Orthodox Church officials, musicians, painters, and writers—most famously Nikolai Gogol (1809–1852, known in Ukrainian as Mykola Hohol)—were able to succeed in the Russian Empire, they did so as part of the Russian establishment. In Gogol's case, for instance, even though many of his stories have clear Ukrainian elements, he wrote in Russian, making his works, including *The Inspector General* (1836), *Dead Souls* (1842), and his various St. Petersburg stories, classics of *Russian* literature.[13] Through both active policy and what might be dubbed malign neglect, Russian-ruled Ukraine was stripped of a Ukrainian-speaking or Ukrainian-oriented elite. In the words of Andrew Wilson, Russification had sucked Ukraine dry, leaving it, in the first part of the nineteenth century, a "cultural backwater."[14]

UKRAINIAN CULTURAL REBIRTH

Although Russian authorities actively discouraged anything that stressed the differences between the "Little" and "Great" Russians, this is not to say that Ukrainians were wholly unable to develop their own culture. In 1798, the first book appeared in modern Ukrainian (Ivan Kotliarevsky's *Eneida*, a take-off on Virgil's *Aeneid*), and writers and folklorists, particularly those associated with Kharkiv University, compiled Ukrainian folk tales and grammars of "Little Russian" dialects. Explorations of folk cultures might seem innocuous enough, but by the 1830s, thanks to the efforts of Mykhaylo Maksymovych, they acquired more of a political cast. Based on his study of Russian and Ukrainian folk songs, Maksymovych concluded that the two peoples were separate, if closely related, nations, and he broke with the official orthodoxy by using the term *Ukrainian* to emphasize Ukrainians' distinctiveness from Russia. He even signed letters to friends as "An Old Ukrainian."[15]

In the 1840s, the center of Ukrainian activity shifted to Kiev and assumed a more explicit political character. In 1845, a group of Ukrainian intellectuals in Kiev founded the Brotherhood of Saints Cyril and Methodius, a secret society in which members discussed radical ideas such as the abolition of serfdom, freedom of the press, and a free federation of Slavic peoples. Such circles, often inspired by socialism or anarchism, were common in other big cities in the empire. Not surprisingly, they were not looked upon favorably by the tsar, who sent his secret police to infiltrate them and arrest their members. In 1847, before it could engage in any serious propaganda work, the Brotherhood was broken up and its members imprisoned or exiled.

The most famous member of the Brotherhood was Taras Shevchenko (1814–1861), a serf orphan who, by virtue of displaying artistic talent at a young age, was sent by his master to study drawing and attend the Imperial Academy of Fine Arts. Shevchenko, however, found fame as a poet. His first collection of poems, *The Kobza Player* (1840), which combined parts of folk songs, the peasant vernacular, and more sophisticated dialects of the Ukrainian language, is considered a milestone in the development of a literary Ukrainian that was accessible to both intellectuals and peasants. Shevchenko's works, however, also had a political cast, as he portrayed Ukraine as a separate nation that has been repressed by both Poles and Russians. In *The Great Vault* (1845), for example, Poland and Russia are portrayed as crows, comparing notes on how to pillage the land. He resurrected myths about the Cossacks, lamenting their failures to create an independent Ukrainian state. After the fall of the Cossacks, "rue, rue has grown and choked our freedom down," but, he predicts:

That glory will revive
The glory of Ukraine,
And a clear light, not a twilight,
Will shine forth anew.[16]

He characterized the Russian tsars as "executioners" and "cannibals," and in his poem *The Dream* (1844), he laments:

It was [Peter] the First who crucified
Unfortunate Ukraine
And [Catherine] the Second—she who finished off
Whatever yet remained.[17]

For his anti-Russian writing, Shevchenko was sentenced to 10 years of service as an army private in central Asia, a punishment that was the equivalent of
hard labor. Shevchenko was pardoned by Tsar Alexander II in 1857, but he was
forbidden to live in Ukraine. Nonetheless, his poetry, which spoke both for the
Ukrainian cause and for social justice for the oppressed peasantry, made him
a hero and an example for many Ukrainians. What distinguishes Shevchenko,
however, is that for him the definition of Ukrainian identity extends beyond
language. It includes a clear political component—the Ukrainian's love of liberty, exemplified in the Cossacks, versus imperialist Russia's desire to enslave
others. He warns in his allegorical poem *Kateryna* (1838):

O lovely maidens, fall in love,
But not with *Moskaly* [a derogatory term for Moscovites]
For *Moskaly* are foreign folk,
They do not treat you right.
A *Moskal* will love for sport,
And laughing depart.[18]

These themes were picked up by other Ukrainian writers, including Semen
Hulak-Artemovskyi (1813–1873), who wrote an opera celebrating the Zaporizhian Cossacks, and Lesia Ukrainka (1871–1913), whose play *The Noble
Woman* portrayed Moscow as a place of coarse manners populated by primitive, Asiatic people compared to a more pious and purer Ukraine. This play,
not surprisingly, was not performed under either Russian or Soviet rule, but
a similar theme emerges in her *Captives of Babylon* (1902), which is an allegory
on Ukraine suffering under Russification. In it, a character condemns:

Those, who in captivity,
Have learned to use the language of our foes.
How shall such understand their native song,
And how can it be sung in alien speech . . .
To suffer chains is shame unspeakable,
But to forget them is far worse disgrace.[19]

In the 1860s, enthusiasts tried to popularize and spread the ideas of Ukraine's
cultural intelligentsia by forming secret *hromadas* (communities). The first *hromada* was formed by students in Kiev in 1861, and the phenomenon spread to
other cities. Shevchenko even co-founded a *hromada* in the imperial capital of

St. Petersburg and started a monthly journal, *Osnova* (Foundation). Members of *hromadas* wore Ukrainian peasant dress, published books in the Ukrainian language, and started Sunday schools for peasants both to teach literacy and to familiarize them with the works of Ukrainian writers.

These developments were not viewed favorably by Russian authorities, who inaccurately viewed the Ukrainophiles as allies of Polish separatists. In 1863, when Poles revolted against Russian rule, the Russian minister of interior affairs issued an order that banned the publication of educational and religious works in the Ukrainian language. Sunday schools were closed, *hromadas* were disbanded, and many Ukrainian activists were exiled to other parts of the Russian Empire. *Hromadas* were reconstituted in the 1870s. Their members created literary circles and took control of some newspapers to print pro-Ukrainian articles. In 1876, however, Russian Tsar Alexander II issued the Ems Decree (so-called because he signed it while vacationing at the German spa of Ems), which banned the publication of all Ukrainian books, their importation from abroad, and the use of Ukrainian in public performances. Activists in the *hromadas* were fired from their jobs, and many were exiled outside of Ukraine. In 1881, the Ems Decree was amended to allow performances of Ukrainian songs and plays, but works in Ukrainian had to be balanced with an equal number of works in Russian.

REFORMS AND SOCIOECONOMIC CHANGE

After Russia's defeat in the Crimean War (1854–1855), the tsar launched a series of reforms to modernize the Russian state and society. The most significant reform, for both Ukraine and the larger empire, was the abolition of serfdom in 1861. Serfs were peasants who were legally tied to the land. They could not move, and they were economically and legally under the control of the owner of the land. They were not technically slaves, but, as land changed hands, the new owners of the land acquired the serfs along with the land. Although a few serfs, such as Shevchenko, were able to make their way in the larger world, most were trapped into rural poverty.

The abolition of serfdom was, in theory, supposed to create new opportunities for the serfs. Henceforth, they would able to own their own land and be able to move off the land and into different professions. By increasing labor mobility, the tsar hoped to advance economic growth and modernization.

Unfortunately, things did not turn out so well for most of the newly freed serfs. They did not acquire land without cost. They were forced to make redemption payments to their former landlords. Few could gain access to credit to purchase farming equipment, and their meager harvests were insufficient to pay their debts. Many were forced to sell their holdings and high rural birthrates and improving health care contributed to overpopulation in the countryside. By 1900, the average size of a peasant landholding in Ukraine had decreased by half compared with the 1860s.[20] Most of the arable land in Ukraine was held by 5,000 noble estates, and many peasants worked on these lands as day laborers. Resentment against landlords fed peasant rebellions throughout the late nineteenth and early twentieth centuries. To escape crushing poverty, many Ukrainian peasants on Russian lands moved, with the government's encouragement, to colonize new lands in Siberia, Kazakhstan, and the Pacific coast.

Although the lot of the average peasant did not significantly improve, Ukrainian agriculture was a crucial component of the economy of the Russian Empire. Despite occasional strife between peasants and landlords, on the eve of World War I, Ukraine produced 90% of the empire's (and 20% of the world's) wheat, as well as sizable harvests of barley and sugar beets. Exports of Ukrainian agricultural products were central to the Russian Empire's economic modernization in the late nineteenth century.[21]

In Ukraine, modernization was overwhelmingly concentrated in eastern regions, particularly the Donbass basin. Railroad construction was the first stage of industrialization, and Ukraine's first railroad was built in 1865 to connect major grain-producing regions with the port of Odessa. The Russian government invested heavily in railroads throughout the empire in the 1870s, and this required production of iron and coal, which were available in the Donbass of southeastern Ukraine. Foreign capital—mainly French, English, and Belgian—spurred the development of mining and metallurgy in the region. The major industrial center of the Donbass, Yuzivka, was named after a Welshman, John Hughes (today it is known as Donetsk). Most of Ukraine's development was based on raw materials—extraction and basic processing of coal and iron—with profits accruing to the foreign investors or those in Russia that produced higher-end finished goods. Most of Ukraine, it should be noted, did not experience this wave of industrialization, and even today eastern Ukraine—particularly in and around the cities of Donetsk, Dniepr-petrovsk, Zaporizhzhe, and Kryvyi Rih, all of which became industrial centers in the late 1800s and early 1900s—remains the country's most industrialized region.

Industrialization transformed the social and demographic fabric. Although some Ukrainians did move off the land and join the working class, most landowners preferred to exploit peasant workers in their fields. Factory managers therefore had to import labor, mostly from Russia itself. For example, 80% of the workers in the 1890s in Yuzivka (Donetsk) were newcomers from the Moscow region, and more than 40% of all the industrial workers in Ukraine had been born elsewhere.[22] Because of the influx of new workers and various assimilationist pressures, by the beginning of the twentieth century Ukrainian speakers were a minority in the region's growing cities, where Russians and

Jews dominated in the administrative and intellectual professions and in trade. The native capitalist Ukrainian economic class remained small, and there was little that was distinctively "Ukrainian" about the trade unions and workers' movements that were forming in the industrial centers.

Thus despite the real changes that had occurred in Ukraine, especially since the 1860s, Ukrainians remained overwhelmingly peasants concentrated in the countryside. This over-concentration in what is usually viewed as the most "backward" section of the economy, and lack of a native ruling class contributed to what some have dubbed Ukrainians' "incomplete social structure."[23] Nonetheless, Ukrainians—in the cities and in the countryside—would be caught up in a wave of sociopolitical mobilization that swept the Russian Empire at the turn of the century.

UKRAINIAN POLITICAL MOBILIZATION

The festering problems of rural poverty, late economic industrialization, and harsh political autocracy brought demands for political and social change. By the 1880s, the emergence of both a cultural intelligentsia and a small working class created groups that had much more potential for political organization than poorly educated, physically dispersed peasants.

No single organization, however, emerged to challenge the authority of the tsar. Rather, in Ukraine, as elsewhere in the Russian Empire, numerous groups developed to offer remedies to economic, political, and cultural problems. Various Marxist and socialist groups offered stinging critiques of the tsarist political and economic system. Among Ukrainians, the most prominent socialist voice belonged to Mykhaylo Drahomanov (1841–1895), a former professor at Kiev University who was exiled to Switzerland. From 1876 to 1882, he published Ukraine's first political journal, *Hromada*. Although he embraced the socialists' focus on class conflict, he also saw Ukraine's problem as a national one, as its peasant base was exploited by the Russian upper classes. He saw socialism, even anarchism, as a solution to Ukraine's problems, advocating the transformation of Ukrainian lands in both Russia and Austria-Hungary into self-governing communes. Drahomanov's influence on Russian-ruled Ukraine remained limited, but he did become a mentor to many younger Ukrainian socialists in Austria-Hungary.[24] In 1891, young activists from Kharkiv established the Taras Brotherhood, so called because it was formed at the grave of Taras Shevchenko in the village of Kaniv. The Taras Brotherhood called for the liberation of all the peoples of the Russian Empire from political repression. More of a social organization than a formal political party, it established branches among Ukrainian students before it was shut down in 1893.[25]

By the end of the 1800s, underground political parties made their first appearance in the Russian Empire. The Russian Social Democratic Workers Party

(1898) was Russia's first party, and it included a more radical Marxist faction led by Vladimir I. Lenin. In 1903, this party would split, with Lenin's faction called the Bolsheviks, derived from *bolshinstvo,* the Russian word for majority. Both factions of the Social Democratic Workers Party, the Bolsheviks and the Mensheviks (taken from *menshinstvo,* the word for minority), courted support among industrial workers, including those in eastern Ukraine. As noted, however, most of these workers were not ethnically Ukrainian and they did not embrace a separate Ukrainian agenda.

The first Ukrainian political party in the Russian Empire was the Revolutionary Ukrainian Party (RUP), founded in Kharkiv in 1900. Like Drahomanov, it attempted to fuse the ideas of socialism and nationalism, producing, as argued by one historian, young men who had Marx's *Communist Manifesto* in one pocket and Shevchenko's poems in the other.[26] One of its founders was Mykola Mikhnovsky (1873–1924), whose pamphlet *Independent Ukraine* (1900) became a sort of manifesto for the party. Recognizing the power of nationalism and arguing that Ukraine had been illegitimately subjugated by Russia, he asserted that Ukraine faced a decisive, historical moment that required the mobilization of the population to create a "free and independent Ukraine from the Carpathians to the Caucasus." This would not be easy, he acknowledged, but he had faith, that even though "numerically we are small, but in our love of Ukraine we are strong!"[27]

The RUP split in 1903–1904 into several factions. A more nationalist-oriented Ukrainian National Party (which included Mikhnovsky) put primacy on the national question, labeling Russians, Jews, Poles, Hungarians, and Romanians as enemies insofar as they dominated Ukraine. In contrast, the more socialist-centered *Spilka* (the Union) cooperated with Russian socialist parties and criticized the nationalists as bourgeois radicals. Finally, there was a rump RUP core, which renamed itself in 1905 the Ukrainian Social Democratic Workers' Party and combined a socialist orientation with a call for Ukrainian autonomy.

More moderate groupings also formed. These included the General Ukrainian Organization (1897), which originated as cultural institution but renamed itself in 1904 as the Ukrainian Radical Democratic Party (URDP). Like the socialists, it argued for a democratic transformation of the empire, but it had a more conservative orientation on social reform. It allied itself with the all-Russian Constitutional Democratic Party, popularly known as the Cadets. Overall, however, all of the Ukrainian political groupings remained small, with most members drawn from students and intellectuals, not the more numerous peasants or industrial workers.

In 1905, the Russian Empire experienced a wave of revolutionary activity including strikes, peasants' uprisings, and army mutinies. In response, the tsar cancelled the peasants' redemption payments and established a limited constitutional regime with an elected assembly, called the Duma. The however, only had limited power vis-à-vis the tsar, and Tsar Nicholas II dismissed the Duma in both 1906 and 1907 and then changed the electoral law to ensure that the landholding elite would receive the majority of seats in future elections. Ukrainian activists, however, also took advantage of the more liberal environment created by the 1905 Revolution to reestablish *hromadas*, educational societies, and peasant cooperatives. Ukrainian newspapers also appeared, but, because of the small number of literate Ukrainians who could afford subscriptions, only one newspaper, *Rada* (Council) of the URDP, managed to exist from 1905 to 1914.

The 1905 Revolution, however, was incomplete and, by 1908, Nicholas II made several moves to reassert his authority. In addition to cowing the Duma, Russian authorities arrested many leading Ukrainian socialists and nationalists and closed many of their organizations. In 1910, the old ban on all Ukrainian publications was reinstalled, with the Russian press justifying such moves to prevent allegedly Austrian-inspired Ukrainian separatist tendencies. Pyotr Struve, a leading Russian liberal, even criticized the Ukrainian movement for its "lack of patriotism," and the Club of Russian Nationalists, backed by the state, was created in Kiev for the purpose of "waging social and cultural war against the Ukrainian movement and defending the foundations of the Russian state in Ukraine."[28] Ukrainian writers, both those composing literary works and those interested in political polemics, were either forced underground or published, as they were forced to do before, in Ukrainian-language outlets in Austrian-controlled Ukrainian lands.

In the 1910s, the Russian Empire launched a series of reforms designed to encourage both more industrialization and agricultural development. In the words of Prime Minister Pyotr Stolypin, these reforms were a "wager on the strong," and included measures to expand credit to peasants and help them consolidate and expand their land holdings. Stolypin, however, was assassinated in September 1911 while attending, with Nicholas II, a performance ...iev's opera house.[29] Stolypin's assassination launched another crackdown ...ependent political groups, and hopes for far-reaching reforms were ...n 1914, Russia was dragged into World War I, a struggle that would ...elp lead to the overthrow of tsarist rule.

...of the outbreak of World War I, Ukrainian consciousness re-...eveloped. Ukrainian political and cultural expressions were ...t Russia; much of Ukrainian society, particularly in urban ...ussified; and the peasants, the vast majority of Ukrainian-...poor and largely illiterate. Focused on life in their village, ...the Russian Empire knew they were not Moscovites, or ..."did not yet have a clear notion of allegiance to a broader [30] If pressed about his identity, the typical peasant would ...that he was a *muzhik*—a peasant—or perhaps that he was

Orthodox, or simply one of the *tuteshni*, "people from here."[31] In this respect, they lagged behind East European peoples such as the Czechs, Serbs, and Croats, as well as their compatriots on Austrian-ruled Ukrainian lands, who are discussed in the next chapter.

Nonetheless, there was at least an embryonic Ukrainian movement that sought to advance a culturally defined Ukrainian nation, something that did not exist when Russian rule descended on Ukraine in the 1600s. Even though many Ukrainians were not self-consciously aware of possessing a nationality different from that of the Russians, one could see signs of incipient national development. An English writer, traveling through Ukraine in the early 1900s, noted:

> The city (Kiev) and the surrounding countryside are, in fact, Little Russian rather than Great Russian, and between these two sections of the population there are profound differences—differences of language, costume, traditions, popular songs, proverbs, folk-lore, domestic arrangements, mode of life, and Communal organization. In these and other respects the Little Russians, South Russians, Ruthenes, or Khokhly, as they are variously designated, differ from the Great Russians of the North . . . I should say that we have here two distinct nationalities, further apart from each other than the English and the Scotch.[32]

When Russian power was weakened during World War I (see Chapter 6), this Ukrainian movement came to the fore to advance a political vision for a Ukraine free from Russian rule, a development, as we know, that would not be realized until 1991.

NOTES

1. Orest Subtelny, *Ukraine: A History,* 3rd ed. (Toronto: University of Toronto Press, 2000), p. 159.

2. Subtelny, 2000, pp. 181–184.

3. Subtelny, 2000, p. 161.

4. Subtelny, 2000, p. 161. See also Orest Subtelny, *The Mazepists: Ukrainian Separatism in the Early 18th Century* (Boulder: East European Monographs, 1981).

5. Subtelny, 2000, p. 172.

6. From Taras Shevchenko, "Taras's Night," translated by the author.

7. Quoted in Andrew Wilson, *The Ukrainians: Unexpected Nation* (New Haven, CT: Yale University Press, 2000), p. 65.

8. Subtelny, 2000, p. 203.

9. Russian itself was not fully codified until the nineteenth century, as readers of Tolstoy's *War and Peace* will know, the upper classes in Russi

early 1800s spoke better French—regarded as a "civilized" language—than Russian.

10. John Doyle Klier, *Russia Gathers Her Jews: The Origins of the "Jewish Question" in Russia, 1772–1825* (DeKalb, IL: Northern Illinois University Press, 1986).

11. Anna Reid, *Borderland: A Journey through the History of Ukraine* (Boulder: Westview, 1997), p. 67.

12. Serhy Yekelchyk, *Ukrainians: Birth of a Modern Nation* (Oxford: Oxford University Press, 2007), p. 57.

13. For more on Gogol with respect to the Ukrainian question, see George S. N. Luckyj, *The Anguish of Mykola Hohol, a.k.a. Nikolai Gogol* (Toronto: Canadian Scholar's Press, 1998).

14. Wilson, 2000, p. 76.

15. Yekelchyk, 2007, pp. 40, 235.

16. Quoted in Wilson, 2000, p. 91.

17. Quoted in Wilson, 2000, p. 92.

18. Quoted in Wilson, 2000, p. 92.

19. Quoted in Wilson, 2000, p. 98.

20. Yekelchyk, 2007, p. 54.

21. Yekelchyk, 2007, p. 55.

22. Bohdan Krawchenko, *Social Change and National Consciousness in Twentieth-Century Ukraine* (Edmonton: Canadian Institute of Ukrainian Studies, 1985), pp. 42–43.

23. Andreas Kappeler, "A 'Small People' of Twenty-Five Million: The Ukrainians *circa* 1900," *Journal of Ukrainian Studies* 18, nos. 1–2 (1993): pp. 85–92.

24. Yekelchyk, 2007, p. 44.

25. John Reshetar, *The Ukrainian Revolution, 1917–1920: A Study in National-*
        'Princeton: Princeton University Press, 1952), pp. 11–12.
            'an Lysiak-Rudnytsky, *Essays on Modern Ukrainian History* (Edmonton:
                Institute of Ukrainian Studies, 1987), p. 139.
                    d in Reshetar, 1952, pp. 2, 16.
                        2000, p. 299.
                        rov, the assassin, was linked to radical leftist groups, but
                            y also have been in the employ of conservative forces who
                            lypin's reforms.
                            7, p. 54.
                            76.

            en'   cKenzie Wallace, 1905, quoted in John Armstrong, *Ukrain-*
                                    edition (New York: Columbia University Press, 1963), p. 6.

5

Western Ukraine under the Habsburg Empire

Although the vast majority of Ukrainian lands were gradually absorbed into the Russian Empire, most of western Ukraine managed to escape Russian rule. This area, which had been subjected to rule by Kievan Rus and the Polish-Lithuanian Commonwealth, remained a part of Poland even as Left Bank Ukraine fell under Russian rule after 1654. By the end of the 1700s, however, Poland was disappearing from the map of Europe. Much of Poland, as noted in the previous chapter, was taken over by Russia; but Polish-ruled areas of Galicia, together with the Ottoman-ruled region of Bukovyna, were incorporated into the Habsburg Empire, whose capital was Vienna. These regions would be ruled by the Habsburgs for more than a century and were forcibly rejoined with the other Ukrainian lands by the Soviet Red Army only during World War II. Although representing only a small portion of today's Ukraine, western Ukraine's different historical experience has direct relevance for contemporary Ukraine. Because this region long avoided Russian and later Soviet rule, its residents were more prone to develop a distinct Ukrainian identity, and it became the main area for Ukrainian nationalist activity both during and after the Soviet period. Unlike eastern Ukraine, western Ukraine can also claim a stronger "European" identity thanks to its experience under the Habsburgs.

THE HABSBURG DOMINION
ON UKRAINIAN LANDS

From the 1500s until the end of World War I, Austria, ruled by the Habsburg Dynasty, was a major European power. Although Germans were the dominant group within the empire, they were not a majority, as the Habsburgs ruled over numerous national groups (e.g., Poles, Czechs, Ukrainians, Hungarians, Croats, Jews, Italians) and displayed, especially compared to the Russian Empire, a respect for diversity. Thanks in part to prudent dynastic marriages and in part to military conquest, the Habsburgs expanded their rule across Central Europe and into the Balkans.

The Habsburgs became rulers of some Ukrainian lands as a result of the partitions of Poland in the late 1700s. Poland was weak and squeezed among three rapacious powers: Prussia, Russia, and Austria. In 1772, Austria acquired eastern Galicia, whose major city was Lviv (known as Lemberg under the Austrians and as Lwow in Polish). In 1774, Austria acquired Bukovyna, a mountainous, ethnically mixed region south of Galicia with a substantial Ukrainian population, from a weakened Ottoman Empire. Transcarpathia, which had been under Hungarian rule since medieval times, remained part of the Hungarian part of the Habsburg Empire (which, after 1867, was known as Austria-Hungary). In 1795, in the final partition of Poland, Austria acquired the rest of Galicia, which was overwhelmingly ethnically Polish, and merged western Galicia (whose center was Krakow) and eastern Galicia into a single province.

The Ukrainian-speaking inhabitants were known as Rusyns or, in the English version, as Ruthenians.[1] As with Ukrainians in the Russian Empire, they were overwhelmingly peasants, as the urban residents, which made up only 10% of the population, were primarily Germans, Jews, and Poles. Most of the Ukrainian peasants were quite poor, farming on small plots and subject to exploitative rule by the nobility, who were largely Polish. Isolated in largely inaccessible villages and using rudimentary farming methods, the average Ukrainian peasant produced only a third of his Austrian counterpart, and food shortages and famine were common. The partition of Poland also cut the peasants off from markets in Russia, making Galicia, especially its eastern, Ukrainian-inhabited area, one of the poorest regions of the Habsburg Empire.[2]

Ukrainians lacked their own landed nobility or merchant classes. The Austrians brought in some German speakers to help administer Galicia and Bukovyna, but local landowners, Poles and Romanians, respectively, retained much of their traditional powers. Commerce was handled mostly by Jews and German speakers. Ukrainians were largely denied access to political or economic power. The closest thing they had to an elite was their clergy. In western Ukraine, much of this clergy was associated with the Greek Catholic (Uniate)

Church. Many of the priests did not live much better than the peasants and were scorned by Polish nobles, but they had strong bonds with the peasants, and the Church became a focal point for Ukrainian communities.

THE POLITICS OF IDENTITY UNDER
THE HABSBURGS

The Habsburgs, unlike the Romanovs, made little effort to force the Ukrainians to assimilate into the dominant culture. Ukrainians, in short, could not be made into Germans or Austrians as easily as they might be made into Russians. Nonetheless, for many Ukrainians, the politics of identity—dominated by questions of who we are and how we fit into the broader political and social environment—were important under the Habsburgs.

Most of the Austrian-ruled Ukrainian lands remained dominated by Polish culture. Even before the arrival of the Habsburgs, of course, Ukrainians in what is today western Ukraine were under great pressure to adopt Polish customs and culture as the only way to become part of the elite. Primary education, until 1818, was exclusively in Polish, and higher education under the Habsburgs was available only in Polish and German. Polonization thus continued even under Habsburg rule, with one scholar of the period noting that "there was more Polonization . . . after 1795 than there had been in the four centuries between 1370 and 1772."[3] Attempts to establish a Ukrainian secondary school in Lviv failed because students themselves preferred an education in Polish or German, and, in the 1830s, some Ukrainians even advocated adoption of the Latin alphabet as a means of broadening literacy and cultural access.

This is not to say, however, that all Ukrainians were under pressure to become Polish. Most Ukrainians had limited schooling, and their social interactions were largely confined to life in their village. Most of them lacked the luxury of being able to "choose" their culture or join the Polish elite. They were and would remain peasants. Of course, this created resentments and peasant attacks on Polish nobles were not uncommon. Myths of the Cossacks—which had been marginal players in Galicia—also kept alive notions of Ukrainian separateness, and much the Greek Catholic clergy worked against Polonization, which included conversion to Roman Catholicism. Thus although some Ukrainians, mostly artisans, did assimilate into Polish culture, anti-Polish feeling provided a reservoir for the growth of more explicit manifestations of Ukrainian identity later in the nineteenth century.

Another option for Ukrainians, however, was to become "political Austrians," in response to cultural and material opportunities—not forced assimilation—offered by royal authorities as an effort, particularly in the late 1800s, to create a counterweight to the Poles. An example of a Galician-Austrian is

Leopold von Sacher-Masoch (1836–1895), who was born in Lviv, learned German, and became a writer of colorful tales of rural life and sexuality (the term *masochism* comes from his name). Austria, however, lacked the resources and coercive capacity to become a full-fledged "nationalizing state." It was always a relatively decentralized empire, granting powers and privileges to provincial elites. By the late 1800s, however, amid fears of Polish separatism, the Austrians did more to develop a local Ukrainian elite, but this was far more a political project to put Ukrainians into the state machinery than a cultural makeover of the Ukrainian populace.

Ironically, Russia was also a source of cultural attraction for some in western Ukraine. This is ironic, of course, because in eastern Ukraine the Russian Empire did much to combat the rise of a separate Ukrainian identity. Given overt efforts by Polish elites to Polonize Ukrainians, however, Russia offered a means of resistance. By the early nineteenth century, Russia, unlike Ukraine, had a relatively well-developed "high culture" and a literary language. It was also a powerful empire with a history of conflict with Poland. True, Russia could obviously be a threat to any notion of a distinct Ukrainian identity, but some Ukrainians argued that the Russian language was derived from "Little Russian" anyway, whereas many peasants arguably looked toward the savior tsar as one who could "devour the Jews, chastise the Poles, seize the land from the lords and dispense it to the local peasants."[4] More seriously, however, Russian patronage suggested the adoption of Orthodox Christianity, meaning that many Ukrainians would have to surrender the foundation for their identity, the Greek Catholic Church, which had been banned on Russian territory. Austrian fears about Russian power—well founded given Russia's activities in the Balkans—combined with increasing realization about Russia's repressive behavior in eastern Ukraine produced a backlash by both Habsburg and local Ukrainians against the spread of Russophilia.

And last of all, under the Habsburgs there was the possibility of developing a separate Ukrainian or "Rusyn" identity. This identity was difficult to realize, however, at least in the early part of the nineteenth century. In addition to active Polish resistance to this idea, the Ukrainians lacked economic resources, political consciousness, a well-established intelligentsia, and even a common language, as there were many dialects of proto-Ukrainian (initially called Slaveno-Rusyn by Habsburg authorities) in Galicia alone and most people spoke *yazychie* (macaroni), a hodgepodge language with no formal grammar.[5] Discussions over language were particularly divisive. Although some advocated that Ukrainians adopt Russian or Polish as their tongue, by the 1830s, the idea of using a local vernacular as "the" Ukrainian/Ruthenian language was winning support and was given form in the folkloric *The Nymph of the Dniestr* (1837) by a group of writers from Lviv known as the Ruthenian Triad, who were in contact with Ukrainian writers in eastern Ukraine. This effort, however, fizzled, thanks in part to opposition from the Greek Catholic Church, which condemned their work as "undignified, indecent, and possibly subversive."[6] Publication of the *Nymph of the Dniestr* was banned in Lviv, forcing the group to publish it in Budapest. "Rus patriotism," such as it existed, remained centered on the Church, which did not think a Ukrainian "high culture" was desirable or necessary. There was, at best, a dim recognition of the broader idea that Ukrainians under the Habsburgs and those under the tsars shared a common bond and might be a single people or nation.

IMPERIAL REFORMS AND SOCIOECONOMIC CHANGE

The modest stirrings of Ukrainian nationalism in the first half of the nineteenth century were given a boost by unexpected events and subsequent government policies. In 1848, national groups throughout Europe, including Italians, Poles, and Hungarians, revolted against their imperial masters in what was dubbed the "springtime of nations." Poles in Galicia organized and formed a Polish National Council to press for Galicia's autonomous, "Polish" status. This development alarmed the Austrian governor of Galicia, Count Franz Stadion, who decided to create a political counterweight among the Ukrainians/Ruthenians, who composed roughly half the population of the province. With participation by the Greek Catholic hierarchy, a Supreme Ruthenian Council, headed by Bishop Hryhorii Yakhymovvych, was formed to counter Polish influence. The council issued a manifesto declaring the Ruthenians a separate people from both the Poles and the Russians but of the same stock as other Ruthenians in the Russian Empire. The council also asked Vienna to recognize Ruthenians as a separate nationality and to split Galicia into two, thereby creating a more homogeneous "Ruthenian" province out of eastern Galicia. The council also published the first newspaper in Ukraine, *Zoria Halytska* (The Galician Dawn) (1848–1857). These actions are dated by some as the first manifestations of modern Ukrainian nationalism.[7]

The council was a success, at least from Vienna's perspective. Ukrainian leaders did not support Polish calls for autonomy. Other reforms, such as the abolition of serfdom in 1848, the establishment of a Department of Ruthenian Language and Literature at Lviv University, support for Ukrainian-language education and publishing, and the calling for a national parliament also helped win over Ukrainians. Although they were relatively poorly organized and inexperienced, Ukrainians managed to elect 25 of the 100 deputies from Galicia. The Supreme Ruthenian Council even tried to organize a militia unit to support the Austrian crackdown in Hungary.

These reforms and the spirit of Austrian-Ruthenian cooperation would be short-lived. After the various revolutions were suppressed, the parliament was disbanded and absolute monarchy was reestablished. The Austrians also began to reach accommodations with the provincial elites, which, in the case of Galicia, meant the Poles. By the 1860s, Polish had replaced German as the language of internal administration and language of instruction at Lviv University and at high schools. In 1859, provincial assemblies were created, but electoral rules favored landowners, meaning that the Galician assembly was overwhelmingly Polish, with Ukrainians, whose numbers roughly equaled the Poles, typically occupying only about one-fifth of the seats.

Disheartened by their position in the Austrian Empire, some Ukrainians began to turn to the east. Although some, particularly in the older generation, embraced Russophilia—Russia aspired to protect Slavs in neighboring states and was reliably anti-Polish—far more significant was the development of a broader Ruthenian/Ukrainian idea. Ruthenians in Galicia, particularly among the youth, began to emphasize their commonalities with "Little Russians" across the border. Those in Galicia that saw themselves as similar to the "Little Russians" but distinct from "Great Russians" were known as the Populists (*narodovtsi*). Like the earlier Ruthenian Triad of the 1830s, they wanted to develop Ukrainian into a modern literary language. Many looked to Taras Shevchenko for inspiration, both for his literary accomplishments and for his orientation to the peasantry (*narod*). The Populists established their own journals, theater troupes, economic cooperatives and credit unions, athletic groups, and cultural organizations, including the Prosvita ("Enlightenment") Society (1868) and the Shevchenko Scientific Society (1873), the latter of which was formed with moral and financial support from eastern Ukrainians.

Reactions to this nascent Ruthenian/Ukrainian awakening varied. Poles were prone to see it as a conspiracy of the Greek Catholic clergy or, ironically given that many Russians viewed it as a Polish ploy, an invention of Russia to gain influence on Polish territory. Russophiles rejected expressions of "Ruthenianism" as creating an artificial wall with longstanding cultural, linguistic, and ethnic ties with Russia. Austrian authorities, however, gradually became worried both about Polish nationalism and possible Russian threats from the east. They supported the Ukrainian orientation against the region's Russophiles and by the 1890s, over Polish objections, recognized Ukrainian as a language for school instruction. Nonetheless, it bears emphasis that despite their moniker as populists, the connections between the emerging cultural intelligentsia and the mass of Ukrainians remained, at least until the 1890s, rather limited.[8]

While Ukraine was experiencing the beginnings of a cultural renaissance, there were also some signs of economic modernization and urbanization on Habsburg-controlled Ukrainian lands in the late nineteenth century. Previously, Vienna had regarded the region as a source of food and raw materials, particularly lumber. In the 1870s, however, foreign capital began investing in oil fields near the villages of Boryslav and Drohobych. These fields produced 4% of the world's oil on the eve of World War I. Lviv grew in population to 200,000 by the early twentieth century, although it was still smaller than more industrialized cities in eastern Ukraine and provincial by European standards. Ethnic Ukrainians, however, constituted less than one-fifth of the region's nascent working class (numbering 230,000 by 1902), which was mostly composed of Poles and Jews.[9] Conditions in the countryside generally remained poor. Some peasants became radicalized, engaging in strikes and other actions against landlords. Others, sensing little opportunity to improve their lot, simply left. Between 1890 and 1914, 717,000 Ukrainians left Austrian lands for the United States, Canada, and Latin America, constituting the first wave of the overseas Ukrainian diaspora.[10]

NATIONAL AWAKENING: FROM RUTHENIANS TO UKRAINIANS

Toward the end of the nineteenth century, Ukrainians began to experience an important "ideological conversion," as the cultural intelligentsia, which had been growing throughout the nineteenth century, abandoned its previous ethnic self-destination as Rusyns, or Ruthenians, and began using a new moniker, Ukrainians.[11] This new term was important, as it stressed the commonality of Ukrainian-speaking peoples in both Austria-Hungary and Russia. This renaming marked a victory of a more modern Ukrainian identity that claimed Ukraine as a nation like Czechs, Slovaks, and Poles as opposed to previous cultural formulations or national "projects" that had existed earlier in the century. During the 1890s, Ukrainian activists, admittedly a small percentage of the population, developed the idea of Ukrainian independence as the ultimate goal of the Ukrainian national movement.

In Austria-Hungary, unlike in Russia, Ukrainian identity was accepted by the authorities. In 1893, the Austrian government recognized literary Ukrainian, in the form that had been developed in eastern Ukraine by Panteleimon Kulish, as the official language of school instruction in Galicia. By 1914, Galicia had more than 2,500 Ukrainian-language elementary schools and 16 state and private high schools. Education in a standardized vernacular language became crucial in reinforcing national identity and producing a new generation of national activists.[12] Publishing in the Ukrainian language was also allowed, and by the early twentieth century, 70 journals appeared in Ukrainian. Moreover, Andrei Sheptytsky, who was born into a noble Polish family but became leader of the Greek Catholic Church in 1900, endorsed Ukrainian nation-building efforts. This position represented a change from previous ambivalence to the secular national project and reaffirmed the Church as a pillar of Ukrainian identity in western Ukraine.

The Ukrainian national-political movement began to take political shape in the 1890s. Part of this, as was the case in the 1860s, was stimulated by contacts with Ukrainians in the Russian Empire, who could publish freely only in Galician journals. They received a receptive audience. For example, the socialist Mykhaylo Drahomanov's ideas were particularly influential on the founders of the Radical Party (1890) in Galicia, which, by 1895, adopted a demand for Ukrainian autonomy and eventual independence. In 1899, a more moderate National Democratic Party emerged that called for independence as the eventual goal but in the short run wanted Galicia to be broken into separate western (Polish) and eastern (Ukrainian) parts. The National Democratic Party became the most popular party in Galicia. Ukrainian Marxists organized a Social Democratic Party in 1899 to represent the interests of the region's small, but slowly growing, Ukrainian working class. Relying on their economic cooperatives, journals, youth groups, and reading clubs, these parties mobilized the broader masses for the nationalist cause. The Austrian government introduced universal male suffrage in 1907, and Ukrainian parties won 22 seats in Galicia (17 by the National Democrats, 3 for the Radicals, 2 for the Social Democrats) for the national parliament, as opposed to only two seats for more Russophile ones. In the Galician provincial assembly, however, where voting favored the landed elites, Poles continued to dominate, stoking more antagonisms between Poles and Ukrainians. Brawls between rival groups on university campuses were not uncommon, and in 1908 a Ukrainian student, Myroslav Sichynsky, assassinated Galicia's Polish viceroy.

The Ukrainian awakening was supported by an impressive group of intellectuals. Most significant was Mikhaylo Hrushevsky (1866–1934), a Russian citizen from eastern Ukraine, who was hired in 1894 as the first professor of Ukrainian history at Lviv University. Hrushevsky's multivolume *History of Ukraine-Rus* traced Ukraine's history back to Kievan Rus and argued for Ukraine's distinctiveness from Russia. As alluded to in Chapter 2, this was of crucial importance to the entire Ukrainian national idea. As Andrew Wilson writes:

> By renaming Rus as "Ukraine-Rus," the Ukrainians no longer had to rely on the antiquarian romanticism of the Coassack myth as the main foundation of their identity. After Hrushevskyi, they could invert prevailing stereotypes and claim that their culture was older than Russia's—insofar as Russia was cultured at all, it was only so in virtue of having stolen Ukraine's birthright.[13]

Hrushevsky soon became both a cultural and political figure and helped transform the Shevchenko Scientific Society into the equivalent of the Ukrainian Academy of Sciences.[14] It united Ukrainian scholars in both Russia and Austria-Hungary and invited many famous European scholars into its ranks. Ivan Franko (1856–1916), a disciple of Drahomanov, was Ukraine's most prolific writer at the time, composing novels, poems, satires, psychological sketches, and social commentaries. The influence of socialist ideas can be seen in novels such as *Boa Constrictor* and *Boryslav is Laughing,* which depict the brutality in the lives of oil workers. In the 1890s, however, together with Hrushevsky, he joined the National Democratic Party. Lviv State University is named after him. Ukrainian geographers and anthropologists developed arguments to support the idea of a separate Ukrainian "space" between Poland and Russia and that Ukrainians and Russians were racially distinct peoples. In contrast to Ukrainians living in Russian-controlled territory, Ukrainian intellectuals in Galicia adopted more than just a cultural program. They had a clear political agenda, exemplified by the slogan adopted by the writer Yuliian Bachynsky (1870–1940), "Ukrainian, Independent, United State."

This is not to say that Ukrainian activists achieved most of their objectives. Galicia was not divided, there was no Ukrainian language university,[15] and, despite, gains, Ukrainian still did not enjoy equality with Polish in public life and education. The national consciousness of the average Ukrainian peasant was still poorly developed, and socioeconomically, Ukrainians still ranked far below German speakers, Poles, and Jews. Ukrainian nationalism did not have a mass following as did Polish or Hungarian nationalism. The larger dream of unifying all Ukrainian lands had seemed distant at best, and even Hrushevsky in 1906 wrote an article entitled "Galicia and Ukraine," suggesting that the divided Ukrainian territories might be fated to go their separate ways.[16]

Nonetheless, thanks to the efforts of Ukrainians such as Hrushevsky and the relatively tolerant atmosphere of the Habsburg Empire, a politically aware Ukrainian nation was emerging by the early twentieth century in western Ukraine. In 1900, it was illegal in Kiev to publish a book in Ukrainian; but in Lviv one found Ukrainian schools, learned societies, newspapers, cooperatives, and political parties. In 1907, the Polish-Jewish general Wilhelm Feldman wrote: "The 20th century has seen many nations rise from the ashes but there are few cases of rebirth so rapid and energetic as that of the Ukrainians of Austria . . . their unexpected and vigorous growth is mostly the result of self-help and hard-fought gains."[17] The historical importance of the leading cultural figures in the late nineteenth century Ukrainian national movement are reflected in the fact that the highest denominations of today's Ukrainian national currency (*hryvnia*) are graced with a representation of Franko (on the 20 *hryvnia* note), Shevchenko (on the 50), Hrushevsky (on the 100), and the writer Lesia Ukrainka (on the 200).

REGIONAL VARIATIONS: TRANSCARPATHIA
AND BUKOVYNA

Until this point, we have mostly discussed developments in Galicia, the most populous of the Ukrainian-inhabited regions of the Habsburg Empire and the most "Ukrainian" in terms of composition of the population. As noted, much of the rise of Ukrainian nationalism was based in Galicia, which Hrushevsky dubbed in 1906 as the "Ukrainian Piedmont," referring to the Italian Piedmont as the region in the mid-1800s that was the agent of Italian unity and the keeper of the true nationalist faith. However, the Galicians were not the only western Ukrainians.

The case of Transcarpathia or "Hungarian Rus" provides an interesting contrast to Galicia. As in Galicia, rival Ukrainophile and Russophile movements emerged in the nineteenth century, but feelings of local exceptionalism, that the Slavs living in this region possessed a distinct "Rusyn" identity, were strongly held.[18] Although both Russians and Ukrainians emphasized the region's connection to Kievan Rus, "Rusyn" history promoted the idea that the region was ruled by a separate kingdom until the 1400s, when it was conquered by Hungary. Would-be Ukrainians in this region had to fight against concerted governmental attempts to turn them into good Hungarians. They were frequently unsuccessful, as the local intelligentsia was overwhelmingly Hungarian-speaking until 1914, and schools increasingly used Hungarian as the medium of instruction. Hungarian rule tended to be less liberal than that of the Austrians, and elections were rigged against non-Hungarians. Separated from the rest of Ukraine by the Carpathian Mountains,[19] Transcarpathia continued to have less of a Ukrainian identity than other parts of today's western Ukraine. Transcarpathia became part of Czechoslovakia after World War I, and was added to the Ukrainian Socialist Republic of the Soviet Union only in 1945. Even in the 1990s, support for Ukrainian nationalism has been relatively low, and voters in the region approved a measure (not implemented) for special regional autonomy in 1991. Transcarpathia today also has both Rusyn and Hungarian political-cultural movements.

The other Habsburg province on modern-day Ukraine was Bukovyna, long a disputed territory among Slavs, Ottomans, and Romanians. Many Romanians argue that it was historically part of Romanian kingdoms, the outermost defense of Western Europe from the Slavic hordes to the east. Ukrainians, on the other hand, claim that long before it was part of a Romanian-speaking Moldovan Kingdom it was an integral part of Kievan Rus and later the Kingdom of Galicia-Volhynia. The Romanians began to exercise control over southern Bukovyna in 1359, but the entire region fell to the Turks in 1514. In 1775, it passed to the Habsburgs.

Under the Habsburgs, Bukovyna had a heterogeneous population composed of, among others, Ukrainians/Ruthenians, Romanians, Jews, Germans, Hungarians, and Slovaks. Ukrainians made up the largest percentage of the population, although there were regional divisions.[20] Northern Bukovyna, which abuts Galicia, was far more Ukrainian; southern Bukovyna was more Romanian, and the capital city, Chernivtsi (Czernowitz in German), was one of the most multicultural cities in the entire empire. "Political Austrianism" had more support here than in Galicia, thanks in large measure to a larger percentage of German speakers and Jews. Romanians constituted most of the landed elite, and, as in Galicia, the Ukrainians were overwhelmingly peasants. Unlike in Galicia, the two communities were linguistically divided (Romanian is akin to Italian; it is not, unlike Polish, a Slavic language), but they were both Orthodox. Ethnic Romanian nationalism received a boost when an independent Romanian state was created in 1858, but Romanian irredentism was resisted by Vienna and Romanians did not have the same political clout as the Poles. Toward the end of the nineteenth century Ukrainian-language schools outnumbered Romanian ones, and a professorship of Ruthenian Language and Literature was established at Chenivtsi University in 1875. Ukrainian nationalist parties, taking a cue from events in Galicia, mobilized in Bukovyna at the end of the 1800s, winning seats in the 1907 imperial elections. After World War I, all of Bukovyna fell under Romanian control, and the local Ukrainian population suffered as the new authorities adopted the idea that the Ukrainians were really Romanians who had forgotten their nationality and native tongue. Bukovyna (along with neighboring southern Bessarabia) was joined to Soviet Ukraine during World War II. Romania disputed this annexation of territory, but Romania and Ukraine signed a treaty in 1997 affirming their borders. Today most of what was Bukovyna is part of the Chernivtsi *oblast* (region) in Ukraine and has only a small minority of ethnic Romanians.

UKRAINIANS AND WORLD WAR I

Ukrainians lived on both sides of the border between Russia and Austria-Hungary, and concerns over Ukrainians created some tensions between the Romanovs and the Habsburgs in the nineteenth century. Russia, in particular, claimed a special interest in the fate of Slavs outside of its empire. With respect to the Ukrainians in Galicia, Bukovyna, and Transcarpathia, the Russians had a desire to annex these "Russian" lands, eliminating a source of Ukrainian nationalism that they believed was spilling over into Russian-controlled Ukrainian lands.[21]

World War I broke out in the summer of 1914, triggered by the assassination of Austrian Archduke Ferdinand by a Bosnian Serb but more broadly the result of increasing nationalism throughout Europe and a series of entangling alliances. Austria and Russia, which had also been rivals in the Balkans in the late 1800s, found themselves on opposing sides. The Russians, taking advantage of superior numbers, moved westward and, by September 1914, occupied all of eastern Galicia and Bukovyna. German and Austrian forces counterattacked; but the Russians remained in control of Lviv for nearly a year, with Tsar Nicolas II even paying the city a visit.

Many Ukrainians on both sides of the border welcomed the war and millions were conscripted into imperial armies. Whereas one could argue that the Ukrainians living in Russia may have feigned enthusiasm given the broad patriotic mood in Russia at the outbreak of the war, many leading Ukrainian figures in western Ukraine embraced the war as a chance to inflict a major blow on Russia and establish a new political order friendly to the Ukrainian cause. The leaders of Ukrainian parties in Austria-Hungary established a Supreme Ukrainian Council, which declared the peoples' loyalty to the crown and called for the creation of an all-Ukrainian military unit to fight against tsarist Russia. More than 28,000 volunteered, but, because of fears of a creating an overly large Ukrainian force, the army command selected only about 2,500 to serve in the Ukrainian Sich Riflemen.

Ukrainians, however, did not fare well during the war. The civilian population suffered, as Galicia was the scene of some of the biggest and bloodiest battles on the Eastern Front. Ukrainians serving on opposite sides of the conflict were ordered to kill each other. When Russian armies advanced, retreating Austrian troops, informed by the provincial Polish administration about the alleged treachery of Ukrainians, took revenge on Ukrainian peasants and priests who were charged with spying for Russia. Some were executed without trial; tens of thousands of others were sent to internment camps in Austria, where they lived in squalid conditions and many perished. Then, the arriving Russian military units, distrustful of expressions of all things Ukrainian, shut down Ukrainian cultural organizations and deported Ukrainian activists to Russia. Efforts were also made to replace Ukrainian with Russian as the language of school instruction and to undermine the position of the Greek Catholic Church, whose priests were deported to Russia and replaced by Orthodox clergy. The Russian authorities were supported in these endeavors with local Russian-speaking populations and the Russian press hailed the "return" of the "ancient Russian lands" of Galicia and Bukovyna to Russian control. Russian rule in Galicia was so harsh that Pavel Miliukov, a noted Russian statesman, denounced it in the Russian parliament (Duma) as a "European scandal."[22]

Farther to the east, in the Russian Empire itself, there was also repression of Ukrainian organizations, and when Hrushevsky, recognized by then as a leading political and cultural figure, returned to Kiev in 1916, he was arrested and exiled to northern Russia. The tsar's foreign minister stated, "Now is exactly the right moment to rid ourselves of the Ukrainian movement once and for all."[23]

In addition to mounting a military counteroffensive in 1915, the Austrians tried to exploit Ukrainian nationalism to their own advantage. They sponsored a group of socialist émigrés from Russian-ruled Ukraine to act as spokespeople for Ukrainians living under tsarist rule. This group, known as the Union for the Liberation of Ukraine, established a publishing house in Vienna, propagated their ideas among Russian POWs of Ukrainian nationality, and sent emissaries to several countries. It called for an independent Ukraine, albeit one that would be exclusively on formerly Russian-ruled lands, not eastern Galicia. The Supreme Ukrainian Council, renamed the General Ukrainian Council, also put forward a similar program for independence of Russian Ukraine and autonomy for eastern Galicia.[24]

As both Moscow and Vienna felt the strains of war and (especially on the Russian side) ineptitude and casualties mounted, national minorities in both empires played an increasingly prominent role. When the Russians retreated from eastern Galicia in 1915, their local allies either fled or were arrested by the returning Austrians. With the pro-Russian minority eliminated, Ukrainian national parties found themselves in a strong position vis-à-vis Vienna. The Austrians, however, would promise limited reforms only when the war was over. This was not enough for many, as some came to believe that the war offered a propitious chance to gain total independence. In Russia, semisecret Ukrainian organizations agitated for constitutional reforms and autonomy for Ukraine. By 1917, Ukrainian elites in both Russia and Austria-Hungary "possessed a clear notion of belonging to a single Ukrainian nation that was entitled to some form of statehood and to the free development of its language and culture."[25]

In neither case, however, did the Ukrainian national movement have the strength to put forward a demand for independence. The end of World War I created auspicious circumstances for other East European peoples (e.g., Poles, Czechs, and Slovaks) to win a state of their own. Ukrainians, however, would not be so fortunate, as they were caught up in the drama of the collapse of the Russian Empire, the Russian Revolutions of 1917, and civil war.

NOTES

1. Throughout this chapter, I will usually refer to "Ukrainians," unless I am referring to a group that explicitly uses the word "Ruthenian" or "Rusyn."

2. Orest Subtelny, *Ukraine: A History*, 3rd edition (Toronto: University of Toronto Press, 2000), pp. 213–214.

3. Roman Szporluk, "Ukraine: From an Imperial Periphery to a Sovereign State," *Daedalus* 126, no. 3 (Summer 1997): pp. 100, 108.

4. Ukrainian historian Yaroslav Hrytsak, quoted in Andrew Wilson, *The Ukrainians: Unexpected Nation* (New Haven, CT: Yale University Press, 2000), p. 107.

5. Wilson, 2000, p. 106.

6. Subtelny, 2000, p. 241.

7. Serhy Yekelchyk, *Ukraine: Birth of a Nation* (Oxford: Oxford University Press, 2007), pp. 46–47.

8. Subtelny, 2000, p. 321.

9. Subtelny, 2000, p. 312.

10. Yekelchyk, 2007, p. 61.

11. Yekelchyk, 2007, p. 62.

12. For the importance of education and languages in the development of modern nationalism, see Ernest Gellner, *Nations and Nationalism* (Ithaca, NY: Cornell University Press, 1983).

13. Wilson, 2000, p. 109.

14. Serhii Plokhy, *Unmaking Imperial Russia: Mykhailo Hrushevsky and the Writing of Ukrainian History* (Toronto: University of Toronto Press, 2005).

15. By 1900, only about 30% of the students of Lviv University were Ukrainian, and there were only 8 Ukrainian professors out of 80 total faculty in 1911. Hrushevsky's appointment, interestingly, occurred because of a compromise between Poles and the central authorities to create an additional Ukrainian professorship at the university. See Subtelny, 2000, p. 326.

16. Wilson, 2000, p. 118.

17. Quoted in Subtelny, 2000, p. 329.

18. The classic work on Rusyns is Paul R. Magocsi, *The Shaping of a National Identity: Subcarpathian Rus, 1848–1948* (Cambridge: Cambridge University Press, 1978).

19. Today, the region is called Transcarpathia (*Zakarpatia*), meaning *beyond* the Carpathians. This would be the perspective from Lviv, St. Petersburg, or Kiev. From the perspective of Budapest or the local Rusyn movement, it made more sense to refer to the region as Subcarpathia (*Pidkarpatia*), *below* the mountains.

20. Wilson, 2000, p. 115.

21. Yekelchyk, 2007, p. 64.

22. Subtelny, 2000, p. 343.

23. Subtelny, 2000, p. 343.

24. Yekelchyk, 2007, p. 65.

25. Yekelchyk, 2007, p. 66.

6

Revolution and the Establishment of Soviet Authority

Although the years before World War I saw the beginnings of Ukrainian political mobilization, it was the collapse of the Russian and Austro-Hungarian Empires in 1917–1918 that created circumstances under which some Ukrainians could act on their feelings of nationalism. Between 1917 and 1920, several entities that aspired to be independent Ukrainian states came into existence. This period, however, was extremely chaotic, characterized by revolution, international and civil war, and lack of strong central authority. Many factions competed for power in the area that is today's Ukraine, and not all groups desired a separate Ukrainian state. Ultimately, Ukrainian independence was short-lived, as most Ukrainian lands were incorporated into the Soviet Union and the remainder, in western Ukraine, was divided among Poland, Czechoslovakia, and Romania. Nonetheless, Ukraine had been established as a geopolitical and cultural unit, and memories of what-could-have-been lived on, allowing some Ukrainians to claim in 1991 that post-Soviet Ukraine was regaining what had been taken away 70 years previously.

THE REVOLUTIONS OF 1917

Developments in Ukraine from 1917–1920 are at times characterized as the "Ukrainian Revolution." Nonetheless, one should emphasize that the genesis of this revolutionary period occurred in Russia's imperial capital, Petrograd, the Russified-name of the city once (and currently) known as St. Petersburg. Food shortages, antiwar feeling, and simmering resentment against tsarist authority led to street demonstrations on March 8, 1917 (February 23 in the Old Style calendar used at the time). Military units stationed in the city sided with the crowds, and the tsar, unable to reestablish his authority, abdicated the throne. Liberal members of the Duma formed a Provisional Government, and more radical workers, soldiers, and intellectuals established the Petrograd Soviet (meaning "council" in Russian) that vied with the Provisional Government for power. Soviets sprang up in other cities, including Kharkiv and Kiev. For much of 1917, Russia was saddled with an uneasy political arrangement of "dual power" between the Provisional Government and the soviets, and continuing economic troubles, as well as setbacks in Russia's World War I military campaign, contributed to still more popular dissatisfaction.

In Ukraine, one could say that there was "triple power," meaning that the all-Russian Provisional Government and the various soviets competed for power with Ukrainian nationalists.[1] On March 17, 1917, only two days after the abdication of the tsar and a day after the formation of a soviet in Kiev, Ukrainian activists from the Society of Ukrainian Progressives set up their own institution, the Central Rada ("council" in Ukrainian). Mykhaylo Hrushevsky, the well-known historian, returned from exile in Moscow and was chosen as its chairman. All of the main Ukrainian political parties, which were now free to engage in political activities openly, sent representatives to the Central Rada.

The collapse of tsarist authority led to a revival of Ukrainian political and cultural life. Within the Central Rada, parties voiced a variety of positions. The Ukrainian Party of Socialists-Federalists was the most moderate, calling for more Ukrainian autonomy within a Russian state and rejecting demands for seizing large landholdings. The Ukrainian Socialist Revolutionary Party (USRP), which Hrushevsky joined, called for more radical land reform and catered to the peasants, who, above all else, wanted land. The USRP became Ukraine's largest party and nominally was allied with similar Socialist Revolutionary (SR) parties across the Russian Empire. Finally, there was the Ukrainian Socialist Democratic Workers' Party, which made stronger appeals to the working class and included younger radicals such as Volodymyr Vynnychenko (1880–1951) and Symon Petliura (1879–1926), a former theological student turned ardent nationalist. Meanwhile, Ukrainian educational and cultural clubs, economic cooperatives, and newspapers reemerged, and Ukrainian activists tried to mobilize the masses for their cause. On April 1, an estimated 100,000 people marched in Kiev under Ukrainian blue and yellow flags for Ukrainian autonomy. A week later, the Central Rada declared that the All-Russian Constituent Assembly, scheduled to convene the next January, should affirm Ukrainian autonomy. In the summer, when the Provisional Government allowed the creation of national military units, 300,000 soldiers from the old Russian army swore allegiance to the Central Rada, which, in addition to calling for more Ukrainian rights, tried to appeal to the masses with slogans of land reform and the end to the war.

The Central Rada, however, was not an elected body. Initially, its membership was small, composed mostly of teachers, clergy, students, and representatives from Ukrainian cultural societies. It was, in other words, hardly representative of Ukrainian society. It did, however, attempt to expand its base, organizing an All-Ukrainian National Congress from April 17–21, which attracted 1,500 participants.[2] The Congress adopted a resolution declaring that only national-territorial autonomy would meet the political, economic, and cultural needs of the people residing in Ukraine; however, this was not a statement in favor of independence. Rather, the Congress asserted that Ukraine should henceforth constitute a component part of a reformed, federal Russia. Throughout the spring of 1917, the Central Rada helped organize other congresses (e.g., the First Ukrainian Peasants' Congress, the First Ukrainian Workers' Congress), which also affirmed the need for an autonomous Ukraine and protection of the Ukrainian language. By summer, an expanded Central Rada included more than 600 representatives and functioned as the revolutionary parliament of Ukraine. It met at the Pedagogical Museum in Kiev, under a portrait of Shevchenko and an Ukrainian flag emblazoned with the slogan, "Long live autonomous Ukraine in a federated Russia."[3]

The Central Rada's appeals for greater Ukrainian autonomy were rejected, however, by the Provisional Government in Petrograd, which, among other objections, noted that the Rada was an unelected body and therefore could not claim to represent the will of the population of Ukraine. In response, the Central Rada issued its First Universal (the name used by Cossack Hetmans for their decrees) on June 23, 1917, and declared Ukrainian autonomy unilaterally. The Universal declared:

> Let Ukraine be free. Without separating themselves entirely from Russia, without severing connections with the Russian state, let the Ukrainian people in their own land have the right to order their own lives. Let law and order in Ukraine be given by the all-national Ukrainian Parliament elected by universal, equal, direct, and secret suffrage . . . From this day forth we shall direct our own lives.[4]

In many respects, this statement was bluster. The Central Rada had little authority on Ukrainian territory, and relied on a voluntary tax to fund its meager operations. What it meant by "autonomy" was never fully spelled out, nor were Ukraine's borders. The Provisional Government tried at first to ignore the First Universal, later issuing an appeal to "Brother Ukrainians" to not "embark upon the heedless path of destroying the strength of liberated Russia."[5] Nonetheless, the Central Rada was undaunted and formed a General Secretariat (in effect, a government cabinet), led by the socialist Vynnychenko. The Provisional Government, which was on the defensive as a result of defeats at the front by Germany and Austria-Hungary, refused to acknowledge the Central Rada itself, but it did recognize the authority of the General Secretariat in five of the nine regions where Ukrainians constituted a majority: Kiev, Chernihiv, Poltava, Podolia, and Volhynia, all in Central or Right Bank Ukraine. Meanwhile, representatives of national minorities, including Russians, Poles, and Jews, were given over a quarter of the seats in another expansion of the Central Rada.

In July, there were elections for city and local councils. Ukrainian parties did well in the countryside, but they received less than 10% of the vote in the larger cities, which were primarily ethnically Russian or Jewish. Ukrainian parties fared particularly poorly in Russified eastern Ukraine, which, with its relatively large working class, gravitated more toward Marxist-oriented parties. In Kiev, where Ukrainian parties controlled less than 20% of the municipal council's seats, anti-Ukrainian groups such as the Gogol League of Little Russians and the Russian National Union actively opposed introduction of Ukrainian language into the schools. The president of Kiev University condemned what he saw as the dangerous moves taken by the Central Rada.[6] Crucially, however, the general secretariat refused to implement land reform, thus failing to satisfy the main demand of the peasants, who arguably were less interested in abstract ideas such as Ukrainian autonomy and more interested in their individual economic status.[7] By fall of 1917, violent seizures of land by peasants were becoming commonplace, and, despite the machinations for political power in Kiev and other major cities, the lack of order in the countryside remained a chronic problem. Meanwhile, Vynnychenko and other Ukrainian leaders, who believed in the socialist idea of the "withering away of the state," failed to create a strong national army or a functioning bureaucracy. Thus despite, or perhaps even because of, the presence of various institutions competing for power, Ukraine suffered from a power vacuum.

This phenomenon held true throughout the erstwhile Russian Empire, and in November 1917 (October in the old calendar), the Bolshevik Party, led by Vladimir Lenin, seized power in Petrograd. In Ukraine, the Central Rada's military forces supported Kiev's Bolsheviks in their successful battles against troops loyal to the Provisional Government. Afterward, the Central Rada declared authority over all nine of Ukraine's provinces and its Third Universal on November 20 announced the creation of the Ukrainian People's Republic (UPR) as an autonomous unit within a future democratic federation of Russia's nationalities. It adopted its own flag, anthem, symbols, and currency, all of which, it is worth noting, would be readopted by Ukraine after the collapse of the Soviet Union. In effect, then, the creation of the UPR was a declaration of Ukrainian independence.

This led to civil war in Ukraine. The Bolsheviks, who commanded strong support in eastern Ukraine, refused to accept any idea of a separate Ukraine. In December 1917, they organized an All-Ukrainian Congress of Soviets that unsuccessfully tried to topple the Central Rada. On December 25, in Kharkiv, they proclaimed creation of the Soviet Ukrainian Republic, which would be loyal to Lenin's government in Russia. Bolshevik forces from Russia, together with pro-Bolshevik Ukrainian forces, marched on Kiev. The Bolshevik detachments, although not large, were well organized and gained support from many Ukrainians because they endorsed a more radical social program. The UPR was much weaker, particularly as it lacked a powerful military force. Pro-Bolshevik rebellions broke out among some workers in Kiev, and in February 1918, after some heavy fighting that included heavy casualties from a unit of Ukrainian schoolboy volunteers, the Bolsheviks took Kiev as the Central Rada, in a futile gesture, passed a law abolishing the right of private land ownership and fled westward to the city of Zhitomir.

The Central Rada, however, took measures to ensure its survival. Since December 1917, it had been secretly negotiating with the advancing Germans about a peace treaty. The Germans and Austrians were favorably disposed to the dismemberment of the Russian Empire and the subsequent creation of smaller, weaker states along their eastern borders. Because only a fully independent state could conclude an international treaty, however, on January 25, 1918, the Central Rada issued its Fourth Universal, which condemned the Bolsheviks for spreading "anarchy, murder, and crime" in Ukraine and officially proclaimed that the UPR as "independent, dependent upon no one, a free sovereign state of the Ukrainian people."[8] On February 9, 1918, the UPR signed a peace treaty with the Germans and Austrians. This treaty recognized the UPR's authority over Ukraine's nine provinces. Secret protocols to the peace treaty, however, stipulated that Ukraine would deliver food to the German and Austrian armies. Repaying what the German negotiator called the Ukrainians' "practical attitude," the Germans compelled the Bolshevik-dominated government of Russia, which was engaged in its own peace talks, to recognize the UPR, withdraw from Ukrainian territory, and cease efforts to establish a Soviet Ukrainian government.[9] The Bolsheviks, who had presided over executions of thousands of "class enemies" in Kiev and elsewhere, withdrew from Ukrainian territory by April 1918. Many of their leaders fled to Russia, where they created the Communist Party (Bolshevik) of Ukraine.

THE GERMAN OCCUPATION
AND THE HETMANATE

The UPR thus returned with German and Austrian assistance to rule over Ukraine, although Hrushevsky assured Ukrainians that German troops would "remain only so long as they will be needed by our government for the liberation of Ukraine."[10] Despite its struggles with the Bolsheviks, however, the UPR remained socialist in orientation. It intended to enforce its decrees mandating an eight-hour working day and banning private land ownership. The latter, which had been hastily adopted in February 1918, was not popular with either landowners, for obvious reasons, or with peasants, who wanted the large estates to be distributed to individual households instead of being nationalized by the state.[11]

This leftward orientation also alienated the conservative German military administration in Ukraine, which was an important patron of the UPR. The UPR was weak, a "virtual state,"[12] lacking the administration to enforce laws, maintain order, and, vitally to the Germans, provide the grain to feed the German army and to export to Germany. By April 1918, the Germans had taken control of the railways, reversed the UPR's decree on land ownership, and introduced martial law. At the same time, the Central Rada signed an agreement with the Germans to provide Germany and Austria-Hungary with, among other items, 1 million tons of grain by the end of July. Vynnychenko lamented that the UPR had forgotten the proverb that warns "you must sing the tune of the person on whose wagon you ride."[13]

It was clear, however, that the Central Rada lacked the means to implement this agreement. As a backup plan, the Germans began meeting with Pavlo Skoropadsky (1873–1945), a Russian-speaking, former tsarist general who was a descendent of an eighteenth-century Cossack hetman. The Germans discussed with Skoropadsky the possibility of creating a Ukrainian monarchy and offered him the throne. Skoropadsky agreed, and on April 29, 1918, the conservative Congress of Ukrainian Landowners proclaimed Skoropadsky Hetman of Ukraine, thereby reanimating the old Cossack title. That same day, the Central Rada adopted a constitution and elected Hrushevsky president of the UPR. A day later, however, the UPR was no more and Hrushevsky had to be smuggled out of Kiev on foot by sympathetic soldiers.

Thanks to German support and the weakness of the UPR, Skoropadsky came to power largely peacefully, with a small regiment loyal to the UPR offering only slight resistance. Skoropadsky, however, remains a controversial figure in Ukrainian history. Some are prone to dismiss him as a German puppet, a reactionary figure loyal to the old social order of tsarist Russia. In part, of course, this is true: Skoropadsky relied on German support and reestablished much of the old tsarist administrative structure. He banned strikes and resurrected censorship. Most of his administrators did not speak Ukrainian, and many favored reestablishing Ukraine within a renewed Russian state. All the major political parties from the Central Rada refused to cooperate with Skoropadsky, deeming his rule illegitimate.

Recent scholarship, however, paints a more sympathetic portrait of Skoropadsky. Although he was not an ethnic Ukrainian nationalist, he was, in his own way, a Ukrainian nation and state-builder, one who "strove to introduce a new concept of the Ukrainian nation that was founded not on knowledge of the Ukrainian language, but on loyalty to the Ukrainian state."[14] Paradoxically, under his reign Ukrainian culture and education advanced, as the government established more than 150 high schools with instruction in Ukrainian and two new universities. Skoropadsky's government established the Ukrainian Academy of Sciences, the National Library, State Archive, the Ukrainian Academy of Fine Arts, and other cultural institutions, many of which are still in existence. In foreign policy, Ukraine established diplomatic relations with a number of European states. In this respect, Skoropadsky did much to establish the legitimacy of the idea of separate Ukrainian statehood.

His rule, however, was short-lived. German expeditions to seize grain led to resentment and peasant rebellions in the countryside. Political opposition consolidated in the Ukrainian National Union, which elected Vynnychenko as its leader. By the fall of 1918, German defeat in World War I seemed imminent, and Skoropadsky's various measures to preserve his power—including negotiations with the Ukrainian National Union and, later, appointment of a pro-Russian cabinet to appease the Western powers who favored a non-Bolshevik Russia—failed. Vynnychenko and Petliura organized a committee, called the Directory after the French revolutionary government of 1795–1799, to overthrow the Hetmanate. Thousands of peasants volunteered to fight for the Directory, and many of the Hetmanate's units defected, sensing that the tide had turned. On December 14, 1918, the Germans left Kiev, and Skoropadsky, disguised as a wounded German officer, fled with them.

DEVELOPMENTS IN WESTERN UKRAINE

As noted in the previous chapter, parts of western Ukraine, including the historical region of Galicia, were part of the Austro-Hungarian (Habsburg) Empire. Thus as the Russian Empire imploded, Ukrainians in these lands were, at most, sympathetic observers to the efforts of Ukrainians to free themselves from Russian rule.

Toward the end of 1918, however, as the Habsburgs faced final defeat in World War I, the authorities offered concessions to the empire's various minority groups, pledging, for example, in October 1918, to create a free federation of peoples. On October 18, Ukrainian deputies of both the imperial and provincial parliaments, together with representatives of major political parties, established the Ukrainian National Council in Lviv. On November 1, with the end of the war only days away, the Ukrainian National Council declared the establishment of an independent Ukrainian state, which was named the Western Ukrainian People's Republic (WUPR).

The WUPR, however, was opposed by Poland, which had its own territorial and national aspirations. Poles claimed all of Galicia, and they were the largest group in the major cities, including Lviv. Street fighting between Poles and Ukrainians broke out in November, and on November 22, the Poles forced the nascent Western Ukrainian government out of Lviv. This conflict turned into a full-fledged Ukrainian-Polish war, which later turned into a Soviet-Polish war. At roughly the same time, the Ukrainian-populated regions of Bukovyna and Transcarpathia were transferred to an enlarged Romanian state and a new country, Czechoslovakia, respectively. This arrangement was confirmed by the June 1919 Treaty of Versailles.

The WUPR, however, did not simply disappear. Thanks in large measure to a relatively liberal political environment under the Austrians, Ukrainian civil society was well organized and unified in the struggle against the Poles, its long-time rival. The WUPR had its own national army, the Ukrainian Galician Army. It included former German and Austrian officers and, interestingly, its two commanders-in-chief were former Russian generals.

The WUPR also looked to the east for support, seeking to unite with the emerging Ukrainian state in former tsarist Russian lands. The Hetmanate had already collapsed, meaning that the WUPR, which, in key respects, had a more conservative orientation, had to turn to the leftist-dominated Directory, which had reanimated the UPR upon disposing the Hetmanate. On January 22, 1919, the two Ukrainian states formally unified, making the WUPR the western province of the larger UPR. In fact, however, in large part due to the military situation, the western regions retained their autonomy and their laws.

This Ukrainian state, however, was "proclaimed to the sound of Bolshevik guns in the east and Polish guns to the west"[15] and never had a good chance of survival. In the west, the Ukrainian Galician Army mounted a counteroffensive against the Poles, but their efforts were unsuccessful. In part, this was because the Poles managed to secure western support for their cause, as the victorious Allies chose to back the Poles as a counterweight to Germany and a Bolshevik Russia. Although the British were more favorably inclined to the Ukrainians, the Americans had the decisive vote. Arnold Margolin, head of the Ukrainian delegation at the post-World War I Paris peace talks, noted that the American side was "as uninformed about Ukrainians as the average European is about numerous African tribes."[16] The Americans sided with the Poles. Self-determination, one of the principles of U.S. President Woodrow Wilson, was thus not applied to Ukrainian lands.

To defeat the Ukrainians, the Poles called on a 100,000 strong army that was trained and equipped in France and sent east to fight Bolsheviks but, instead, was put to use against Ukrainian forces. Peasant rebellions, fueled by the authorities' failure to enact land reform, together with a pro-Bolshevik uprising in Drohobych, western Ukraine's main industrial center, also undermined the WUPR. In July 1919, a month after the Treaty of Versailles gave "temporary" control over Galicia to the Poles, what remained of the Ukrainian Galician Army crossed the Zbruch River, the traditional boundary between Austria-Hungary and Russia.

The western Ukrainians tried to turn to the leaders of the UPR for assistance, but to little avail. The UPR, as noted later, was on the retreat in its own battles against various military forces. The two Ukrainian governments also had different geopolitical orientations. Whereas western Ukrainians hoped their compatriots to the east would help them in their struggle with the Poles, leaders of the Directory, which controlled the UPR, considered Poles allies in their own struggles with the Russian-dominated Bolsheviks. The Ukrainian Galician Army did fight alongside the forces of the Directory through most of 1919, even occupying Kiev at the end of August. Amid heavy fighting with both Red (communist) and White (anticommunist) armies as part of the larger "Russian" civil war and the onslaught of deadly typhus epidemics, however, the Ukrainian Galician Army surrendered to White forces in November. Meanwhile, Polish forces, which had made a separate peace with the Ukrainian Directory, advanced farther into western Ukraine, occupying the provinces of Volhynia and Podolia.

Although fighting between Polish and Soviet forces occurred in western Ukraine in 1920 and Polish forces even reached Kiev in May, the WUPR could not be resurrected. Soviet forces eventually pushed the Polish forces back, and by the terms of the Treaty of Riga of March 1921, the Soviets recognized Polish control over Galicia and western Volhynia.

THE DIRECTORY AND CIVIL WAR

When the Directory entered Kiev in December 1918, it reanimated the UPR; however, this incarnation of the UPR was different from the previous one. The Central Rada was not reconvened and Hrushevsky was not invited back to play a political role. Instead, the five-person Directory assumed supreme executive and legislative authority, operating like a modern-day military junta. The Directory itself was dominated by two men from the Ukrainian Social Democratic Workers' Party: Vynnychenko, a committed socialist who had served in the earlier version of the UPR, and Petliura, who had a more nationalistic orientation.

Vynnychenko attempted to steer the Directory to the left, proposing the confiscation of large estates and worker's control of factories. In January 1919, the Directory convened a Labor Congress in Kiev, which acted as an unelected parliament and approved the government's measures. The Directory established Ukrainian as the official language and proclaimed the autocephaly (independence) of the Orthodox Church in Ukraine, which had been a part of the Russian Orthodox Church. As noted, in January 1919, the UPR organized a ceremony in Kiev that formally joined together the western and eastern Ukrainian republics.

The main problem for the Directory, like the WUPR, was its precarious military situation. The situation in Ukraine was unsettled, even chaotic. Peasant armies, led by self-proclaimed Hetmans or *otamany* (some of whom, at least according to legend, were female), controlled large parts of the countryside. The largest force was controlled by Nestor Makhno (1884–1934), an anarchist, who, famously, issued his own coinage but printed a disclaimer that allowed anyone for counterfeit it.[17] French forces, intent on ridding Russia of Bolshevism, landed in Odessa in support of White (anticommunist) forces. Last of all, and perhaps most seriously, the Bolsheviks had regrouped and were invading from the north. Vynnychenko tried unsuccessfully to negotiate with the Bolsheviks. The largely peasant forces that had supported the Directory against the Hetmanate evaporated back to the villages. Kiev fell to the Bolsheviks in February 1919—an event vividly recounted in *The White Guard* (1924), a novel by Kiev-born writer Mikhail Bulgakov (1891–1940)—as Ukraine itself became a prime battlefield in the Russian civil war, a moniker that fails to capture the fact that many of the forces involved in this struggle were not Russian.

After the fall of Kiev, Petliura became chairman of the Directory. In an effort to win favor with the allies, Petliura resigned from the Social Democratic Workers' Party and created a nonsocialist cabinet. This arrangement, however, failed to convince the Allies, who saw the White forces as the better bet. By April 1919, at about the same time that Polish forces were moving in from the west and pushing the Ukrainian Galician Army to the east, the Directory was in full retreat to the west, losing control over most Ukrainian lands to Bolshevik and White forces. Hrushevsky, among others, advocated negotiations with the Bolsheviks to preserve some type of Ukrainian autonomy. Petliura, who retains a reputation as a bandit among Russians to this day, refused this course.

The Bolsheviks set up the Ukrainian Socialist Soviet Republic to administer territories under control of the Red Army. It reestablished Russian as the language of education and administration. It sent out armed detachments to collect grain from the countryside and began forcing peasants into state-run collective farms. In cities, the secret police, the Cheka, ferreted out alleged counterrevolutionaries and class enemies. Bolshevik rule was unpopular in many quarters, especially in the countryside. Peasants wanted land of their own, not collective farms, and peasant rebellions—directed, at various times and places, against foreign forces, Ukrainian nationalists, Bolsheviks, and Whites—became even more widespread.

Amid the chaos, anti-Jewish pogroms occurred throughout Ukraine in 1919, claiming more than 30,000 lives and ranking, in pre-Nazi Europe, as the greatest modern mass murder of Jews. All sides—Whites, Reds, *otamans*, the Directory—were guilty of atrocities. Despite the contention that the UPR had a "good record of treating its national minorities" and was the first modern state to establishment a ministry of Jewish affairs and guarantee the rights of Jewish culture, evidence indicates that a large number of pogroms were carried out by the forces of the Directory under Petliura, which puts him, together with Khmelnytsky, into the pantheon of Ukrainian historical figures condemned by world Jewry. Petliura would later be assassinated in Paris in 1926 by a Jew who had served with the Red Army. Despite standing over Petliura's body with a smoking gun, he was acquitted after a three-week trial.[18]

The Bolsheviks, however, could not maintain control over Kiev. By August, a combination of White forces from the south and Petliura, assisted by the Ukrainian Galician Army, from the west, occupied Kiev. The Whites, intent on reestablishing a unified Russia, had no intention of recognizing a separate Ukrainian state. They ordered the Galician forces, which they viewed as foreigners, to withdraw. They did so, and the Whites tried to undo the actions of the Bolsheviks by imposing aspects of the prerevolutionary social order on lands under their control. This included bans on publications in Ukrainian and transfer of lands back to their former owners.

White rule proved no more popular than the Bolsheviks, and the Directory declared war on the Whites. The Ukrainian forces, however, were short on guns and then decimated by disease. In November, as noted previously, the Ukrainian Galician Army surrendered to the Whites. At the same time, Petliura, desperate to fight off Russian forces, reached an agreement with the Poles, thereby ensuring a rupture between western and eastern forces.

As Polish forces advanced into formerly Russian-held lands, the Directory disintegrated. It was attacked by peasant bands, and its treasury was stolen. Petliura, who had proclaimed himself dictator, fled to Warsaw. Meanwhile, farther to the east, Bolshevik forces, blessed by superior organization, were beating back the Whites. In December 1919, they took Kiev for the third time. Learning from past mistakes, this time they were not so harsh: Lenin agreed to policies that would recognize the Ukrainian language and be less forceful vis-à-vis the peasantry, granting them individual allotments of land. Ukrainian Bolsheviks also formed an alliance with a splinter group from the Ukrainian Socialist Revolutionary Party, giving the Bolshevik-run government more of an "Ukrainian face." The Bolsheviks managed to establish control over eastern Ukraine, although the Whites, diminished as a military force, managed to hold out in Crimea until November 1920.

The final denouement of this revolutionary period was the brief Soviet-Polish War of 1920–1921. Petliura, now in Warsaw, managed to win Polish support for an expedition against the Bolsheviks. Petliura's move, however, was condemned by, among others, Hrushevsky and his erstwhile ally Vynnychenko as final proof that he was willing to betray socialism for the pursuit of blind, egotistical nationalism. Vynnychenko was unsparing, calling Petliura an "unhealthily ambitious maniac, soaked up to his ears in the blood of pogromized Jewry, politically illiterate . . . a pernicious and filthy gladiator-slave of the Entente [Western allies]."[19] The anti-Russian Poles happily used Petliura, hoping to create a buffer state between them and communist Russia. Polish and Ukrainian forces retook Kiev in May 1920, and the last incarnation of the UPR was established there. In June, however, the Bolshevik's Red Army pushed the Poles and Ukrainians out, driving them all the way back to Warsaw. After a Polish counteroffensive, the two sides agreed to peace, with Poland gaining eastern Galicia and western Volhynia and recognizing Bolshevik rule to the lands farther to the east.

FORMATION OF THE SOVIET UNION

The dream of Ukrainian statehood was thus shattered. The Bolsheviks, thanks to force of arms, good organization, backing by forces from Russia, and the weaknesses and mistakes of their various rivals, gained control over most of Ukraine. Although the Bolsheviks had supporters not only among Russians but also among some ethnic Ukrainians—it is important to recall that socialist ideas had animated the UPR as well—the victory of Bolsheviks and the subsequent imposition of communism meant the reestablishment of Russian rule over Ukraine.

Although both tsarism and communism were centered in Russia and, as it turned out, disastrous (if not deadly) for many in Ukraine, communist rule did not take the same form as Russian monarchism. Communism created a new economic and social order, and, instead of a political system in which one person ruled with the assistance of a secret police and a giant, unwieldy bureaucracy, the Bolsheviks established a political system in which one party ruled with the assistance of a secret police and a giant, unwieldy bureaucracy. Many of these aspects of communist rule are covered in the next chapter. For purposes of this chapter, the key difference is the territorial/institutional form of rule in Ukraine.

Under the Russian tsars, Ukrainian lands had been divided into nine different provinces. There was no "Ukraine." Like the Germans in 1918, the Bolsheviks had to recognize that there was now something called Ukraine.[20] Thus in 1919, they proclaimed the Ukrainian Socialist Soviet Republic, which was technically an independent state, managing to win diplomatic recognition from several European states. True, this republic was ruled by the Communist Party of Ukraine, which was a branch of the Russian Communist (Bolshevik) Party, and its authority was established and preserved thanks to the efforts of the Red Army. It was not, in other words, a purely, or even mostly, Ukrainian creation; however, Lenin, recognizing that Russification was not the answer, acknowledged that it would have to have some Ukrainian content. He formulated a nationalities policy that allowed non-Russian parts of old Russian Empire under Bolshevik control to be "national in form, socialist in content," meaning that the main priority was maintenance of communist or socialist ideology.

Thus when the pretense of an independent Ukrainian state was dropped in 1922 after the Soviet Union was created, Ukraine did not disappear. Instead, the Soviet Union was initially composed of four separate, ethnically defined republics, one for Russia, one for Belarussia (White Russia), a Transcaucasian Federative Republic (which included Armenia, Georgia, and Azerbaijan), and a Soviet Ukrainian republic.[21] Soviet Ukraine would have its own government (communist, of course, and, until 1934, based in Kharkiv, closer to the Russian border than Kiev), but it could control certain economic enterprises and cultural and scientific institutions to help develop Ukrainian language and culture. Khristian Rakovsky, head of Soviet Ukraine's government from 1919–1923, turned from denial of the Ukrainian nation's existence to a defender of its interests and institutions, including clashing with future Soviet dictator Joseph Stalin over rights for separate republics.[22] Ukrainian nationality (citizenship was "Soviet") was recognized under the law, thereby maintaining the notion of a separate Ukrainian identity. Notably, the Ukrainian Soviet Socialist Republic (as it was known after 1936) retained the right to secede from the Soviet Union. For a long time, this was of no consequence, as secession was politically impossible and, at least according to Soviet ideology, unnecessary, as the Soviet Union was a fraternal union of various peoples and preexisting national differences would gradually disappear under communism. This development, of course, did not occur and in 1991, Soviet Ukraine finally was able to act on its right to secede from the Soviet Union.

THE OUTLIER: WESTERN UKRAINE UNDER POLISH RULE

As noted, not all of present-day Ukraine fell under Soviet control in the early 1920s. Seven million Ukrainians, one of the largest stateless minorities in Europe, found themselves in a reconstituted Polish state, in the new state of Czechoslovakia, and in an expanded Romania. Five million Ukrainians became Polish citizens, as Galicia, the most populated part of Austrian-ruled Ukraine, together with the parts of the adjacent region of Volhynia, were incorporated into Poland. Ignoring Ukrainians' desire for self-rule, the League of Nations recognized Polish sovereignty over these lands in 1923. The division of Ukrainian territory between the Soviet Union and Poland between World War I and World War II is pictured in Map 6.1.

As might have been expected, however, many Ukrainians, particularly in Galicia, resented being under Polish rule. Polish-Ukrainian tensions had not only been simmering in Galicia for centuries, but the two sides had violently clashed from 1918–1920. Ukrainian nationalism and identity, it is worth recalling, was also arguably more developed in Galicia than anywhere else. The reconstituted Polish state, whose population was 14% Ukrainian, promised the League of Nations that it would grant Ukrainian lands an autonomous administration, allow use of the Ukrainian language in government, and create an independent Ukrainian university. None of these promises were fulfilled. Polish governments became increasingly authoritarian and nationalistic, especially after Josef Pilsudski, hero of the war against the Bolsheviks, seized power in a military coup in 1926. Ukrainian schools were closed or made Polish-speaking, Ukrainian professorships at Lviv University—which remained, as before, overwhelmingly Polish—were abolished, newspapers were subjected to censorship, Ukrainians were barred from government jobs, and Ukrainian candidates and voters removed from electoral rolls. Orthodox churches were demolished or converted to Roman Catholicism, and up to 200,000 ethnic Poles were moved into Ukrainian villages and were the primary beneficiaries of the government's land reform program. The goal was to turn these lands into ethnically Polish territory, as the government in Warsaw began to call Galicia "Eastern Little Poland" (*Małopolska Wschodnia*).[23]

These moves generated resistance among many Ukrainians. The largest Ukrainian political party, the Ukrainian National Democratic Union (UNDO), unsuccessfully sought compromise with Warsaw in the late 1920s. Many institutions that backed the UNDO, such as Ukrainian literary societies, cooperatives, and newspapers, were repressed by the Polish government. As a consequence, the public mood shifted in favor of those urging confrontation with Poland. Some on the left pushed for unification with Soviet Ukraine, and covert Soviet assistance was funneled into the region to support Ukrainian groups and institutions. Local communist groups organized, and, even though the Communist Party was officially banned, their front organization, the Workers' and Peasants' Socialist Union, fared well in 1928 elections, especially in Volhynia. By the mid-1930s, however, when it was clear that Ukrainians in the Soviet Union were subjected to harsh repression (an issue covered in the next chapter), pro-Soviet sentiment largely evaporated. As a consequence, the most important and longest lasting challenge to Polish rule came from the nationalist right, which embraced

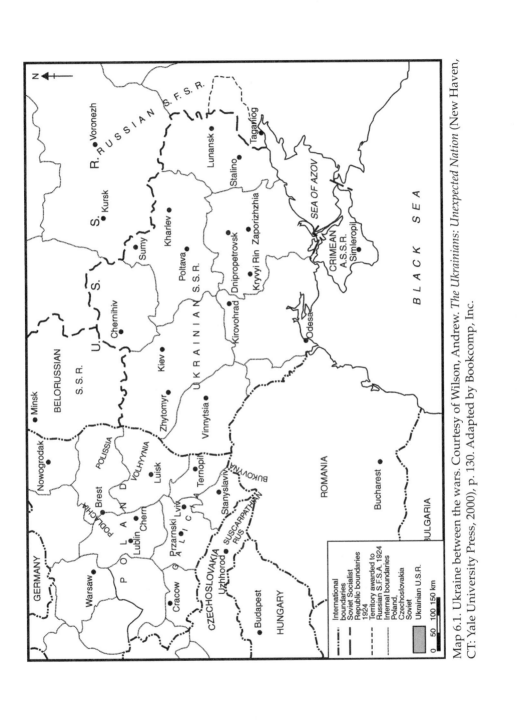

Map 6.1. Ukraine between the wars. Courtesy of Wilson, Andrew. *The Ukrainians: Unexpected Nation* (New Haven, CT: Yale University Press, 2000). p. 130. Adapted by Bookcomp, Inc.

political violence. For example, as early as 1921, nationalists tried to assassinate Pilsudski during his visit to Lviv. In Vienna in 1929, various military organizations, student radicals, and émigré groups formed the Organization of Ukrainian Nationalists (OUN), which became a major source of political instability within Poland.

The OUN was led by Yevhen Konovalets, a veteran of the Polish-Ukrainian conflict and former backer of the Hetmanate, and its chief ideologue was Dmytro Dontsov (1883–1973), an émigré from eastern Ukraine. A former socialist, Dontsov preached what is known as "integral nationalism," a doctrine that elevated the ethnically defined nation as the supreme form of human organization. Dismissive of ideas of both democracy and socialism, his slogan was "The Nation Above All."[24] Influenced by the rise of fascism in Italy and later sympathetic to Nazism in Germany, he supported the idea of a supreme leader (*vozhd*) that would ensure the nation's survival. He was critical of Ukraine's nineteenth-century literary-cultural revival and enjoined Ukrainians to move away from the "reason, evolution, and cosmopolitanism" of the older generation and embrace the "fire of fanatical commitment" and the "iron force of enthusiasm."[25] For Dontsov, ethnicity was key, and his vision was of an ethnically pure Ukraine that had no place for minorities such as Russians, Poles, and Jews. The OUN won support across Ukraine, especially among youth. "Its stress on revolutionary action, radical solutions, and the creation of a new breed of 'super' Ukrainians appealed to youths who felt victimized by the Polish government, frustrated by lack of employment, and disillusioned by failures of their elders."[26] The OUN infiltrated economic, educational, and youth organizations; organized protests and boycotts of Polish goods; and enlisted writers and poets in its propaganda activities. A crucial component of its resistance, however, was violence, frequently directed against Polish landowners in the Ukrainian countryside, with more than 2,000 attacks recorded in the summer of 1930 alone.

In response to OUN activities, the Polish government launched a counteroffensive in Ukrainian villages. Villagers who were deemed to be uncooperative were beaten by Polish soldiers. Ukrainian libraries, artwork, and stores were destroyed, and Ukrainian priests were forced to pledge publicly their loyalty to the Polish state under the threat of physical assault. Thousands of individuals were arrested, and many activists, including Ukrainian members of the Polish *Sejm* (House of Representatives), were put on trial. In turn, the OUN stepped up its campaign, killing Polish officials and Ukrainians it accused of being disloyal to the cause. Its most prominent victims, both killed in 1934, were Bronislaw Pieracki, the Polish interior minister, and Ivan Babii, an Ukrainian high school principal who forbade his students to join the OUN. Polish authorities upped the ante and imprisoned hundreds of suspected militants in the newly built Bereza Kartuzka concentration camp.[27]

In addition to political violence, the region also suffered from economic difficulties. Polish rule did little to develop the economy, whose mainstay was still agriculture. During the Great Depression, when agricultural prices collapsed, many people in the region were pushed into poverty on their small plots of land. Rural penury helped fuel nationalist discontent. Many Ukrainians also emigrated to Europe, Canada, the United States, and Argentina to escape their plight.

The OUN, however, failed to achieve its goal of an independent Ukrainian state. Both the UNDO and, crucially, the Greek Catholic Church, the most important Ukrainian institution in interwar Poland, condemned its campaign of violence. In 1935, the Polish government began to work more constructively with the UNDO, and its leader, Vasyl Mudry, was selected as vice-speaker of the *Sejm*. In 1938, Konovalets of the OUN was killed by a Soviet agent in Holland. Afterwards, the OUN split into two, with one faction led by more moderate émigrés in Europe and a more radical group, based in Galicia and led by Stepan Bandera (1909–1959). The OUN, however, was involved in the formation of the short-lived Carpatho-Ukrainian state formed in 1939 in the far eastern region of Czechoslovakia. Carpatho-Ukraine, however, fell to Hungarian forces that were supported by Nazi Germany, as Hitler's forces took control of Czechoslovakia.

Likewise, Poland could not preserve its independence in the face of threats from Nazi Germany and the Soviet Union. On September 1, 1939, Germany forces invaded Poland, starting World War II in Europe. On September 17, Soviet forces invaded from the east and asserted control over Ukrainian-populated territories. Later, fighting among Nazis, Poles, Soviets, and Bandera's OUN group, together with Nazi-led efforts to annihilate Jews, would devastate western Ukraine, an important episode detailed in the next chapter.

The chaos of interwar western Ukraine was captured in literature by two Jewish writers from the region, Joseph Roth (1894–1939), who wrote in German, and Bruno Schulz (1892–1942), who wrote in Polish. In *The Radetzky March*, Roth paints an unflattering portrait of Galicia. "Any stranger coming into this region was doomed to gradual decay. No one was as strong as the swamp. No one could hold out against the borderland."[28] Schulz's surrealist portrayal of his native Drohobych featured flying pots and pans, parades of crocodiles in the streets, and people turning into insects. Both authors, albeit in very different ways, lamented the passing of the old order and reflected the uncertainty of the new, presenting, especially in Schulz (who, unlike Roth, remained in Galicia) the tensions in the region resulting from the presence of a variety of ethnicities. Confined to the Jewish ghetto of Drohobych after the city was occupied by the Germans in 1941, Schulz was shot dead by a German officer.

NOTES

1. Serhy Yekelchyk, *Ukraine: Birth of a Modern Nation* (Oxford: Oxford University Press, 2007), p. 68.

2. John Reshetar, *The Ukrainian Revolution, 1917–1920: A Study in Nationalism* (Princeton: Princeton University Press, 1952), p. 49.

3. Reshetar, 1952, pp. 52–53.

4. Quoted in Reshetar, 1952, p. 61.

5. Reshetar, 1952, p. 64.

6. Reshetar, 1952, p. 137.

7. Andrew Wilson, *The Ukrainians: Unexpected Nation* (New Haven, CT: Yale University Press, 2000), pp. 124–126.

8. Quoted in Reshetar, 1952, p. 111.

9. Reshetar, 1952, p. 116.

10. Quoted in Reshetar, 1952, p. 119.

11. Yekelchyk, 2007, p. 73.

12. Wilson, 2000, p. 124.

13. Quoted in Reshetar, 1952, p. 119.

14. Ukrainian historian Yaroslav Hrytsak, quoted in Yekelchyk, 2007, p. 74.

15. Yekelchyk, 2007, p. 77.

16. Arnold Margolin. *From a Political Diary: Russia, the Ukraine, and America, 1905–1945* (New York: Columbia University Press, 1946), p. 41.

17. Wilson, 2000, p. 125.

18. Yekelchyk, 2007, p. 81, and Anna Reid, *Borderland: A Journey through the History of Ukraine* (Boulder: Westview, 1997), p. 102.

19. Quoted in Reshetar, 1952, p. 306.

20. Richard Pipes, *The Formation of the Soviet Union: Communism and Nationalism, 1917–1923* (Cambridge: Harvard University Press, 1923).

21. As the Soviets gained control over more territory, the number of republics grew, eventually reaching 15.

22. Yekelchyk, 2007, p. 91.

23. Anna Reid, 1997, p. 105, and Yekelchyk, 2007, p. 123.

24. Yekelchyk, 2007, p. 127.

25. Wilson, 2000, p. 131.

26. Orest Subtelny, *Ukraine: A History*, 3rd ed. (Toronto: University of Toronto Press, 2000), p. 444.

27. Yekelchyk, 2007, p. 128.

28. Quoted in Reid, 1997, p. 109.

7

Ukraine under Soviet Rule

For most of the twentieth century, most Ukrainians lived in the Soviet Union, a communist state made up of 15 different union republics, one of which was the Ukrainian Soviet Socialist Republic. Although on paper union republics reserved certain rights, most of the fundamental decisions were made by Russian-dominated leadership of the Soviet Communist Party, prompting many in Ukraine to consider Soviet rule a continuation of earlier Russian rule. Ukraine was fundamentally transformed, however, during the Soviet period, experiencing extensive industrialization, urbanization, and wider social change. Communism, in theory, promised both freedom and economic plenty. It did not live up to this promise, however, as Ukrainians (and other Soviet citizens) suffered political repression and famine. Ukraine was also devastated by World War II, and its Jewish population fell victim to the Holocaust perpetrated by Nazi Germany and its allies. Despite Soviet expectations that nationalism would recede, the Ukrainian national idea did not go away. Dissidents emerged to press for both individual and national freedoms. Although they were repressed by the communists, their voices would help fuel the push for independence in the 1980s.

UKRAINIANIZATION OF THE 1920s

Ukraine was devastated by World War I, conflict with Poland, and civil conflict among Bolsheviks (Communists), Whites (anticommunists), nationalist forces, and motley peasant bands. The 1921 Treaty of Riga ended fighting between the Poles and Bolsheviks and established the western border for the new Soviet state. The Ukrainian Socialist Soviet Republic (after 1936 the Ukrainian Soviet Socialist Republic, Uk SSR) was one of the four original constituent parts of the Soviet Union, formally created in December 1922.

Upon establishing their authority throughout much of the former tsarist empire, the communists were faced with the massive task of rebuilding the country and creating a communist political, economic, and social system. The harsh and rapid movement to communism under War Communism (1918–1921), which included forced seizures of grain and movement of peasants into collective farms, had generated political resistance and ruined the economy. Starting in 1921, therefore, Vladimir Lenin (1870–1924), the leader of the Soviet Union, changed course and adopted what was called the New Economic Policy (NEP), envisioned as a less forceful, more gradual path to communism.

NEP lasted through the 1920s.[1] Rather than nationalizing all property, the state allowed small-scale private business to exist. Prices were set for various products, but peasants were allowed to sell their surplus production on the free market. The government backed off of earlier plans to establish collective or state farms, thus allowing the peasants to retain their own land. Lenin expected that NEP would produce economic growth and that workers and peasants would voluntarily embrace communist institutions such as collective farms. Although economically somewhat liberal, politically the system remained a dictatorship, with only one political party—the Communists—and a secret police to arrest "class enemies" and others who might be opposed to communism.

NEP principles were put into place in Ukraine, although they came too late to prevent a famine in 1921 that claimed hundreds of thousands of lives. By 1923, however, the economy showed signs of recovery, based on agricultural production, small shops, leased enterprises, and state investment in larger industrial projects, which helped create a larger Ukrainian working class. By 1927, the Ukrainian economy had recovered to pre-World War I levels, and living standards were noticeably improving. Despite this success, however, Soviet authorities objected to the ideological effects of NEP, which were creating a relatively prosperous class of peasants (derided as *kulaks* in Russian *or kurkuly* in Ukrainian) in the countryside. In 1927 and 1928, the state launched campaigns against the *kulaks*—always a loosely applied term—to force them to sell more of their grain to the state to feed workers in the cities and to export abroad for needed capital for investment in industry.

Politically, the Uk SSR was ruled by the Communist Party of Ukraine (CPU), which had been created in April 1918 and followed the lead of the all-Soviet Communist Party led by Lenin. In 1922, the CPU had only 56,000 members, about 0.2% of the population. Most of its members were ethnically Russian and Jewish; less than a quarter were ethnically Ukrainian and only 11% knew the Ukrainian language.[2] The CPU, therefore, had to establish both a broader and more indigenous membership. Already in 1920–1921, the CPU folded into its ranks some pro-Bolshevik splinter groups from other Ukrainian parties, and other parties, including various socialist and nationalist organizations, were formally banned. In 1923, the Communists adopted a policy of indigenization (*korenizatsiia*) to promote local leaders and thereby give the Uk SSR a more prevalent "Ukrainian" face. Subsequent Ukrainianization was resisted by ethnically Russian leaders in Ukraine, but in 1925 Lazar Kaganovich, a Ukrainian Jew who was allied to Joseph Stalin (1879–1953), the general secretary of the Soviet Communist Party, became leader of the CPU. He promoted officials with roots in Ukraine, including some who had been purged by the previous Russian-dominated leadership. In 1927, ethnic Ukrainians constituted, for the first time, more than half of both party members and government officials.

Ukrainianization extended beyond politics. The government took active steps to promote the Ukrainian language in education, media, and the arts. The mantra was "nationalist in form, socialist in content," meaning that one could express things in Ukrainian as long as the expression itself did not deviate from the prescribed ideological line. By 1927, 70% of the Uk SSR's business was being conducted in Ukrainian, as opposed to only 20% in 1925. Some people, however, caution that not too much should be made of this claim, as research has shown that a minority of top officials knew Ukrainian well. More impressively, perhaps, by 1929, 83% of elementary schools and 66% of secondary schools offered instruction in Ukrainian, and almost all ethnic Ukrainian students were enrolled in Ukrainian schools, which, it bears emphasizing, were banned under the tsars.[3] Similarly, by the end of the 1920s, most of the books and newspapers in the Uk SSR were in Ukrainian, and Soviet investment in education meant that literacy rates grew to more than 50% by 1927. The arts—including theater, music, literature, painting, and film—experienced a renaissance, thanks in part to government subsidies. Significantly, in 1924 Mykhaylo Hrushevsky was invited back from his self-imposed exile in Europe to become a member of the Ukrainian Academy of Sciences. Hrushevsky also became the editor of *Ukraina*, the leading journal of Ukrainian studies. The communists even tolerated religion, particularly the Ukrainian Autocephalous (Independent) Orthodox Church (UAOC), which had been created in 1919, and, with the support of the authorities, took over St. Sophia Cathedral in Kiev. National councils were also set up for Jews, Poles, Germans, Greeks, Czechs, and other smaller nationalities, who were given rights to publish and use their language for government business.

Ukrainianization, however, was not without its critics. Several "national communists," who believed in promoting both socialism and nation-building, made authorities in Moscow uneasy. For example, Oleksandr Shumsky, the Ukrainian minister for education, argued in 1925 for an ethnic Ukrainian head of the CPU, the forcible Ukrainianization of Russian speakers in Ukraine, and greater economic and political autonomy for Ukraine. The communist leadership in Moscow rejected this position, removing him from office while accusing him of "deviationist" thinking and of attacking both Soviet and Russian culture.[4] Other writers, who broached the idea that Ukraine was being subjected to colonial exploitation by Moscow and that Ukrainian art should become more "European," were similarly reprimanded and forced to denounce their views. In 1928, Kaganovich was recalled to Moscow. Rather than replacing him with an ethnic Ukrainian, as "national communists" would have favored, Stanislav Kosior, an ethnic Pole and Stalinist loyalist, was made head of the CPU.

UKRAINE UNDER STALIN

Lenin died in 1924 without naming a successor and, after a power struggle among top communist leaders, Stalin, thanks to his ruthlessness and control over the party bureaucracy, assumed supreme leadership of the Communist Party by 1929, engineering the removal of those who might oppose him. Although an early supporter of NEP, Stalin became one of its harshest critics, claiming that NEP was moving too slowly and was too capitalist. Instead, by the end of the 1920s, he advocated total state control over the economy, including rapid industrialization and creation of collective farms. By using harsh methods of political repression and terror, Stalin would make the Soviet Union into a powerful but totalitarian state.[5]

Industrialization

One of Stalin's primary points of emphasis was industrialization, as he believed that "backwards" Russia had to modernize to survive against hostile capitalist states. Rather than rely on NEP, Stalin favored a "command economy" entailing both state ownership and planning. The state would control all aspects of the economy, determining what was produced, the prices of products, and how to distribute goods and services. A state planning agency, Gosplan, was established in 1928, and in 1929 the Soviet leadership retroactively approved a first year (1928–1932) plan that envisioned enormous increases in Soviet industrial production.

Ukraine played an important role in Stalinist industrialization. Ukraine was showered with resources. State investment in Ukrainian industry nearly tripled from 1928 to 1932. Four hundred new industrial plants were constructed in Soviet Ukraine. Most of the industrialization occurred in eastern and southern Ukraine, regions that had already been subject to some industrialization in the late tsarist period. Examples included the Dniprohes hydroelectric dam (Europe's largest) on the lower Dnieper, the giant Kharkiv tractor factory, and steel mills in Zaporizhzhe and Kryvyi Rih. The Donbass region remained a center for coal mining. By 1932, Ukraine supplied more than 70% of the Soviet Union's coal, iron ore, and pig iron.[6]

Although precise figures of economic growth are disputed (Soviet authorities exaggerated their accomplishments), there is no doubt that Ukraine and, more generally, the Soviet Union, had impressive industrial growth. Ukraine's urban population doubled in the 1930s. Many peasants moved into cities and industrial centers in search of employment. Ethnic Ukrainians became both a majority of the republic's industrial workforce and, for the first time, of all urban residents. Although the rate of industrialization slowed during the second (1933–1937) and third (1938–1941—unfinished because of World War II) five-year plans, by the end of the 1930s, Ukraine was one of Europe's leading industrial centers, producing more metal and machines than Italy and France and nearly as much as Great Britain.[7]

These accomplishments were not cost-free. Much of the capital for industrialization came from the export of grain that was seized—at great human cost—from the peasants. Several Soviet construction projects relied on veritable slave labor, people who had been sent to labor camps for alleged resistance to Soviet authority. Problems during the industrialization process (e.g., faulty construction, missed targets, slowdowns) were blamed on wreckers or saboteurs, who were also placed on trial. While production of steel, coal, chemicals, tractors, and other industrial products increased, food was rationed throughout the 1930s, housing remained a problem, and shortages of consumer goods (e.g., clothing, household products) were chronic, as Soviet planners did not put a priority on individual consumption. Tough laws were passed to ensure labor discipline. Those concerned about Ukrainian economic sovereignty noted that Stalinist economic centralization meant that Ukrainian industry, which in the 1920s had been largely controlled by Ukrainian authorities, was primarily subordinated to ministries in Moscow. Ukrainian economists in 1932 even complained that Ukraine was getting a bad deal under Soviet planning, as it supplied raw materials, but Russian industries were more responsible for the production of finished goods.[8]

The Great Famine

One might be able to view some features of industrialization under Stalin as examples of modernization or progress, but one should also recognize that Stalin is held responsible for the greatest tragedy to befall the Ukrainian people: the Great Famine of 1932–1933. Thanks to government policy that forcibly seized grain and other food from Ukrainian peasant households, millions of people—the leading scholar of the famine makes a "conservative estimate" of 5 million[9]—starved to death. Note that this was not because of crop failures or war, the usual causes of famine. Instead, for political and ideological reasons, the government allowed people to starve, taking food away from them while exporting grain abroad to procure funds it could use for its industrialization program.

Several motivations lay behind the famine. First, the Soviet government sought control over the peasantry. Under NEP, it was assumed that peasants could be offered incentives to sell grain to the state and that they would voluntarily give up their private land holdings and enter into ideologically correct collective or state farms.[10] Grain procurement, however, was a chronic problem, and peasants showed no enthusiasm for collective farms. Stalin came to power promising that he would no longer coddle the peasants. Instead, he used coercion to force peasants to surrender grain to the state, and in 1930 began a massive campaign to push peasants into collective farms. Many resisted, killing their cows or chickens rather than surrendering them to collective farms. These resisters were labeled *kulaks* by Stalin, who ordered their eradication as a class enemy. Millions of people throughout the Soviet Union were arrested as *kulaks*, executed on the spot or sent to labor camps in Siberia and the Far North. Soviet propaganda, exemplified in the film *The Earth* (released in 1930 and directed by Oleksandr Dovzhenko), celebrated the collectivization as a form of modernization. Although brutal, it was effective: by 1932, 70% of Ukrainian peasants were working, usually for meager wages, on collective farms.

The second motivation behind the famine was to attack Ukrainian nationalism. In 1929, the secret police began to arrest Ukrainian intellectuals, accusing them of membership in illegal Ukrainian nationalist organizations. In 1930, a parade of fake cases against political figures (many of whom had belonged to noncommunist parties), writers, priests, and students began in Kharkiv. In 1931, Hrushevsky, Ukraine's most distinguished public figure, was forced to move to Moscow, and many of his associates in the Academy of Sciences were sent to labor camps for alleged membership in illegal organizations. These moves served to "decapitate" Ukraine of its intellectuals. Stalin, however, knew that the base of Ukrainian nationalism lay in the peasantry. One of the aims of collectivization (and, by extension, the famine itself) was "the destruction of Ukrainian nationalism's social base—the individual land-holdings."[11]

The immediate cause of the famine was the Soviet government's demand for grain delivery from Ukraine in 1932. Although the target, 7.7 million tons of grain, was criticized by officials within the Ukrainian Communist Party as being excessive and unrealistic—meaning that if that amount of grain was transferred to the state, there would not be enough to feed the peasantry in the countryside—officials in Moscow would brook no compromise. Vyacheslav Molotov, a top Soviet official, told a meeting of the Ukrainian Communist Party that talk of lowering the grain quota was "anti-Bolshevik" and that there would be "no concessions or vacillations in the problem of fulfillment of the task set by the party and the Soviet government." That settled the matter. Thus "on Stalin's insistence, a decree went out which, if enforced, could only lead to the starvation of the Ukrainian peasantry."[12]

The decree was enforced. A government decree in August 1932 declared all collective farm property—including animals and agriculture produce—as state property and proscribed harsh punishments for those who would requisition it for their own use. Party officials, often aided by the military, sent out teams to the countryside to acquire grain from the peasants. The normal harvest from the farms would not be enough; officials were sent to peasants' homes to check for hidden grain and food. Those caught "hoarding grain"— even a few sacks—were sent to labor camps or shot. Local party officials that failed to deliver their quotas of grain were considered soft or unreliable and replaced. Throughout the winter of 1932, the government, despite all its efforts, failed to meet the grain quota. The Party-controlled media and top Party officials blamed *kulaks* and saboteurs for these failures and called for even harsher methods against the alleged class enemy. In December 1932, a government decree prohibited shipment of any goods and granting of credits to areas that were behind on their grain deliveries.

The result was mass starvation. People were left with literally nothing to eat. Some tried to flee, but international borders and, significantly, the border with Russia was closed. Peasants were legally barred from cities, but some managed to move there, even though food was rationed. Notably, stores of grain were available in silos throughout the countryside—restricted for use in an emergency—and some peasants rebelled and seized them. Party officials, even those in the Ukrainian countryside, had plenty to eat. Grain was also available in Russia, although famine did occur in some Russian regions, but its importation into Ukraine was barred. Top Soviet officials knew of the famine. Nikita Khrushchev, who worked in Ukraine and later became General Secretary of the Soviet Communist Party, conceded in his memoirs that he knew that "people were dying in enormous numbers." Stalin allegedly dismissed one brave official who brought the issue to his attention by accusing the man of concocting "fairy tales." One communist activist recalls:

With the rest of my generation I firmly believed that the ends justified the means. Our great goal was the universal triumph of Communism, and for the sake of that goal everything was permissible—to lie, to steal, to destroy hundreds of thousands and even millions of people, all of those who were hindering our work or could hinder it, everyone who stood in the way . . . In the terrible spring of 1933 I saw people dying from hunger. I saw women and children with distended bellies, turning blue, still breathing but with vacant, lifeless eyes. And corpses—corpses in ragged sheepskin coats and cheap felt boots; corpses in peasant huts, in the melting snow of the old Vologda, under the bridges of Kharkov . . . I saw all this and did not go out of my mind and commit suicide. Nor did I curse those who had sent me out to take away the peasants' grain in the winter, and in the spring to persuade the barely walking, skeleton-thin or sickly-swollen people to go into the fields in order to fulfill the Bolshevik sowing plan in shock-worker style.[13]

Peasants sold whatever they could to get money to buy food, and the Soviet government allowed this, offering a loaf of bread or a pound of butter for gold coins, antiques, or foreign currency. Still, people resorted to eating bark, pine nettles, worms, dogs, cats, and each other. Grisly accounts of cannibalism range from scavengers to those who trapped children for food to elderly parents who implored their children to eat them when they died.

Ultimately, millions suffered horrible deaths. Most were in Ukraine, but millions died under similar conditions in parts of Russia and Kazakhstan as well. The Soviet government, of course, denied that there was a famine, at most conceding that there were food shortages because of sabotage and slack workers. In Stalin's time, those who spoke of famine were subjected to arrest themselves, and Soviet leaders after Stalin did not encourage investigation of the issue. The famine, however, was reported in many Western newspapers, although some apologists for Stalin—most notoriously the British socialists Sidney and Beatrice Webb and the *New York Times* correspondent Walter Duranty, all of whom were in the Soviet Union at the time—parroted Stalin's claims that there was no famine. Yet, one Western reporter, writing in May 1933, observed a "battlefield" composed:

On the one side [of] millions of starving peasants, their bodies often swollen from lack of food; on the other, soldier members of the GPU [secret police] carrying out instructions of the dictatorship of the proletariat. They had gone over the country like a swarm of locusts and taken away everything edible; they had shot or exiled thousands of peasants, sometimes whole villages; they had reduced some of them most fertile land in world to a melancholy desert.[14]

Was this a genocide, a term coined after World War II by Raphael Lemkin, a Polish Jew who had studied law in Polish-ruled Ukraine at Lviv University? Lemkin himself thought so, as do many Ukrainian activists who have framed the event as a planned eradication of the Ukrainian people and culture. Robert

Conquest and James Mace, the two greatest Western scholars of the famine, use this term.[15] In today's Ukraine, commemoration of the famine (*holodomor* in Ukrainian, literally "death by hunger") is a major event. The Ukrainian Parliament has issued declarations affirming that the famine was a genocide, an opinion shared in statements and resolutions made by 25 other countries, including the United States and Canada but not, of course, Russia. Critics would contend that the famine, although tragic, was not technically genocide because other groups besides Ukrainians suffered, urban populations were not targeted, and/or that it was a result of the ideologically driven collectivization campaign.[16] Considering Stalin's hostility to Ukrainian nationalism—that collectivization in Ukraine was already largely complete by 1932, that importation of grain from Russia into Ukraine was expressly banned, and that the region in Russia that suffered the greatest was the Kuban, an area in the North Caucasus that is heavily populated by ethnic Ukrainians—there is solid reason to label the famine a genocide, a monstrous event that rivals the Holocaust as one of the twentieth century's greatest cataclysms.

Purges and the Great Terror

With Ukraine still suffering from the famine, Stalin launched a purge against officials in the CPU. Of course, as noted previously, many Ukrainian officials were treated with suspicion by Stalin, and some of the braver ones tried to speak out or at least do something to prevent the famine. In 1933, top Ukrainian party officials were arrested for allegedly participating in Ukrainian military organizations that were supposedly financed by Polish landlords and German fascists. Arrested figures included Matvii Yavorsky, the chief party watchdog over Ukrainian intellectuals, and Mykhailo Yalovy, chief editor of the Ukrainian state publishing house. Hundreds of writers, scientists, and intellectuals were denounced as anti-Soviet agitators who were "hiding behind the back" of Mykola Skrypnyk, who had served as Ukrainian minister of education since 1926 and tried to defend aspects of Ukrainian language and culture. Rather than face arrest, Skrypnyk committed suicide, later being called a "nationalist degenerate" by the state-controlled press.[17] Throughout 1933–1934, all leading Ukrainian cultural institutions—the Academy of Sciences, theaters, media, scientific institutes—were purged of allegedly anti-Soviet, counterrevolutionary elements. Thousands were sent to harsh labor camps, where they perished. The general policy of Ukrainianization of the 1920s was reversed. Russian was promoted as the lingua franca of the Soviet Union, and Ukrainian-language publishing declined.[18]

From 1935–1938, all of the Soviet Union was engulfed in a wave of purges and mass terror. The pretext was the assassination in December 1934 in Leningrad (formerly St. Petersburg) of Sergei Kirov, a popular Communist Party official. His murder, however, was ordered by Stalin, who used the event as a pretext to weed out alleged traitors from within the party apparatus. Tens of thousands of party members were arrested. Leading party officials were put on rigged "show trials" and then executed. People were encouraged to turn each other in. Anyone could be arrested for any reason. Torture by the police elicited confessions and denunciations of neighbors, colleagues, and family members. Millions of people were sent to labor camps, where many perished in harsh conditions.[19] The Soviet media portrayed victims as spies, saboteurs, and counterrevolutionaries, praising Stalin, who masterminded the process, as being a benevolent, almost godlike figure.

In Ukraine, both party officials and average citizens were victims.[20] Most of those who died were alleged to be *kulaks,* who, it seems, had somehow survived mass deportations and famine and were still engaging in sabotage against collective farms. As part of Stalin's "Great Purge" after the murder of Kirov, hundreds of local communist leaders and rank-and-file collective farm workers were put on trial, accused of crimes that they did not, in fact, commit. Leading Ukrainian party officials, often accused of nationalist or anti-Soviet attitudes, were also killed off, on a scale greater than that elsewhere. At the Congress of the CPU in 1938, the new Central Committee of 86 top leaders had only three from the previous year's gathering, all the others replaced and/or killed. Nikita Khrushchev (1894–1971), Stalin's ally and an ethnic Russian who had been born in Ukraine, became the head of the CPU in 1938 and faithfully carried out orders to complete the elimination of alleged enemies within the party.

Stalin's actions may seem irrational, even crazed. He literally destroyed the Communist Party and killed or imprisoned millions of innocent people. He created a climate of fear throughout the country. On economic terms, collectivization led to less efficient farms and chronic food shortages. Despite the building of immense steel or chemical plants, the average person lived worse in 1939 than in 1928. But Stalin was in control. He was assured of the party's loyalty. No one would or could challenge him. He had built a totalitarian state.

UKRAINE DURING WORLD WAR II

The greatest accomplishment under Stalin's rule, however, something for which he is still celebrated, was the Soviet victory over Nazi Germany in World War II. Stalin's push for industrialization, it is argued, allowed the Soviets to have the wherewithal to stand up to the Nazi war machine, even as the Soviet Union suffered horrible human and material losses in the war. Ukraine was an important battleground during that conflict. Soviet victory meant that Moscow was able to assert control over all Ukrainian lands, thereby unifying a people that had for centuries been divided among various states and empires.

The Soviets Invade Western Ukraine

World War II started on September 1, 1939. That August, as part of the notorious Molotov-Ribbentrop Pact, the Germans and Soviets agreed to divide Poland between themselves. On September 1, Germany invaded Poland from the west, prompting Great Britain and France to declare war. On September 17, Soviet forces invaded Poland from the east, in the process overrunning much of what today is Belarus and western Ukraine.

The Soviets moved quickly to consolidate their authority in western Ukraine.[21] They portrayed the invasion as the reunification of Ukraine. A pro-Soviet "Ukrainian National Congress," elected under dubious circumstances immediately after the invasion, convened in late October and asked that western Ukraine be admitted to the Uk SSR, a request that was approved by the latter's parliament on November 15. Many Ukrainian newspapers and journals that published under Polish rule were shut down by the Soviet authorities, who set up their own pro-Soviet media. Leaders from noncommunist Ukrainian political parties were arrested and not seen again. Communist youth organizations were established. Authorities also tried to set up collective farms. Tens of thousands of party, state, and military officials (overwhelmingly ethnic Russians) were sent by Moscow to administer western Ukraine. The Soviets deported up to a million people—mostly Poles and Jews but also ethnic Ukrainians—to Siberia, Central Asia, and Arctic regions of Russia because of their social background, political past, or suspected anti-Soviet sentiments.[22] A similar pattern held in the summer of 1940, when, as part of arrangement with Germany and Romania, Soviet forces occupied northern Bukovyna.

In Galicia, however, the Soviets did not try to impose all aspects of the totalitarian model. They criticized the Greek Catholic Church and seized some of its properties, but they did not arrest its leaders or ban it altogether, a reflection of the fact that they did not want to alienate the population entirely. The Ukrainian language was given greater scope than it had under Polish rule, with Lviv University effectively "Ukrainianized" in language and personnel. Cultural and educational exchanges were promoted between western and eastern Ukraine, although by 1940, it became clear to the authorities that west Ukrainians were not enamored with what they saw in Soviet Ukraine and those from eastern Ukraine risked being contaminated with the virus of bourgeois nationalism.

The Ukrainian nationalist movement was pushed underground, lacking the wherewithal to resist Soviet power. Some leaders of the Organization of Ukrainian Nationalists (OUN) who did not manage to flee from the advancing Soviets were tracked down, put on trial, and sentenced to death for anti-Soviet activities. The heart of the OUN, however, survived in both Western Europe and Poland. Many OUN officials were sympathetic to Nazi Germany and in

1940, mounting tensions between older and younger members of the OUN led to a split in the organization, with Stepan Bandera assuming leadership of the more radical, militant faction (OUN-B) and Andrii Melnyk, who had taken over leadership of the OUN after the assassination of Konovalets in 1938, heading the more moderate faction (OUN-M). In early 1941, Germany began to provide military training to Ukrainians, many from the OUN-B, in German-occupied Poland in anticipation of an attack against the Soviet Union.

German Invasion and Occupation

On June 22, 1941, German forces attacked the Soviet Union. Stalin was surprised at Hitler's betrayal, and Soviet forces were ill-matched against the better-armed and organized Germans. By June 30, German forces reached Lviv, although not before the Soviets killed 4,000 Ukrainian political prisoners being held by in the secret police's prison.[23] Thousands of others were deported eastward, and Soviet officials as well as Jews retreated to the east to avoid capture and death. Many in western Ukraine welcomed the Germans, figuring they would treat the population better than the Soviets had treated them.

Forces attached to the OUN-B moved in with the Germans. In Lviv on June 30, 1941, they declared the creation of a sovereign Ukrainian state. In their declaration, the OUN-B called on all Ukrainians to join in the fight against "Moscovite occupation" and to press forward to seize Kiev, which would be the capital of independent Ukraine.[24] Yaroslav Stetsko declared himself chief of state, as Bandrea himself was compelled by the Germans to remain in Poland. The call for Ukrainian independence won the approval of the Greek Catholic Church. Metropolitan Sheptytsky issued a letter declaring that "we greet the victorious German Army as a deliverer from the enemy" and that he recognized Stetsko as head of the new Ukrainian entity.[25] Groups from the OUN-B moved farther into Ukraine to set up a separate Ukrainian administration.

The attempt to create a separate Ukrainian state, however, would not succeed. The Germans, although initially exhibiting some tolerance for the Ukrainian activists, arrested leaders of the OUN-B, including Stetsko in Lviv and Bandera in Poland. Groups loyal to the OUN-M began to move into German-occupied Ukraine. In August, leaders from the OUN-M were assassinated in Zhytomyr in central Ukraine, and many blamed the OUN-B, although some evidence suggests that the Soviets may be to blame.[26] In any event, neither the OUN-B nor the OUN-M had the resources to set up an effective administration, and it also became clear that the Germans had their own plans for Ukraine. Whereas some German officers argued that allowing non-Russians a measure of self-government would help win the Germans civilian support, Nazi racial ideology held that the Ukrainians, like other Slavs, were *Untermenschen* ("subhuman"). Hitler made the German position clear in September 1941, declaring that Germany had no interest in a free Ukraine.[27]

Meanwhile, German armies swept eastward. They captured most of south-eastern Ukraine in August. Kiev fell on September 19 in a bloody battle. Soviet losses in Kiev alone were 600,000 dead and 600,000 taken prisoner.[28] In October, Odessa fell to invading Romanian forces and Kharkiv was occupied by the Germans. Crimea held out against the Germans until the summer of 1942, when, in a series of battles for Sevastopol and the Kerch Strait, the Soviet Red Army was defeated and forced to retreat. Millions of Ukrainian civilians fled to Russia. Before retreating, the Soviets blew up dams, bridges, and factories; flooded mines; and burned the fields, desiring to leave nothing for the Germans. Some factories were dismantled, and equipment was placed on trains and shipped east, where it could be reassembled and used to make material to support the war effort.

German occupation of Ukrainian lands entailed repression and extermination. Mobile killing units, called *Einsatzgruppen,* followed German armies and rounded up Communists, Roma (Gypsies), and, especially, Jews for execution. In many parts of Ukraine, the Germans found willing collaborators who helped identify, track down, and kill Jews.[29] One of the largest massacres of Jews took place at the end of September 1941, when 33,771 Jews from Kiev were taken out of the city, herded by local auxiliary police into Babi Yar, a ravine outside of the city, and killed by men from *Einsatzgruppen* C. Successive waves of victims were forced to lie on the bodies of those who were forced into the ravine ahead of them. In all, up to one-and-a-half million Ukrainian Jews are estimated to have died in the Holocaust, shot by *Einsatzgruppen* and their collaborators or sent to death camps, most of which were in Poland. Some Ukrainians risked death to shelter Jews during Nazi occupation, and 1,984 have been honored by Israel as "Righteous Gentiles" for their heroism.[30] Nonetheless, Soviet authorities did not erect any special monument to acknowledge Jewish victims of the Holocaust. For example, at Babi Yar, where from 1941–1943 more than 150,000 people (including Jews, prisoners of war, communists, and Ukrainian nationalists) were executed, the Soviets erected a memorial in 1966 to "citizens of Kiev and prisoners of war," denying the fact that many of those who were killed at Babi Yar were killed only because they were Jewish. In 1991, Jewish groups set up their own memorial, a 10-foot high menorah at Babi Yar.[31]

Although not singled out for extermination like the Jews, ethnic Ukrainians were subjected to discrimination and repression. German-only schools, restaurants, and public transport appeared in many Ukrainian cities. Local medical services were curtailed and schooling above the fourth grade was shut down, as Germany intended to make Ukraine an agricultural colony and saw no need to educate the local population. The Germans took over the collective farms, and independent food shipments to cities were banned, leading to starvation and a population exodus to the countryside. More than two million young workers were rounded up and sent to Germany to work in factories as virtual slave labor. Conditions were somewhat better for Ukrainians in Nazi-occupied Poland (which included Galicia), where the Germans preferred dealing with ethnic Ukrainians over the Poles. Even so, political terror and economic exploitation remained staples of German policy.

There was determined resistance to German rule. Some of this was by Soviet partisans who operated in Ukraine behind German lines. Some estimate that as many as 200,000 pro-Soviet insurgents or guerilla fighters—most of whom were ethnically Ukrainian—attacked German supply and communication lines during the occupation. In 1942, the Ukrainian Insurgent Army (UPA), a small group organized initially to fight against the Soviets, began attacking the Germans. Both the OUN-B and OUN-M established military units to fight the Germans as well. In 1943, these various groups came together under the banner of the UPA, a 40,000-person force, which, at various times from 1942–1945, fought Germans, Soviet partisans, regular Soviet Red Army troops, and Polish guerilla forces.[32]

The End of the War

By early 1943, the tide turned against the Germans on the eastern front. Soviet forces, at the cost of up to a million dead, repelled the Germans at the Battle of Stalingrad and began to push German armies back westward. Just to the north of Ukraine in the summer of 1943, the Soviet Red Army won the Battle of Kursk, the largest battle ever in terms of men and armaments. By that August, Soviet forces had liberated Kharkiv in eastern Ukraine, and in November they took Kiev. In July 1944, the Soviets took Lviv, and in October 1944 the Red Army rolled into Transcarpathia, leading the Soviet press to declare the liberation of all Ukrainian lands.

Liberation, of course, came at a high cost, as Ukraine once again was turned into a battlefield. Cites were razed, fields were burnt, and in many cases the Germans wiped out entire villages for alleged collaboration with Soviet forces or partisans. Although the Soviets launched a propaganda campaign to win over the Ukrainian population, this was relatively short-lived, especially when Soviet forces entered western regions of Ukraine. There, they encountered resistance from the UPA and other nationalist forces. During 1944–1945, as the Red Army pushed into Poland and later Germany, thousands of Soviet security forces were deployed in western Ukraine to squash the UPA and other manifestations of the Ukrainian nationalism. The Greek Catholic Church and the UAOC were repressed and later banned, as the Soviet government grudgingly agreed to support the Russian Orthodox Church, which was free of Ukrainian nationalist sentiment. Many in western Ukraine fled westward with the departing Germans, and even many of the Ukrainian workers and prisoners of war in Germany refused to come back to Ukraine because they feared Soviet repression. In Crimea (then under Russian, not Ukrainian jurisdiction), the Soviets deported the Crimean Tatars, more than 200,000 people, who were collectively punished because some Tatars collaborated with the Germans during the occupation. They were sent to central Asia, and nearly half perished because of disease and malnutrition both in transit and in resettlement camps.

Once the war was over, Stalin insisted that all Ukrainian lands be unified under Soviet rule. This meant that Galicia, Volhynia, northern Bukovyna, and Transcarpathia were taken from Poland, Romania, and Czechoslovakia and formally merged with the Uk SSR. The movement of the Ukrainian border westward entailed sizeable population transfers between Ukraine and Poland, with more than 800,000 Poles moving to Poland and nearly 500,000 ethnic Ukrainians moving from Poland into Ukraine.[33] For the first time in modern history, all the Ukrainian lands were united, albeit in a state that was ruled from Moscow. Stalin had also created a separate Ukrainian ministry of defense and foreign affairs, and used these essentially hollow structures to argue successfully for a separate Ukrainian seat at the United Nations (the same was done for Belorussia as well).

POSTWAR UKRAINE: REBUILDING AND REPRISALS

The imposition of Soviet rule after World War II entailed its own difficulties. Ukraine, like other parts of the Soviet Union, was devastated by the war. The deaths of up to 8 million Ukrainians—soldiers and civilians—meant that there was an acute labor shortage. Famine, a result this time of wartime devastation and drought, killed hundreds of thousands—precise figures vary widely and run up to a million people—in 1946–1947.

There was, however, no real change in the Soviet model. Agriculture remained collectivized and was relatively neglected in terms of state investment. The Soviet administrative system, built on a single party with control over all aspects of political, economic, and social life, was reestablished The Soviets, again relying on state planning, rebuilt most of the industry in eastern Ukraine, so that by 1950 industrial output already exceeded prewar levels. The Russian Orthodox Church, which was allowed greater freedom during the war, was again subjected to state control, although it was not banned outright.

Matters were more difficult and in many respects more brutal in Western Ukraine, however, which had not been under Soviet control before World War II and was the scene of fighting between Soviet and local nationalist forces during the war. Afterwards, the UPA, which secretly received American and British support, continued to attack Soviet forces. Soviet security sweeps in Galicia and Volhynia pushed the UPA into eastern Poland, where

they were suppressed in 1947 in Operation Wisla, a joint Soviet-Polish campaign. Sporadic fighting and sabotage against the Soviets continued into the
early 1950s.[34] In response to the fighting, the Soviets also deported more than
200,000 western Ukrainians, mostly family members of nationalist fighters.
Khrushchev later acknowledged that Stalin had wished to treat the western
Ukrainians in the same manner as the Tatars, but mass deportation was never
attempted because "there were too many of them and there was no place
to which to deport them."[35] The Greek Catholic Church, however, was shut
down. Many of its priests were imprisoned and its property was handed over
to the Russian Orthodox Church. Ideological purification campaigns were
launched against suspect Ukrainian writers, historians, and theater directors
to purge Ukraine both of Western and nationalist influences. Agriculture was
collectivized—which, as during the 1930s, prompted some resistance—and
some investments were made to develop industry in the region, including
mineral extraction and bus and radio production in Lviv. There was not, however, a mass influx of ethnic Russians, and western Ukraine kept its Ukraine-
language schools and media. Membership in the Communist Party remained
low. Even though the Soviets firmly controlled it, western Ukraine would
remain one of the "least Soviet" and "least Russian and least Russified" parts
of the Soviet Union.[36]

STIRRINGS OF OPPOSITION

Joseph Stalin died in 1953. After a brief power struggle, Nikita Khrushchev,
who had served as head of the CPU at various times between 1938 and 1949,
became the General Secretary of the Communist Party of the Soviet Union.
Khrushchev quickly acquired a reputation as a reformer, denouncing several
of Stalin's policies in a secret speech to party leaders in 1956.

Khrushchev's rule brought some positives for Ukraine. Because he considered Ukraine his power base, he promoted several officials from Ukraine into
the all-Soviet leadership in Moscow. For the first time since the 1920s, ethnic Ukrainians were also picked to head the republic-level CPU, and ethnic
Ukrainians dominated the high ranks of the CPU hierarchy. The economy was
decentralized, giving Ukrainian ministries more control over Ukrainian economic enterprises. In an effort to raise living standards, Khrushchev funneled
more state investment into the agricultural sector. In the 1950s, both food supplies and rural incomes increased. Construction of apartment blocks in the
cities relieved housing shortages. Artistic expression of various kinds was
given greater freedom, and political figures, artists, and writers who had been
condemned under Stalin, including Mykola Skrypnyk, the symbol of Ukrainianization, were rehabilitated. Many political prisoners were also released,
including some fighters from the UPA. Some began to discuss, however gin-
gerly, the need to protect the Ukrainian language against attempts to make

Russian the predominant language in the republic. Although some of these reforms would later be reversed by Khrushchev's successors, one measure literally changed the map of Ukraine. In 1954, to mark the three hundredth anniversary of the Treaty of Pereiaslav, Crimea was transferred from the Russian Republic to the Uk SSR, even though most of the population of Crimea were ethnic Russians, most of whom moved to the area after the Tatars had been deported. Under Soviet rule, this territorial adjustment had little import, but in 1991, when Ukraine became independent, Crimea, despite its demographic makeup, historical connection to Russia, and the presence of important Soviet military bases, was (and is) part of Ukraine.

Khrushchev, however, never consolidated his authority as Stalin had done. He survived one attempt to oust him in 1957, but his foreign adventurism (e.g., instigating the Cuban Missile Crisis, souring relations with Communist China) and domestic failures (e.g., his obsession with planting corn contributed to bad harvests in the 1960s) led more conservative figures in the Soviet leadership to look for a replacement. In 1964, they managed to force Khrushchev to resign his post, bringing in Leonid Brezhnev (1906–1982) as party leader.

Like Khrushchev, Brezhnev was an ethnic Russian who was born in and developed his party career in Ukraine. Brezhnev, however, had less appetite for reform. Never a supreme leader like Stalin, Brezhnev ruled by consensus, often relying on patronage networks he had built during his time in Ukraine, sometimes derided as the "Dniepropetrovsk mafia." His priority was on political stability, although by the 1970s, it was clear that the price for stability was economic stagnation and corruption.

Brezhnev found himself in conflict with Petro Shelest (1908–1996), an ethnic Ukrainian who had become leader of the CPU in 1963. Although Shelest supported the ouster of Khrushchev, he clashed with Brezhnev and the leadership in Moscow because he was a strong advocate of Ukraine's economy and culture. Shelest was no dissident or anticommunist figure, but for him "Soviet Ukraine meant a strong Ukraine with a fully developed economy and national culture."[37] A former industrial manager, Shelest insisted that Ukraine receive a fair share of Soviet investment, and he protested policies that diverted funds from Ukrainian coal and metallurgy to Siberian oil and gas. He spoke Ukrainian as his native language and praised the Ukrainian language and heritage in public speeches. He refused to launch mass arrests against outspoken intellectuals. As Brezhnev acquired more power in the late 1960s and early 1970s, he began to move against Shelest and other republican leaders. Shelest was stripped of his position in 1972 and forced into complete retirement a year later. He was chastised in the Soviet press for various mistakes, including idealizing the Ukrainian past and abetting nationalist deviations.

While Shelest was leader of the CPU, many younger Ukrainian intellectuals, who came of age during the relatively more liberal period of Khrushchev, began to press for less party control over artistic expression and more respect for Ukrainian culture. Known as the *shistdesiatnyky* (literally, the "sixtiers" or generation of the sixties), they included poets such as Ivan Drach, Lina Kostenko, and Dmytro Pavlychko; prose writers such as Volodymyr Drozd and Valerii Shevchuk; theater director Les Taniuk; and literary critic Ivan Dziuba (1931–), whose manuscript, *Internationalism or Russification?* (1965), was personally submitted to Shelest and became the most celebrated work of Ukrainian dissent. In it, he argued that the Soviet authorities had abandoned Leninist nationality policy in favor of pushing assimilation into Russian culture, the latter of which he compared to tsarist Russia. The work of Dziuba and others was published illegally as underground or self-published work (known as *samvydav* in Ukrainian, *samizdat* in Russian) and smuggled out of the country, where it was published in several languages. Dziuba himself escaped arrest, in large part because he was calling for reforming the Soviet system, not its overthrow. Other writers of *samvydav,* however, were arrested and put on trial, and their plight led others, including the journalist Viacheslav Chornovil (1937–1999), to begin to lobby for human rights and civil liberties.

There were other calls for reform and expressions of dissent. The most controversial novel of the 1960s, *The Cathedral* (1968), was written by Oles Honchar, an older, establishment writer who was chairman of the Ukrainian Writers' Union. The book chronicled the efforts of residents in a town in eastern Ukraine to save an old Cossack church from being torn down, a clear plea that Ukraine should preserve the monuments from its pre-Soviet past. The book was banned, although that only made it more popular among the intelligentsia. Other figures, such as historian Valentyn Moroz and journalist Stepan Khmara, took their cues from the legacy of the UPA and were more explicitly anti-Soviet, condemning the nondemocratic, repressive nature of the Soviet state and the damage it did to Ukrainian culture. In the late 1970s, after the Soviet Union signed the Helsinki Accords, in which it pledged to protect human rights, including rights of free expression, various "Helsinki" groups appeared to press the government to honor its commitments. The leader of the Ukrainian Helsinki Group was Mykola Rudenko, a Soviet war hero who had become a critic of the Soviet system. Underground components of the Greek Catholic Church appeared in western Ukraine, and labor activists tried to create an independent trade union in eastern Ukraine in 1978. Crimean Tatars petitioned for the right to return from their exile in central Asia.

The Soviet Ukrainian government, both under Shelest and even more so under his successor, Volodymyr Shcherbytsky (1918–1990), cracked down on dissent. Activists were monitored by the secret police; some lost their academic or cultural positions; many were arrested. Dziuba was arrested in 1972 and released only when he publicly recanted his criticisms. Others were not so lucky, dying while in prison or serving their time until the late 1980s. By the early 1980s, Ukrainians were the largest ethnic group among all Soviet political prisoners (including the Russians). Many of the dissidents, including Dziuba, Chornovil, Moroz, Khmara, and Drach, reemerged in the late 1980s as leaders they pushed for Ukrainian independence.

This is not to suggest that the dissidents had a large following, particularly outside of western Ukraine and Kiev. One survey counted fewer than a thousand dissidents.[38] Most Ukrainians, like most Soviet citizens, were not willing to risk antigovernment political activity. Although Khrushchev's promise to overtake the United States in terms of living standards went unrealized, people could expect a steady job and provision of basic goods. More and more people enrolled in higher education. By the late 1970s, for the first time, most of the population of Ukraine lived in cities. Many Ukrainians, particularly those living eastern and southern Ukraine, spoke primarily Russian and were attracted in some ways to and indoctrinated in other ways into the idea of a greater Soviet/Russian culture. As noted, however, the Soviets made fewer inroads into western Ukraine, where Ukrainian language schools predominated and memories of the pre-Soviet period were within popular memory. Ukraine, as a political unit, was thus united under Soviet rule. Identity—Soviet, Russian, Ukrainian, or some sort of mix—remained split and increasingly regionalized,[39] a phenomenon that would manifest itself both during the push for Ukrainian independence and in post-Soviet Ukraine.

NOTES

1. Definitive works on the NEP include Stephen Cohen, *Bukharin and the Bolshevik Revolution* (Oxford: Oxford University Press, 1980) and Moshe Lewin, *Political Undercurrents in Soviet Economic Debates* (Princeton: Princeton University Press, 1974).

2. Serhy Yekelchyk, *Ukraine: Birth of a Modern Nation* (Oxford: Oxford University Press, 2007), p. 90.

3. Yekelchyk, 2007, pp. 93–94.

4. Robert Conquest, *Harvest of Sorrow: Soviet Collectivization and the Terror-Famine* (New York: Oxford University Press, 1986), p. 81.

5. Sources on Stalin are legion. For general coverage of Soviet history and Stalin in particular, see Ronald Suny, *The Soviet Experiment* (Oxford: Oxford University Press, 1998) and Robert Conquest, *Stalin: Breaker of Nations* (New York: Penguin, 1992). For a work devoted to Ukraine, see Hryhory Kostiuk, *Stalinist Rule in the Ukraine: A Decade of the Study of Mass Terror* (New York: Praeger, 1961).

6. Yekelchyk, 2007, p. 105.

7. Yekelchyk, 2007, p. 106.

8. Yekelchyk, 2007, p. 105.

9. Conquest, 1986, pp. 306–307.

10. Karl Marx had foreseen collective farms, under which property was owned by a group of agricultural workers, as akin to a worker-owned factory in the countryside and thus compatible with communism. Under the Soviet Union, real control of these farms resided with the state, not the workers themselves.

11. Conquest, 1986, p. 219.

12. Conquest, 1986, p. 223. Much of the account of the famine comes from Conquest, 1986, pp. 223–261.

13. Quoted in Conquest, 1986, p. 233.

14. Conquest, 1986, p. 260.

15. Conquest, 1986, p. 272. Mace (1952–2004) worked with Conquest on his book, wrote many articles on the famine, and was the lead author of the U.S. government's examination of the Great Famine. See *U.S. Commission on the Ukraine Famine, Report to Congress* (Washington, DC: United States Government Printing Office, 1988). A monument has been built in Kiev honoring Mace.

16. Mark B. Tauger, "The 1932 Harvest and the Soviet Famine of 1932–1933," *Slavic Review* 50, no. 1 (Spring 1991): pp. 70–89. For an alternative view, see Yaroslav Bilinsky, "Was the Ukrainian Famine of 1932–1933 Genocide?" *Journal of Genocide Research* 1, no. 2 (1999): pp. 147–156.

17. Conquest, 1986, pp. 267–268.

18. Yekelchyk, 2007, p. 116.

19. A premier source for these events is Robert Conquest, *The Great Terror: A Reassessment* (Oxford: Oxford University Press, 1990).

20. The best source on Ukraine specifically is Kostiuk, 1961.

21. John Armstrong, *Ukrainian Nationalism*, 2nd ed. (New York: Columbia University Press, 1963), pp. 63–70.

22. Yekelchyk, 2007, p. 133.

23. Armstrong, 1963, p. 77.

24. Armstrong, 1963, pp. 79–80.

25. Armstrong, 1963, p. 81.

26. Armstrong, 1963, pp. 94–96.

27. Yekelchyk, 2007, p. 139.

28. Yekelchyk, 2007, p. 136.

29. Martin Dean, *Collaboration in the Holocaust: Crimes of the Local Police in Belorussia and Ukraine, 1941–1944* (New York: St. Martin's, 2000).

30. Yekslchyk, 2007, p. 139.

31. James Waller, *Becoming Evil: How Ordinary People Commit Genocide and Mass Killing*, 2nd edition (Oxford: Oxford University Press, 2007), pp. 92–97.

32. Yekelchyk, 2007, pp. 144–45.

33. Yekelchyk, 2007, p. 147. In 1947, in Operation Wisla, the Polish government moved to remove vestiges of previous Ukrainian settlement in areas such as Kholm and Peremyshl.

34. The best source on this period is Armstrong, 1963, pp. 290–321.

35. Yekelchyk, 2007, pp. 148–149.

36. Roman Szporluk, *Russia, Ukraine, and the Breakup of the Soviet Union* (Stanford, CA: Hoover Institution Press, 2000), p. 267.

37. Yekelchyk, 2007, p. 159.

38. Andrew Wilson, *The Ukrainians: Unexpected Nation* (New Haven, CT: Yale University Press, 2000), p. 153.

39. Wilson, 2000, pp. 147–148.

8

The Drive for Ukrainian Independence

In 1985, the year Mikhail Gorbachev became leader of the Soviet Union, few could have seriously imagined an independent Ukraine. True, many in Ukraine and in the Ukrainian diaspora had dreamed of such an event, but given the repressive nature of the Soviet Union, this seemed to be a very unlikely outcome. Gorbachev's reform program, however, brought significant changes to Soviet political and social life. Although he did not intend to do so, Gorbachev unleashed a tide of nationalism that swept away the seemingly mighty Soviet state. In only six years, Ukraine became an independent state, a development affirmed by a referendum on December 1, 1991, in which 90% of Ukrainian voters expressed their support for independence. The achievement of an independent Ukrainian state was hailed by many as the most significant event in the entire history of Ukraine.

GORBACHEV AND THE EMERGENCE
OF NATIONALISM IN THE SOVIET UNION

One needs to begin the story of Ukraine's drive for independence in Moscow, Vilnius, Tallinn, and Riga, not Kiev, Lviv, or Donetsk. True, Ukrainian dissidents had courageously fought for more democracy and cultural freedoms, but their efforts had little practical effect. Soviet leaders in the 1970s and early 1980s confidently asserted that they had solved the Soviet Union's nationalities question by creating a common Soviet people among the Russians, Ukrainians, Kazakhs, Armenians, Estonians, etc. Few could imagine that the Soviet Union would collapse as a result in large measure of revolts from what seemed to be its largely quiescent national minorities.[1]

Few, however, could have predicted the effects of reforms enacted by Mikhail Gorbachev, who became General Secretary of the Soviet Communist Party—in effect, the leader of the country—in March 1985.[2] Gorbachev was a new type of Soviet leader: young (54), Western-oriented, and aware that the Soviet Union needed to make serious reforms to overcome its economic difficulties and gain the confidence of its citizens. Calling the years of Leonid Brezhnev the "time of stagnation," Gorbachev insisted that the Soviet Union faced a grave crisis, one that threatened its status as a global superpower. He recognized that the Soviet Union had much to do to catch up with the United States economically, especially in the field of technology, and he was aware of the debilitating effect of military spending on the Soviet economy. Unlike most Soviet leaders, who studied engineering, he had studied law. While in university, he befriended figures in various "reform communist" movements. His family had also been victimized by Stalin's collectivization policies, so he had a personal connection to the repressive policies that had been adopted under Soviet rule.

Gorbachev was a protégé of Yurii Andropov, former head of the Soviet KGB who briefly (1982–1984) served as General Secretary. Andropov fashioned himself a reformer, although he was far from a liberal democrat or capitalist. Andropov emphasized issues such as worker discipline and attacking corruption, and Gorbachev, in his first year in office, put forward a plan of "acceleration" that built on some of Andropov's undertakings. By 1986, however, Gorbachev realized that this style of reform would not be enough; something far more radical was in order.

From 1986 to 1988, Gorbachev advocated three major reforms: *glasnost* (openness), *perestroika* (economic restructuring), and *demokratizatsiia* (democratization). *Glasnost*, perhaps his best known reform program, meant less censorship of the media and encouraging the discussion of new ideas. Gorbachev hoped this program would win him some measure of popular political support, involve more social actors in the reform process, generate better reform proposals, and give him a weapon—an invigorated press—with which he could combat corrupt and more conservative elements within the Communist Party. He foresaw *perestroika* as a means to encourage economic initiative from below by limiting the power of central planners and giving more authority to managers and workers in economic enterprises. *Demokratizatsiia* evolved over time, starting off as a means to offer citizens a choice between communist candidates for office (previously voters were given a "choice" of only a single candidate) and becoming, by 1989–1990, a program that allowed noncommunist organizations to field candidates for office. The goal, however, was not capitalism or Western-style democracy. Instead, Gorbachev envisioned a modernized, less repressive communist system that enjoyed the active support of its citizens.

We need not dwell on the details of what transpired next. Suffice it to say that matters did not turn out as he intended. *Glasnost* went further than he intended, as some in the Soviet Union began to attack Gorbachev and communism itself. *Perestroika* created confusion and led to more economic difficulties. *Demokratizatsiia* provided a mechanism by which groups hostile to Gorbachev and, in some cases, to the Soviet Union itself came to power. Our interest lies in how Gorbachev's reforms, taken as a package, encouraged the growth of nationalist movements among the peoples of the Soviet Union.

The Ukrainians were not the leaders in this process; the Baltic peoples—Estonians, Lithuanians, Latvians—were. Estonia, Lithuania, and Latvia had all been independent states after World War I. They were absorbed into the Soviet Union in 1940, a result of the Moltov-Ribbentrop Pact that in 1939 had allowed the Soviets to seize present-day western Ukraine from Poland. Like western Ukrainians, the Baltic peoples had resisted Soviet rule, and, as a consequence, they were singled out for punishments after World War II. Many Russians moved into the Soviet Baltic republics after World War II. They received many of the top political and economic positions. Local languages were given secondary status, as knowledge of Russian became mandatory in many fields. Many Balts felt themselves a colonized people.

Gorbachev's *glasnost*, which encouraged more open discussions of Stalin's crimes and allowed people to voice complaints against Soviet authorities, gave impetus to Baltic peoples who felt they were captive nations that had been illegally annexed by Moscow. They not only wanted a hearing to air their grievances, but they also wanted to rectify the situation. Initially, demands centered on preserving local languages and other aspects of their culture. Eventually, these grew into calls for sovereignty within the USSR and then, finally, complete independence. *Perestroika* played into this because the Baltic republics, ranking as some of the richest in the Soviet Union, believed that economic decentralization would be advantageous for them. Many therefore pushed for more economic autonomy. Finally, *demokratizatsiia* provided a means for nationalist groups both to organize and contend for power—they won 1990 republican-level elections in all three Baltic republics—and to create an incentive for local communist leaders to become more nationalist if they hoped to gain popular support. Although it started relatively slowly in 1986–1987, a wave of nationalism quickly gained strength in the Baltics, and both local elites and authorities in Moscow proved unable or unwilling to stop it. The example of the Baltics would spread elsewhere in the Soviet Union, including Ukraine.[3] By 1989–1990, the situation, from Moscow's perspective, was dire in a number of republics. Gorbachev was like the Sorcerer's Apprentice in the movie *Fantastia*, as he unwittingly released the genie of nationalism, which he then simply could not put back into the bottle.

The Chernobyl Factor

Most of the initial nationalist activity took place beyond Ukraine's borders, but one significant event occurred in Ukraine in the early part of Gorbachev's tenure: the meltdown of a nuclear reactor at the Chernobyl nuclear power plant, located 60 miles north of Kiev. Ironically, articles about Chernobyl's inadequate safety procedures, poor worker morale, and shoddy construction were some of the earliest examples of *glasnost* in the Soviet Union.[4]

Few, however, could have imagined what happened at Chernobyl early in the morning of April 26, 1986. One of the complexes four nuclear reactors exploded and released into the atmosphere 120 million curies of radioactive material, about a hundred times the radiation produced by the atomic bombs dropped on Japan in 1945. Two workers were killed in the initial explosion. More than two dozen workers and firemen died the next week from the immediate effects of the explosion. Although a full count of victims is impossible, between 6,000 and 8,000 deaths have been attributed to the radiation, and thousands more have suffered cancers and birth defects.[5] Of interest, the explosion was not the result of human error or equipment failure. Rather, it occurred because the reactor's automatic shutdown system was turned off during an experiment that went tragically wrong.[6]

On one level, Chernobyl was simply an environmental disaster. Because of inept handling by Soviet authorities, however, it became a political crisis, a symbol for the government's disregard for its own people. Firefighters and cleanup crews lacked protection against radiation. The day after the explosion, life—including soccer matches and outdoor weddings—went on as usual in the immediate vicinity of the power plant. It took the Soviet government two-and-a-half days to make any official announcement about the accident, and even then this occurred only after repeated inquiries by the Swedish government, which detected a cloud of radiation over its territory. Volodymyr Shcherbytsky, the leader of the Ukrainian Communist Party, called Gorbachev and asked if the May Day celebrations in Kiev should be canceled. Allegedly, Gorbachev said no and threatened him with expulsion from the party.[7] Consequently, outdoor May Day festivities, including participation by Shcherbytsky, went on as usual in Kiev, even though radiation levels in the city were well above safe levels. It was only on May 6, ten days after the explosion, that the Ukrainian health minister issued a warning, after which a quarter of million people evacuated temporarily from Kiev. Top party officials, meanwhile, had secretly sent their families out of the city days earlier. Gorbachev himself issued no statement until May 14, and then he mainly condemned Western media for spreading lies about the accident. For years, Soviet authorities prevented independent investigations of the effects of the accident. When faced with data that residents in a region near Chernobyl had an abnormally high level of cancers and birth defects, the state-run Center for Radiation Medicine in Kiev suggested that the mouth cancers were due to poor dental work and the deformities a consequence of inbreeding! Yurii Shcherbak, a doctor who later became an environmental activist and independent Ukraine's ambassador to the United States, stated, "Chernobyl was not like the communist system. They were one and the same."[8]

Chernobyl had social and political repercussions in Ukraine and indeed throughout the Soviet Union. It clearly exposed the limits of *glasnost* and provided new impetus for brave journalists and writers to push for more political openness. It helped spearhead an environmental movement. It revealed to all the extent of Moscow's control over Ukraine, adding credence to the claims of Ukrainian nationalists that Ukraine was a mere colony of Russia. Many therefore began to question seriously both communism and Ukraine's place in the Soviet Union. Yurii Kostenko, who became Ukraine's minister for the environment, conceded that Chernobyl "shattered my final illusions about the totalitarian system."[9] Anniversaries of Chernobyl would later become cause for anticommunist and anti-Soviet demonstrations. In the words of one observer, Chernobyl "traumatized the population, and then galvanized it."[10] It became a potent symbol during later popular mobilizations for sovereignty and independence. As Roman Solchanyk explained:

> In the aftermath of the nuclear catastrophe, Ukrainian writers and journalists began to talk in terms of a "linguistic Chernobyl" or a "spiritual Chernobyl" when discussing the consequences of the seventy-odd years of the Soviet experiment for the Ukrainian language and culture. In short, for Ukrainians, Chernobyl became identified with the duplicity and failure, indeed the complete bankruptcy, of the Soviet system as a whole.[11]

UKRAINIANS MOBILIZE FOR CHANGE

The first major stirrings of the Ukrainian nationalist movement began in the immediate wake of Chernobyl. In June 1986, at the congress of the Ukrainian Writers' Union, delegates broached the issue of Ukrainian national rights while offering implicit criticism of the communist authorities, particularly First Secretary of the Ukrainian Communist Party Volodymyr Shcherbytsky. Oles Honchar, the most senior Ukrainian literary figure of the day, offered an endorsement of Gorbachev's call for reform and new thinking while also noting the importance of safeguarding the Ukrainian linguistic and cultural heritage. The poet Ivan Drach, a member of the Communist Party, went further, linking Chernobyl to the famine and what he called a "virtual ethnocide," manifested by a lack of Ukrainian-language schools and publishing and use of Russian as the main means of public communication. A joke from the late Soviet period captures the problem rather well: "You could teach a Jew to speak Ukrainian in no time, a Russian in two or three years. But for an ambitious Ukrainian, it would take forever."[12] For many, the culprit was Shcherbytsky, who zealously attacked anything that hinted at Ukrainian nationalism. Drach would later remark, "In Moscow they clip your nails, but in Kiev they cut your fingers off."[13] Drach's 1986 speech, despite *glasnost*, was sanitized in the press, but his colleagues would later recall his words as the "first trumpet call in the Ukrainian national revolution."[14]

This plea for national revival—which surely would have earned Drach a prison term during the Brezhnev Era—was picked up by other groups in Ukrainian society. Most of these groups were informal organizations, independent of the Communist Party. Several included dissidents from the 1960s and 1970s, many of whom had been released as part of Gorbachev's political thaw in 1986–1987. A prominent example was the Ukrainian Helsinki Union (UHU), which was officially created in March 1988 and viewed itself as a successor to Ukrainian human rights groups in the 1970s. Levko Lukianenko, who had been a prisoner of conscience for 26 years, was elected its first president. In "What Next?," an essay he wrote in 1988, Lukianenko lamented that Ukraine was "crucified, pillaged, Russified, and torn" and that *perestroika* meant "life or death for our nation."[15] Although many in the UHU wished for Ukrainian independence, such a position was considered too radical to win broad social support. Instead, the UHU's Declaration of Principles in 1988 emphasized promotion of human rights, democratization, protection for the Ukrainian language, and devolution of authority to the republic-level.

The founders of the UHU were also behind the creation of the Ukrainian Association of Independent Creative Intelligentsia, an independent version of the communist-dominated Writers' Union, and the Ukrainian Culture and Ecology Club. Although the primary focus of both of these organizations was Ukrainian cultural revival, their work addressed more political and controversial concerns. For example, they demanded the reburial of Ukrainian writers who had perished in Soviet prison camps during the Brezhnev Era, as well as official publication of their works. Their calls to examine "blank spots" of Ukrainian history, such as the famine, and to celebrate the millennium of Kievan Rus's adoption of Christianity did little to endear them with the authorities.

Thus even though all of these organizations saw themselves as allies of Gorbachev insofar as they opposed the conservative communist establishment, they found themselves subjected to official harassment and attacks in the state-controlled press. For example, when the Ukrainian Culture and Ecology Club organized a protest in Kiev in 1988 on the second anniversary of Chernobyl, the authorities used loudspeakers to drown out the speakers and arrested 17 people. The media claimed that "a group of extremists . . . tried to whip up unrest, interfere with street repairs, and obstruct the flow of traffic."[16]

Students also organized their own organizations. The *Tovarystvo Leva* (Lion Society) was formed in Lviv in 1987 as an ecocultural youth organization that was committed to "the revival of a Ukrainian Sovereign State through Culture and Intellect."[17] Although this organization was less explicitly political—among its campaigns were church and cemetery renovations, instruction in traditional pottery, workshops on environmental awareness, and concerts and performances by Ukrainian artists—it struggled against the authorities for two years before it could be officially registered. In Kiev, students formed *Hromada* (Community), an independent student organization that took its name after Ukrainian cultural societies from the nineteenth century. It published an underground (*samvydav* or *samizdat*) journal, organized a boycott of mandatory military instruction classes at Kiev University, and campaigned for the restoration of the Kiev-Mohyla Academy, whose grounds were occupied by a military school. By the fall of 1988, *Hromada,* together with the environmental group Green World Association, was able to organize in Kiev a demonstration of 10,000 people for the formation of a Ukrainian Popular Front and opposition to nuclear power, and it issued an open letter to the communist leadership that called for the removal of Shcherbytsky and his clique for their responsibility for the state of Ukrainian culture and language. After this, the authorities became sufficiently alarmed by its activities that many members of *Hromada* were expelled from the university.

Religious organizations, long suppressed under Soviet rule, also began to take up the national cause. One concern of both the religious faithful (which was a minority) and nonbelievers was that the 1,000-year anniversary of the adoption of Christianity by Volodymyr the Great of Kievan Rus was planned to be celebrated as a *Russian* event. Many Ukrainians felt that part of their own history was taken from them. In western Ukraine, the priests and faithful of the Greek Catholic Church, which had been banned, openly campaigned for the relegalization of their church. The revival of the Ukrainian Autocephalous Orthodox Church, which also had its traditional stronghold in western Ukraine, also began as a consequence of *glasnost,* and a number of priests from the Russian Orthodox Church in western Ukraine defected to it. In 1989, both of these churches were given official recognition to resume their activities, and battles then began over church property, which had been placed by Soviet authorities into the hands of the Russian Orthodox Church. Religion therefore became a field in which Ukrainians could assert their national and cultural rights.

By 1988, there were efforts to copy the successful national-democratic mobilization in the Baltic states by bringing the various Ukrainian cultural, religious, environmental, and youth organizations together in a Popular Front. The largest turnouts in favor of a Popular Front were in Lviv, where some local communist officials exhibited some sympathy for this approach. The Democratic Front in Support of Perestroika, a precursor to the later *Rukh* movement, grew out of the assemblies of between 20,000 and 50,000 people who met in the summer of 1988 in front of Lviv University. The government, however, sent in the militia to break up the meetings and later denied the demonstrators the right to assemble. Smaller-scale assemblies were likewise broken up in Kiev. Thus although one could say that some elements of Ukrainian society had been awakened, they lacked the means to make a decisive political or social breakthrough.

DEMANDS FOR INDEPENDENCE GROW

The initial activation of Ukrainian society was largely supportive of Gorbachev and his agenda to remake the Soviet Union. No doubt, some dreamed of an independent Ukraine, but most Ukrainian groups tended to couch their demands for greater cultural self-expression and democratic self-government within a remade, perhaps looser, Soviet Union. In 1989, however, momentum began to build for Ukrainian independence, and, by 1990, large segments of the Ukrainian population were politically mobilized and making political, economic, and cultural demands against the communist authorities.

Three events in 1989 would help push the drive for Ukrainian independence forward. In February 1989, the Popular Movement of Ukraine for Restructuring (known as *Rukh*, or "Movement") issued its draft program. Discussions of forming a broad-based popular movement, based on organizations such as Lithuania's *Sajudis* or the Estonian and Latvian Popular Fronts, had been going on since 1988. The driving force behind the creation of *Rukh* was the Ukrainian Writers' Union and the Taras Shevchenko Ukrainian Language Society, which had been officially founded in early 1989; but other organizations such as the UHU, Green World, and various cultural associations also played an important role. Although the official line from Moscow saw creation of Popular Fronts as consistent with the spirit of *glasnost* and democratization, the more conservative communist leadership in Kiev was skeptical. The Writers' Union—which included many Communist Party members and whose paper, *Literaturna Ukraina*, was the foremost example of *glasnost* in Ukraine—pushed ahead, however, advocating adoption of Ukrainian as the republic's language, investigations into the crimes of the Stalinist era, and measures to protect the environment. *Rukh's* February 1989 draft program described the organization as a "mass, voluntary organization based on the patriotic initiative of citizens of Ukraine" that was committed to "fundamental socialist renewal in all spheres of state, public, and economic life." Although statements such as these were, from the perspective of the communist authorities, harmless enough, the document went on to declare that *Rukh's* aim was to redefine Ukraine's position vis-à-vis the Soviet federal government and to transform Ukraine into a sovereign republic. Although *Rukh* did not yet go so far as to push for outright independence, it did declare that Ukraine should control its own resources and enterprises and that the Ukrainian people had the right to determine their own destiny. In a direct challenge to the Communist Party, *Rukh* declared that it would take an active part in election campaigns and propose its own candidates for office.[18]

Rukh would have its first opportunity to test its political strength in March 1989, when elections were held for the Soviet Union's Congress of People's Deputies. Gorbachev had envisioned the Congress as part of a democratized Soviet system, and, although a third of the seats were reserved for members of the Communist Party and its affiliated organizations (e.g., trade unions), the remainder of the seats could be contested by noncommunist organizations. In practice, the communist apparatus did all it could to place bureaucratic hurdles in front of its rivals to prevent voters from having a real choice of candidates, but in some districts noncommunists did manage to get their names on the ballot. *Rukh* was denounced by communist leaders in Kiev, who also developed a plan for stifling it. Public protests, particularly in Kiev and Lviv, did much to bolster *Rukh's* position, and several members of *Rukh* ran as candidates for the Congress. The elections themselves produced a modest victory for the noncommunist opposition. Several of its candidates won in constituencies in Kiev and in western Ukraine. Several communist officials who ran unopposed did not receive the requisite 50% of the votes (voters crossed their names out instead). Some communists, such as Borys Oliinyk, who were sympathetic to the nationalist cause, were elected as well. By April 1989, Rukh and its allies were organizing large protests in Lviv, during which banned yellow and blue Ukrainian flags appeared in the crowd.

The communist authorities were rightfully nervous. Popular Fronts had done well in elections in the Baltic states and were pushing ahead with demands for sovereignty, and in April Soviet troops killed nationalist protesters in Georgia. Authorities in Moscow called for stronger action against nationalists and others who were, in their view, exploiting *perestroika* as an excuse to violate law and order. Authorities in Kiev were concerned about their loss of authority and legitimacy, not just because of the elections but also because many individuals were resigning from the CPU. They blocked Ivan Drach, a leader of *Rukh,* from running in a run-off election in Lviv and sought to discredit other *Rukh* candidates. These actions precipitated more popular mobilization and protest. Meanwhile, Shcherbytsky chastised communists who had effectively sided with the opposition and declared that *Rukh*'s program was "essentially separatist," "destructive," and "extremist."[19] Leonid Kravchuk, in charge of the Ukrainian Party's Ideological Department, reaffirmed that the "dirty and bloody symbols" of the Ukrainian blue and yellow flag and trident would remain prohibited and warned that *Rukh* was in danger of being taken over by anti-Soviet forces.

In June and July 1989, the Congress of Peoples' Deputies met in Moscow. While complaints of all types—nationalist, economic, political, environmental—were voiced, the body itself was under the control of the Communist Party and Gorbachev, who unceremoniously turned off the microphone of Andrei Sakharov, the Soviet Union's best known dissident and champion of human rights. Nonetheless, the Congress did serve as a chance to air many grievances, and it was broadcast live on Soviet television. Those in favor of greater Ukrainian rights met and formed informal alliances with their like-minded colleagues in other republics.

On September 8, 1989, *Rukh* opened its inaugural congress in Kiev. It was attended by more than 1,100 of the elected 1,158 delegates. At that time, *Rukh* claimed a membership of 280,000, impressive perhaps, but still less than a tenth of the membership of the CPU. Kiev's Polytechnical Institute, the site of the congress, was adorned with Ukrainian national symbols and regional emblems, and a Ukrainian Cossack march served as its musical theme song. Although some speakers called for independence—Levko Lukianenko of the UHU call on *Rukh* to "abolish this empire [the USSR] as the greatest evil of present-day life"[20]—most called for the development of Ukrainian culture and language, broader political and economic sovereignty, and for the Soviet Union to become a confederation. What this would mean—one speaker called for an "independent Ukraine within a constellation of free states"—was unclear.[21] Many speakers also went out of their way to appeal to Ukraine's ethnic minorities—Russians, Jews, Poles, Tatars—to support their efforts to democratize Ukrainian society. The congress made an effort to be as representative as possible, bringing together representatives from all regions of Ukraine. Even so, 72% had higher education, whereas only 10% were workers, and only 2.5% were collective farm workers. Half the delegates came from western Ukraine and almost one-fifth were from Kiev.[22]

This regional aspect of the nascent Ukrainian national movement deserves emphasis. Most of the national-democratic activity was centered in western Ukraine and in the capital, Kiev, which would be the natural focus for any political mobilization. Western Ukraine, in particular the historic regions of Galicia and Volhynia, had many features that made it distinct from the rest of the country. Its initial incorporation into the Soviet Union in 1939 was a result of the Molotov-Ribbentrop Pact, which provided cover for Soviet troops to enter what was then eastern Poland. Nationalists in western Ukraine, echoing claims made by the Baltic peoples who similarly suffered a Soviet invasion as a result of the Molotov-Ribbentrop Pact, maintained that the Soviet entry into the region was illegitimate and illegal. Anti-Soviet partisan fighting continued in the region until the 1950s. In large part because western Ukraine was not part of the Russian Empire, its population was overwhelmingly Ukrainian-speaking. Many were also Greek Catholic or members of the Ukrainian Autocephalous Orthodox Church. Geographically, western Ukraine was closer to Europe and to the anticommunist activity going on in countries such as Poland. More than others in Ukraine, western Ukrainians were prone to see Soviet rule by the oppressive *moskali* (Moscovites) as imperialistic and a threat to their indigenous culture. Well-attended protests in western Ukraine in the late 1980s and early 1990s "illustrated the phenomenal growth of the Ukrainian national movement as well as its limits."[23] In part for this reason, Andrew Wilson labeled Ukrainian nationalism a "minority faith," as the more populous regions of the southern and eastern Ukraine did not embrace Ukrainian nationalism or independence with the same fervor as those in the west.[24] In the aftermath of the *Rukh* congress, delegates from Kharkiv in eastern Ukraine resigned in response to what they viewed as its extremist agenda. Even by late 1989, the majority of Ukrainians did not favor creation of a separate Ukrainian state.[25]

This is not to suggest that all was quiet in other regions of Ukraine. The second transformative event in 1989 was a series of miners' strikes that broke out across Russia and the Donbass region of eastern Ukraine in the summer of 1989.[26] These strikes were primarily economic in character; workers demanded higher wages, better working conditions, and more products in the stores, especially soap. The strikes were a reaction to the deteriorating economic conditions brought about by the confusion of *perestroika*, and, like the various Popular Fronts, the miners portrayed themselves as advocates for reform. They were not nationalist in orientation, however, and treated the few local representatives of *Rukh* or the UHU with suspicion or even hostility. The Donbass was (and is) a heavily Russified region of Ukraine. Ethnic Russians make up more than 40% of the population, and Russian is the predominant language even among the region's ethnic Ukrainian population. Eastern Ukraine was the locale of much of Ukraine's "heavy industry" (e.g., steel and chemical factories, mines, defense plants). The industrial workers of the region were, in official Soviet discourse, the favored class, and heavy industry received a large share of the state's budget resources. *Perestroika* promised to change this, and many in eastern Ukraine began to fear for their future. In 1989, miners organized their own independent strike committees to protest government and factory-level policies. They returned to work at the end of July only after Moscow met their demands, including more self-management for the mines. That workers felt compelled to organize themselves against a self-proclaimed workers' state spoke volumes about the population's faith in the authorities.

Although one could write off these strikes, which occurred again in 1990 and 1991, as concerned purely with bread and butter issues, they did assume a national dimension, even though few of the Donbass strikers would have described themselves as Ukrainian nationalists.[27] Socioeconomic considerations eventually became a "motor force for independence,"[28] as many began to argue that rule from Moscow was disadvantageous to the Ukrainian economy. The central government controlled virtually all of Ukraine's economy, directing investment and tax decisions and taking all of the republic's hard currency (foreign currency) earnings. Far less was spent on culture, housing, and scientific research in Ukraine than in Russia. The poor environment—which, in addition to Chernobyl, included horrendous air and water quality, especially in eastern Ukraine—was responsible for poor public health, including a decline in life expectancy and a high (40%) frequency of miscarriage. At the same time, many made the argument that Ukraine would be economically better off with more economic autonomy, if not complete independence. Ukrainian Prime Minister Vitold Fokin, a lightning rod for criticism among the nationalist activists, conceded in 1990 that "our only hope, our only chance of improving the situation is economic independence."[29]

The third development was the removal of Shcherbytsky as leader of the CPU in September 1989, two weeks after *Rukh's* inaugural congress and after the CPU had launched a campaign against the organization. Many had long speculated that Shcherbytsky, a protégé of Brezhnev's and one of the leading conservatives on the Politburo, the top political body in the Soviet Union, would be a target for the reform-oriented Gorbachev. Gorbachev tolerated Shcherbytsky, or perhaps hoped he would endorse his program, but by 1988–1989, it was clear that Shcherbytsky was not going to ameliorate his previous hard-line positions. His fall in 1989, portrayed as a retirement by the Soviet press, was a result of intervention by Mikhail Gorbachev, who recognized that Shcherbytsky's conservatism and resistance to reforms was a liability. The groundwork for this move had been laid in early 1989, when Volodymyr Ivashko, a more conciliatory figure, had, at Gorbachev's insistence, become the second-in-command of the Ukrainian Communist Party. Ivashko took over from Shcherbytsky, who died in early 1990. Ivashko never consolidated his own authority the way Shcherbytsky had done, and he resigned his post in July 1990 to take a new party posting in Moscow. Shcherbytsky's ouster, however, "removed one of the major obstacles to the development of a nationalist movement by permitting the hitherto monolithic Party elite to divide into pro-and anti-*perestroika* factions."[30] A month after Ivashko assumed power, the Ukrainian Supreme Soviet adopted a language law that made Ukrainian the official language and proposed measures to gradually increase the use of

Ukrainian in government, media, and education, although provisions were also made to ensure that Russian would remain an important language of communication. Eventually, top figures within the party, most notably Leonid Kravchuk, would become "national communists," late converts to the idea of national independence.

Consistent with the idea of a wave of nationalism, nationalist mobilization grew throughout the Soviet Union and in Ukraine in 1990, which Motyl and Krawchenko describe as the "decisive year."[31] In the first half of 1990, the Baltic states, controlled by nationalist forces, made clear their intentions to secede from the Soviet Union. Other republics, including Russia itself, debated the merits of declaring sovereignty.

In Ukraine, the year started with a dramatic example of popular mobilization. On January 22, 1990, the anniversary of the declaration of independence of the short-lived Ukrainian Peoples' Republic in 1918, *Rukh* called on Ukrainians to replicate the Baltic "human chain," in which two million people joined hands in 1989 to commemorate the signing of the Molotov-Ribbentrop Pact. In Ukraine's case, 450,000 Ukrainians came out and joined together on the roads linking Lviv and Kiev, but, not surprisingly perhaps, no farther.

A decisive event was the March 1990 elections to the republic-level Ukrainian Supreme Soviet. Forty independent groups banded together to form the Democratic Bloc, which called for Ukrainian political and economic sovereignty, a new constitution, democratization, national rebirth, and an end to nuclear power. The Democratic Bloc organized numerous campaign rallies, including some in eastern Ukraine, where disillusionment with communist rule was spreading. Although these elections were far freer than those typical of the Soviet-era, there were some problems, such as the lack of election monitors and the authorities' refusal to register *Rukh* as an organization until after the deadline for registering candidates had passed. Nonetheless, the Democratic Bloc did quite well, winning approximately 25% of the seats. It won an overwhelming majority (43 of 47) of the seats in Galicia and a solid majority (16 of 22) in Kiev. It performed less well in eastern Ukraine, but did win some seats in Kharkiv and Donetsk. Although the Communist Party remained in charge of national politics, many within it recognized that the party would have to take into account citizen demands, forging "real rather than ascribed relations with the people it claimed to represent."[32]

Local elections were held at the same time. The Democratic Bloc won majorities on regional councils in Galicia, with the former prisoner Vyadcheslav Chornovil, a leading figure in both UHU and *Rukh* becoming head of the Lviv *oblast* (regional) council. The communists' monopoly on political power was broken. At its first session, the Lviv council described itself as an "island of freedom" that was committed to the "end of the totalitarian system" and "the fulfillment of the eternal vision of our nation for an independent, democratic

Ukrainian state."[33] After the Lviv council issued decrees that replaced Soviet symbols with Ukrainian ones, legalized the Greek Catholic Church, registered a variety of independent noncommunist groups, and closed down communist cells in factories and institutions, the authorities in Kiev warned about "destructive elements" that had taken over in western Ukraine.

Momentum, however, was on the national-democrats side. Thousands, especially in western Ukraine, began to leave the Communist Party. By the end of 1990, more than 250,000 individuals resigned from the party, compared with only 6,200 in 1989.[34] The Lviv branch of the *Komsomol* (communist youth organization) defected in its entirety to the opposition as the Democratic Union of Lviv Youth. *Rukh*'s membership grew to 500,000. Popular mobilization and electoral success helped ensure a secure space for the growth of Ukrainian civil society. Even though members of the national-democratic opposition were a minority in the Ukrainian Supreme Soviet, they were well organized and took advantage of the national broadcast of the parliamentary sessions to spread their message to a broader audience. Although more than 385 members of the Communist Party were elected to the 450-seat Ukrainian Supreme Soviet, by the time the parliament convened, the communists could only form a narrow majority of 239 representatives. Ivashko, who had been appointed chairman of the Ukrainian Supreme Soviet, abruptly resigned in July, putting the Communist Party more on the defensive. Meanwhile, more moderate members of the Communist Party demonstrated a willingness to work with the opposition. Within the Supreme Soviet they formed a separate bloc, the Democratic Platform, which endorsed democratization and economic reform. It also began to use *Rukh*'s rhetoric about the need for Ukrainian sovereignty.

Whereas western Ukraine was in the hands of noncommunist forces (although ultimate authority still belonged to Kiev and Moscow), in eastern Ukraine there was another round of strikes and demonstrations in the summer of 1990. The miners' predicament had, despite promises from Moscow, deteriorated from 1989 as the general crisis of the Soviet economy was getting deeper and deeper. This time the miners were more radical in their demands: the resignation of the Ukrainian government, liquidation of local party organizations, and the nationalization of property controlled by the Communist Party. Some workers also voiced support for Ukrainian sovereignty and independence.

With many groups in Ukraine demanding change, the Communists lost the political initiative. On July 16, 1990, the Ukrainian Supreme Soviet, by a vote of 355 to 4, issued a Declaration of Sovereignty, a month after a similar declaration had been made by the Russian Republic under the leadership of Boris Yeltsin. The document borrowed many of the ideas expressed at *Rukh*'s founding congress, asserting that Ukrainian laws would have precedence over federal laws, that Ukraine was economically autonomous with the right to create, if it so desired, a separate currency and banking system, and that it had the right to develop separate armed forces. Still, however, it was not a declaration of independence, as the declaration repeatedly referred to the Ukrainian Soviet Socialist Republic and envisioned the development of a new Union Treaty to reform the Soviet Union. Both sides claimed victory. *Rukh* members and their allies saw this as a first step toward independence. The communists tended to view it as a step toward a renewed Soviet Union.

The autumn of 1990 witnessed more polarization in Ukraine. The communist authorities, nervous that they were losing the ability to control events, banned demonstrations near parliament, limited the ability of the opposition to appear on television, and developed new laws to limit the power of local councils. Troops were massed outside of Kiev, and one nationalist deputy, Stepan Khmara, was arrested on trumped-up charges. Some feared that the Declaration of Sovereignty would never be implemented. In October 1990, however, the opposition, led by student hunger strikers who took over a square in downtown Kiev, fought back, demanding democratization, economic reform, and fulfillment of the pledges of Ukrainian sovereignty. University students throughout Ukraine went on strike, and on October 16, 1990, 150,000 people—students, workers, veterans of the was in Afghanistan, and members of the intelligentsia—marched on parliament and their demands were broadcast on radio and television. The government refused to negotiate, but on October 18, a large column of workers from Kiev's Arsenal factory joined the students. Vitalii Masol, Ukraine's prime minister, resigned, and his successor, Vitold Fokin, promised a series of reforms.

By the end of 1990, it was clear that there would be major changes in Ukraine's relationship with the federal government in Moscow, but the prospects for complete independence did not look certain. At its second congress in October 1990, *Rukh* removed mention of *perestroika* from the organization's name and came out unambiguously for independence, but with 57% of its delegates coming from Galicia or Kiev, one could doubt that *Rukh* spoke for most Ukrainians. The moderate Democratic Platform tried to forge a middle ground, making a plausible appeal to the silent majority for something between Ukrainian and Soviet nationalism. The problem, however, was that the silent majority remained silent; with the exception of Crimea, where popular demands for an autonomous republic were granted in March 1991, ethnic Russians and Russian-speaking Ukrainians did not mobilize. Many citizens in Galicia were marching in the streets or joining civic organizations, but citizens of Kharkiv, Dnipropetrovsk, Zaporizhzhe, and Kirovohrad were far less politically active. Nonetheless, *Rukh,* unlike the Popular Fronts in the Baltics, lacked the national support necessary to dominate Ukrainian politics.

The key player in this standoff was Leonid Kravchuk, chairman of the Ukrainian Supreme Soviet and formerly the Communist Party official in charge of ideology.[35] As the Communist Party and Ukraine as a whole began to split in 1990, Kravchuk tried to carve out a middle ground. Although he had previously been the scourge of nationalist dissidents, he understood the new reality. Embracing democracy and sovereignty gave political elites a better claim for political legitimacy than following Soviet orthodoxy. He appropriated the idea of Ukrainian sovereignty, although again in practice what this would mean was unclear. Already by October 1990, Stanislav Hurenko, the new head of the Ukrainian Communist Party, claimed that Kravchuk "belonged only nominally to the party."[36] Because Ukraine had no president, Kravchuk, as head of the parliament, began to act like the head of state. In November 1990, he invited Boris Yeltsin to Kiev, and the two leaders, acting as if the entire Gorbachev-backed Union framework was irrelevant, signed a broad-ranging treaty between their republics. Kravchuk also came out against the use of force against pro-independence groups in Lithuania, and he openly opposed Gorbachev's plans for a new Union Treaty.

SOVIET ENDGAME AND UKRAINE'S DECLARATION OF INDEPENDENCE

By early 1991, the future of the Soviet Union looked bleak. The Baltic states had declared independence, numerous republics, including Ukraine, had declared their sovereignty, and the economy continued to decline. Across the country, there was a growing divide between nationalist and democratic forces and the communist authorities. Gorbachev had little support, either with the public or within the party. The specter of civil war was raised by many Soviet citizens.

Gorbachev, however, wanted to preserve the Soviet Union, albeit with a reformed federal structure. In March 1991, Soviet citizens voted on a new Union Treaty that asked if they would support the preservation of the Soviet Union as a "renewed federation of equal sovereign states." Six republics that were committed to complete independence—Lithuania, Latvia, Estonia, Moldova, Georgia, and Armenia—refused to participate. In Galicia, civic organizations urged a boycott of the vote on the Union Treaty and offered voters a different question: Did they wish Ukraine to be an independent state? Meanwhile, Kravchuk had succeeded in getting an additional question on the Ukrainian ballot: "Do you agree that Ukraine should be a part of the union of Soviet sovereign states on the principles of the Declaration of State Sovereignty of Ukraine?"

The results of the vote were a modest victory for Gorbachev. Across the nine republics that voted on the Union Treaty, 78% voted to retain the Soviet Union. In Ukraine, more than 80% of eligible voters came to the polls. A solid majority, 70.5%, voted in favor of Gorbachev's proposal. Later, this vote would be used by some to claim that the dissolution of the Soviet Union did not reflect the will of the Soviet or Ukrainian people.

Significantly, however, 80.2% voted in favor of Kravchuk's question. Both proposals used the word sovereignty, and what precisely either measure would mean in practice was still unclear. Kravchuk, however, was able to use his "victory" as a means to argue that Gorbachev's vision of a "Federation of Sovereign Republics" would have to be a "Union of Sovereign States." He claimed that the results of the all-Union voting had "no meaning" for him. Gorbachev talked of 9+1 (nine republics plus a weaker central government), but Kravchuk preferred a 9+0 option (no center), which was still an arrangement that would be short of Ukrainian independence. Thus, although 88% of the voters in Galicia opted for independence in their own poll in March 1991, sovereignty "remained the limit of most political imaginations."[37]

Events through the spring of 1991 reflected a more radicalized atmosphere. Many in Galicia used their vote for independence to try to push for Ukraine to follow other republics and formally leave the Soviet Union. The miners in eastern Ukraine launched another round of strikes, demanding the resignation of Gorbachev and constitutional status for Ukraine's Declaration of Sovereignty. Kravchuk tried to hold a middle ground between Gorbachev and more radical elements in Ukraine, claiming he wanted a union of sovereign states. Nonetheless, nationalist parties such as the Ukrainian Republican Party (an offshoot of the UHU) threatened to call for a general strike if a new Union Treaty was signed, and student leaders pledged they would renew hunger strikes as well. Meanwhile, the Ukrainian government was embarking on its own state-building efforts, including establishing a presidential form of government, nationalizing industries, and creating a National Bank that would issue a separate Ukrainian currency.

Ukrainian statehood, then, looked like a real possibility. Some were alarmed by this prospect. Ethnic Russians tried, without much success, to create Interfront organizations like those in the Baltic states to rally for the preservation of the Soviet Union. Many in Moscow were puzzled at the notion that the Ukrainians, fellow Slavs, would want to separate from Russia. The American President, George H. W. Bush, went to Kiev in August 1991 and delivered his notorious "Chicken Kiev" speech, in which he warned against the dangers of "suicidal nationalism."

Just as the ascension of Gorbachev was the event that triggered the rise of Ukrainian national-democratic movements, the final major event in the struggle for Ukrainian independence occurred in Moscow. On August 19, 1991, the day before a new Union Treaty was to be signed in Moscow (Kravchuk was not planning to attend), conservatives forces in the Communist Party and security forces formed an Emergency State Committee and put Gorbachev, who was vacationing on the Black Sea, under house arrest. Yeltsin, who managed to escape capture, rallied democratic and anticommunist forces outside the Russian parliament. The coup, which was poorly organized, fell apart when the Soviet military sided with Yeltsin, who, emboldened from this victory, banned the now widely discredited Communist Party.

During this dramatic event, Kiev was relatively calm compared to Moscow. Ukrainian Party leader Stanislaw Hurenko, unsurprisingly, supported the coup, and the party called on local party leaders to rally all patriotic forces and ban all demonstrations and protests. Kravchuk, however, was more circumspect. On Ukrainian television, he stated that "our position is deliberation and once again deliberation." One interpretation of these remarks is that Kravchuk was ready to support whatever the outcome was in Moscow.[38] As matters turned out, Kravchuk did not have to sit on the fence for long, and the defeat of the coup plotters put the more orthodox communists on the defensive.

On August 24, 1991, three days after the coup collapsed, the Ukrainian Supreme Soviet, by a vote of 346 to 1, issued a Declaration of Independence. This was followed up by measures—also overwhelming approved—to assert Ukrainian control over all defense forces on Ukrainian territory and introduce a Ukrainian currency. *Rukh* and its allies had pushed for a quick vote on independence, realizing that their opponents were on the defensive. The communists, aware that they no longer commanded a majority (there were more defections from the party caucus immediately after the coup), voted in favor of the measure, which significantly was not accompanied by any concerted effort to de-communize Ukrainian government and society. The CPU was officially banned on August 30, but communist members of the Ukrainian Supreme Soviet kept their seats and many joined the newly formed Socialist Party. In other words, the Ukrainian communists gave the national-democratic opposition what the latter truly wanted, but, by voting for independence, it helped fend off other measures that, potentially at least, would have harmed themselves directly and potentially advanced the cause of democracy and economic reform in Ukraine. Kravchuk, for his part, received emergency powers and was without question the frontrunner to become Ukraine's first president. Volodymyr Hrynov, deputy chairman of the parliament, warned:

> I am not against the independence of Ukraine. But I see a terrible danger today if we pass this Act on its own. Without a decision on the problem of the decommunization of Ukraine, this act will just be a piece of paper. We are building a totalitarian Communist society in Ukraine, I propose that we pass this Act only as part of a package together with [other] measures by which the totalitarian society in Ukraine will be demolished.[39]

Although this failure would handicap the newborn post-Soviet Ukrainian state (see Chapter 9) many people were not looking ahead. Instead, many celebrated the fact that independence, which was nothing but a dream a few years before, looked to be achieved.

Ukraine's Independence Referendum

Two important questions lingered. Did Ukraine's Declaration of Independence enjoy the support of most Ukrainians? In other words, was it legitimate, based on popular will? Second, amid the confusion of a rapidly dissolving Soviet Union, on what basis would Ukraine relate to other post-Soviet republics? Put differently, how would the Soviet divorce be managed?

The answer to the first question was resolved on December 1, 1991, when Ukrainians voted in an independence referendum and also for their first president. Since the August Declaration of Independence, which was uncontested by Soviet or Russian authorities, Ukraine had acted as if it were an independent state, and all major political parties and mass media in Ukraine staked out a pro-independence platform. Ukrainian independence was supported in all the regions of Ukraine, as seen in Table 8.1. Not surprisingly, those in eastern Ukraine overwhelmingly approved it, but so did voters in the east and south. Even residents of Crimea, the only region with an ethnic Russian majority, opted in favor of Ukrainian independence, albeit by a much lower figure than in all other regions of Ukraine. These results, however, did not mean that all Ukrainians were ardent nationalists. Surveys revealed that economic concerns were foremost in the minds of voters, with issues such as cultural revival of Ukraine or securing Ukraine's political sovereignty ranking much lower. Surveys also showed ethnocultural divides, with ethnic Russians, other minorities, and members of the Russian Orthodox Church significantly less supportive of independence than ethnic Ukrainians or those who claimed to be Greek Catholic or members of the Ukrainian Autocephalous Orthodox Church.[40] Nonetheless, that the vast majority of Ukrainians had embraced what, only six months earlier, would have been viewed as a "radical" idea showed how much things had changed in the latter half of 1991.

Table 8.1. Results of Voting on December 1, 1991

Region	% for Independence	% for Kravchuk	% for Chornovil
West	97	37	50
Central	95	69	17
East	88	71	13
South	87	71	14
Crimea	54	54	5
Total	90	62	23

Source: Adapted from Taras Kuzio and Andrew Wilson, *Ukraine: Perestroika to Independence* (New York: St. Martin's, 1994), pp. 187, 189.

Six candidates ran for the Ukrainian presidency. The main two contenders, however, were Kravchuk and Chornovil, who by this time had become *Rukh*'s most prominent political figures. Kravchuk portrayed himself as a man of experience and stability. While pledging to uphold Ukrainian independence, his background as a high official in the Communist Party was useful to reassure those who did not want Ukraine to move in a radical direction. Because most of the media was in the hands of the national communists, Kravchuk enjoyed both more coverage and more favorable coverage than his opponents. Kravchuk, who had no one running to his left, also received support from the Socialist Party and smaller leftist parties that were based primarily in eastern Ukraine. Chornovil's base of support was more limited, and many viewed him as a radical or uncertain choice. Chornovil did well in western Ukraine, particularly in Galicia, but, as seen in Table 8.1, Kravchuk won handily, carrying all regions but western Ukraine.

Although the new Ukrainian leaders would have to make many important decisions (e.g., what to do with nuclear weapons on Ukrainian territory, how to reform the economy, what symbols to adopt for the new state) in the wake of gaining independence, one issue required immediate attention: ensuring that the collapse of the Soviet Union remained peaceful. Ukraine's declaration of independence in August had already largely sealed the fate of the Soviet Union. After December 1, there was no possibility of reviving the union. Not only did Ukraine want out, but, perhaps even more important, so did Russia. Between August and December, Yeltsin, elected president of Russia in July 1991, rebuffed Gorbachev's efforts to refashion relations among the republics. Even central Asian republics, where there was little nationalist mobilization, were intent on leaving the Union. On December 8, 1991, after a night of heavy drinking, Yeltsin, Kravchuk, and Belarussian leader Stanislaw Shushkevich, meeting in Brezhnev's old dacha in western Belarus, agreed to dissolve the Soviet Union. Citing the fact that their three republics were the original founders of the Soviet Union in 1922, they claimed the right to disassemble it. In its stead, they created the Commonwealth of Independent States (CIS), a grouping that was supposed to promote a civilized divorce among post-Soviet states by preserving political, economic, security, and cultural ties. Other post-Soviet states (but not the Baltics) would later join the CIS. The precise functions and powers of the CIS were not spelled out concretely, but it was clear—and Kravchuk emphasized this point—that it was not a reformed union. It was, instead, a purely voluntary organization of independent countries. Kravchuk returned to Kiev and briefly feared that forces from the old center—the military or the KGB—would intervene, but these organizations were being taken over by Yeltsin. The Soviet Union ceased to exist on December 25, 1991. Ukraine was now independent.

NOTES

1. The most commonly cited exception is Helene Carriere d'Encausse, *Decline of an Empire* (New York: Newsweek Books, 1980), who mistakenly argued that the main problem would be Muslim uprisings in central Asia. Even as late as 1990, many leading scholars thought the breakup of the Soviet Union was unlikely. See various contributions in Alexander Motyl, ed. *Thinking Theoretically about Soviet Nationalities* (New York: Columbia University Press, 1992).

2. The best treatment of Gorbachev is Archie Brown, *The Gorbachev Factor* (Oxford: Oxford University Press, 1997).

3. Mark Beissinger, *Nationalist Mobilization and the Collapse of the Soviet State* (Cambridge: Cambridge University Press, 2002).

4. Bohdan Nahaylo, *The Ukrainian Resurgence* (London: Hurst and Company, 1999), pp. 57–58.

5. Anna Reid, *Borderland: A Journey through the History of Ukraine* (Boulder: Westview, 1997), p. 201

6. Reid, 1997, pp. 194–195.

7. Serhy Yekelchyk, *Ukraine: Birth of a Modern Nation* (Oxford: Oxford University Press, 2007), p. 179.

8. Reid, 1997, pp. 194, 204.

9. "Waiting for the Next Chernobyl," *Financial Times*, April 21, 1993.

10. Nahaylo, 1999, p. 60.

11. Roman Solchanyk, *Ukraine: From Chernobyl to Sovereignty* (New York: St. Martin's, 1992), p. xiii.

12. Reid, 1997, p. 205.

13. *Literaturna Ukraina*, July 9, 1987.

14. Nahaylo, 1999, pp. 62–63.

15. Quoted in Taras Kuzio and Andrew Wilson, *Ukraine: Perestroika to Independence* (New York: St. Martin's, 1994), p. 66.

16. Quoted in Kuzio and Wilson, 1994, p. 71.

17. Kuzio and Wilson, 1994, p. 74.

18. Nahaylo, 1999, pp. 172–173

19. Nahaylo, 1999, pp. 192–193.

20. Kuzio and Wilson, 1994, p. 111.

21. Nahaylo, 1999, p. 218.

22. Kuzio and Wilson, 1994, p. 111 and Nahaylo, 1999, p. 218.

23. Ilya Prizel, "Ukraine Between Proto-Democracy and 'Soft' Authoritarianism," in Karen Dawisha and Bruce Parrott, eds. *Democratic Changes and Authoritarian Reactions in Russia, Ukraine, Belarus, and Moldova* (Cambridge: Cambridge University Press, 1997), pp. 338–339.

24. Andrew Wilson, *Ukrainian Nationalism in the 1990s: A Minority Faith* (Cambridge: Cambridge University Press, 1996).

25. Alexander Motyl and Bohdan Krawchenko, "Ukraine: from Empire to Statehood," in Ian Bremmer and Ray Taras, eds. *New States, New Politics: Building the Post-Soviet Nations* (Cambridge: Cambridge University Press, 1997), p. 246.

26. A good source for worker mobilization in Ukraine is Sue Davis, *Trade Unions in Russia and Ukraine, 1985–1995* (New York: Palgrave, 2001).

27. Members of the Donbass Regional Strike Committee were present at *Rukh's* founding congress, but the relationship between the miners and the intellectuals and political prisoners involved with *Rukh* was always tenuous. For example, the miners' movement agreed with *Rukh* about republican sovereignty, but it expressed reservations about the use of Ukrainian national symbols, which subsequently were not adopted as the official symbols of *Rukh*.

28. Motyl and Krawchenko, 1997, p. 244.

29. *Literaturna Ukraina,* April 5, 1990.

30. Motyl and Krawchenko, 1997, p. 247.

31. Motyl and Krawchenko, 1997, p. 248.

32. Andrew Wilson, *The Ukrainians: Unexpected Nation* (New Haven, CT: Yale University Press, 2000), p. 160.

33. Kuzio and Wilson, 1994, p. 127.

34. Yekelchyk, 2007, p. 184.

35. Wilson, 2000, pp. 163–165.

36. Yekelchyk, 2007, p. 186.

37. Nahaylo, 1999, p. 352, and Wilson, 2000, p. 165.

38. Wilson, 2000, pp. 166–167.

39. Wilson, 2000, p. 168.

40. Kuzio and Wilson, 1994, p. 190.

9

Post-Soviet Ukraine, 1991–2004

Ukraine's declaration of independence ended the country's participation in the Soviet Union, but it would be the start of a long difficult process to undo many aspects of Soviet rule and establish a strong, stable, democratic state. Post-Soviet Ukraine faced a variety of challenges, including state-building, democratization, economic reform and revival, and overcoming regional divisions to create a more coherent national identity. On some fronts, there was progress in the 1990s. On many issues, however, Ukraine did not fare so well: the economy collapsed, political reform was slow, and the population grew disillusioned with independence. By the early 2000s, Ukraine found itself embroiled in a deep political crisis, with the president implicated in the murder of a journalist and a host of other crimes. This chapter assesses developments in Ukraine during the presidencies of Leonid Kravchuk (1991–1994) and Leonid Kuchma (1994–2004).

SECURING THE UKRAINIAN STATE

Ukraine became an independent state "without a modern nation or united political community enclosed within its borders."[1] Constructing a fully independent state out of what was a territory within the Soviet Union was thus a major, if not primary, challenge for Ukrainian elites. Ukraine inherited much (e.g., a bureaucracy, laws, locally stationed military forces and equipment) from the Soviet Union. The task, however, was to make these things *Ukrainian* and to make Ukrainian statehood a reality both in the international arena and for the population, which suddenly found themselves citizens of a new state.

State-building had a number of components, from the highly pragmatic (e.g., border security, creating a new constitution) to the symbolic (e.g., resurrecting national myths, choosing a national anthem). Both Leonid Kravchuk, the former communist who was elected president in December 1991, and the national-democratic opposition in *Rukh* and other parties agreed in the early 1990s on the need to build strong state institutions. Some things were done rather quickly. For example, Ukraine entered into negotiations with Russia and other post-Soviet states on dividing up the Soviet military. Ukraine's position was that troops and equipment stationed in Ukraine should become part of Ukrainian military forces, and the 800,000 soldiers inherited from the Soviet Union were expected to swear allegiance to defend Ukraine. On this score, two sticking points with Russia arose: what to do with nearly 200 nuclear-armed missiles stationed on Ukrainian territory and how to divide the Black Sea Fleet, which was based in Crimea. Ukraine's refusal to simply hand over these assets to Russia complicated relations both with Russia and Western states, which were concerned about the security of the Soviet nuclear arsenal. For its part, Ukraine sought both financial compensation for the missiles and security guarantees from both Russia and Western states, suggesting it might keep the weapons for self-defense should such guarantees not be issued.

Ukraine also sought international recognition for its statehood, thereby legitimizing its independence in the eyes of the world. In practical terms, this meant establishing Ukraine's separateness from Russia, which was promoting the Commonwealth of Independent States (CIS), a multilateral arrangement among most of the post-Soviet states, as a vehicle to preserve political and economic integration. Ukrainian leaders were at best lukewarm about the CIS and were unwilling to cede it powers over Ukraine. They wanted the world to recognize Ukraine as truly independent, not simply as part of some other institution. Most states, including the United States, Canada, Poland, and Germany, complied quickly with this request, and Russia's President Boris Yeltsin also said he recognized Ukraine's independence. The problem, as noted more later, was that several members of the Russian parliament did not agree, claiming that all or parts of Ukraine (e.g., Crimea) should remain with Russia.

Kravchuk also took steps domestically to strengthen the state and Ukraine's national identity. One measure was to promote the use of the Ukrainian language, as new elites understood that making the Ukrainian state more "Ukrainian" was importance in securing real separation from Russia. Although "Ukrainianization" was envisioned to be gradual, such moves did encounter resistance from the Russified eastern and southern regions while winning Kravchuk kudos in western Ukraine. Kravchuk also promoted use of the blue and yellow Ukrainian flag (which he himself had repressed as a communist leader), the state emblem (a trident used in Kievan Rus), and the anthem, "Ukraine Has Not Yet Perished." Kravchuk also backed the Ukrainian Orthodox Church (Kiev Patriarchate) over the Russian Orthodox Church. Meanwhile, schools and media began promoting a distinctly *Ukrainian* national history, including claiming that Kievan Rus was a proto-Ukrainian state and celebrating the Cossacks as freedom-loving democrats.

Kravchuk made a remarkable transformation from "guardian of the Soviet state to guardian of the Ukrainian state, from supporter of all things Soviet to critic of all things Soviet, from enemy of Ukrainian nationalism to Ukrainian nationalist *par excellence.*"[2] He appropriated much of the program of the anti-communist national-democrats, many of whom, in turn, became his vocal supporters. For example, the Republican Party, led by former dissident Mikhaylo Horyn, drew upon lessons of history from the post-World War I period and maintained that "the underestimation of the role of the state and inadequate attention to its development resulted in the loss of national statehood, compel the Republicans . . . to support the state,"[3] which, in effect, meant that President Kravchuk, who portrayed himself as a Ukrainian George Washington, was the man who secured Ukrainian statehood.

Kravchuk, however, did not push through significant economic or political reforms. In November 1992, Ukraine did issue its own temporary currency, the *karbovanets* (also called *kupon*), thereby leaving the Russian-dominated ruble zone. Broader marketization and privatization, however, was not on Kravchuk's agenda, and the economy began to collapse for a variety of reasons, including corruption, an uncertain legal environment, hyperinflation, and the loss of economic ties with other post-Soviet republics. The introduction of a permanent new currency was repeatedly postponed. Politically, Kravchuk wanted to centralize authority in his own hands and did little to democratize the state or encourage the formation of independent groups. He called on "all patriotic forces to consolidate around the task of state-building," to "overcome personal ambition," and to "neglect insignificant tactical discrepancies for the sake of a greater strategic goal."[4] He fended off criticism by wrapping himself up in Ukrainian statehood, so that those who might oppose him risked being labeled unpatriotic. At one point, he openly declared, "We are the state."[5] Some national-democrats, as noted, were willing to go along, as they saw Kravchuk as a guarantor of statehood and preferable to a parliament that was still dominated by former Communist Party members.[6] Critics, however, maintained that some national-democrats had developed a "fetish for the state" and therefore were complicit in Kravchuk's attempts to co-opt and muzzle dissent, including turning the media into a mouthpiece for the president.[7]

In 1994, Ukraine held presidential elections. Kravchuk, who could not run on a positive economic record or as a committed democrat, was forced to run as a nationalist. In the run-off election he faced Leonid Kuchma, a former director of a Soviet missile factory who served as prime minister from 1992 to 1993. Kuchma, who spoke poor Ukrainian, appealed to voters in eastern and southern regions and eschewed much of the Ukrainianization program. He was vilified by some as a person who would surrender Ukrainian sovereignty to Russia. Kuchma, however, ultimately prevailed, and it fell to him to complete many aspects of the state-building project. In 1996, Kuchma pushed through both a new constitution and a new, permanent currency, the *hryvnia*. Kuchma concluded a deal whereby Ukraine gave up its nuclear weapons, and he also divided up the Black Sea Fleet and concluded a Treaty of Friendship with Russia. By the mid-1990s, Kuchma had established his bonafides as a state-builder, and he was viewed positively by many in the more nationalist-oriented western parts of the country. Like Kravchuk, however, one could doubt both his commitment to democracy and to economic reform.

DEMOCRATIZING THE UKRAINIAN STATE?

Ukraine's declaration of independence secured the country statehood, but there was no broad political housecleaning to remove the Soviet-era leadership. Elections had been held in 1990, but national-democrats performed well primarily in western Ukraine and Kiev. Most members of the legislature were communists, and even though the CPU was formally banned in August 1991, the individual parliamentarians remained in place. Kravchuk did become more of a nationalist, but he did little to democratize the state, preferring to concentrate power in the executive branch, bypass the parliament, and co-opt or repress opposition. He did not join or lead a political party, but critics accused him of creating a "party of power" that substituted the slogans of nationalism for those of communism. Others, including many ardently committed to Ukrainian statehood, found this justifiable or desirable because democratic development needed to be secondary to the demands of state-building. One writer in the ostensibly liberal Ukrainian Language Society newspaper lamented that democracy "does not teach national consciousness, does not create it, does not stimulate a de-nationalized population to solidarity in the national organism." The solution, therefore, was for the state to promulgate "the" national idea and unite society.[8] Political parties, which present alternative programs and compete for votes, were derided, in Kravchuk's terms, for "speculating on workers and advancing private interests."[9]

By 1993, however, it was clear that the country was in political crisis. A constitution had yet to be approved, and there were battles for authority between Kravchuk and the *Verkhovna Rada* (parliament). Political parties were weak.

Political opinion expressed little confidence in any government body. Deteriorating economic conditions produced a wave of strikes, led by coal miners from eastern Ukraine. In addition to economic demands such as higher wages, they wanted new elections. Presidential and parliamentary elections were held in 1994. Many candidates ran for parliament as independents, a reflection of the weaknesses of political parties, and once in parliament various factions formed, producing a very fractured parliament. As seen in Table 9.1, national-democratic parties such as *Rukh*, however, fared poorly compared to those tied to the communist past (including the Center Party, *Yednist*, and the Inter-Regional Reform Bloc); and poor voter turnout, a reflection of growing disillusionment with politics, meant that only 338 of 450 seats could be initially filled in 1994.[10] Commenting after these elections, former dissident Levko Lukianenko lamented the close ties between democratic parties and the "party of power," which, in his view, had compromised both the democratic parties and the idea of democracy.[11] One analyst noted that Kravchuk's

Table 9.1. 1994 Elections in Ukraine

| Parliamentary Elections* | | Presidential Elections | |
Party/Faction	Number of Seats	Candidate	% vote Rd.1/Rd. 2
Communists	97	Leonid Kuchma (Independent)	31.2/52.2
Center Party	37	Leonid Kravchuk (Independent)	38.4/45.1
Reform Group	36	Oleksandr Moroz (Socialist)	13.3
Yednist (Unity)	34	Volodymyr Lanovoi (Independent)	9.6
Inter-Regional Bloc for Reforms	32		
Rukh	29		
Socialist Party	27		
Others	124		

*These figures include results from by-elections through 1996, at which time 34 seats remained unfilled. Data from Economist Intelligence Unit Country Profile, 1996–1997.

approach to governance resembled that of the old Soviet system and that it was a "recipe for stagnation, corruption, and the growing abuse of power of the state."[12] Still, in the 1994 presidential contest, the national-democrats did not even run a candidate, opting instead to back Kravchuk. Kravchuk, however, was defeated by Kuchma, who was seen as the candidate of the Soviet managerial class, in the run-off between the top two vote-getters.

Ukraine, however, did have a change in leadership, something that few other post-Soviet states could claim in the 1990s. One could question, however, whether there was real change in either the style or substance of governance or whether the shift from Kravchuk to Kuchma represented simply the victory of one faction of the "party of power" over another. Kuchma, like Kravchuk, put a priority on consolidating his power. A central political concern in the first years of Kuchma's reign was passage of a new constitution. The main sticking point was the division of power between the president and the parliament, which was dominated by leftists and, by 1995, had come to oppose many aspects of Kuchma's economic reforms and his foreign policy, both discussed in more detail later in the chapter. After a prolonged stalemate with parliament that produced political paralysis, Kuchma broke the impasse by threatening to hold a referendum to pass a law that would allow him to disband parliament. Mostly out of concern for its self-preservation, the *Verkhovna Rada* passed a new constitution on June 28, 1996. The constitution gave the president considerable power, including the right to appoint and dismiss the prime minister and other state officials (e.g., judges, state prosecutors, heads of state-run media and the privatization agency). Kuchma retained the right to issue decrees with the force of law. In other respects, however, the constitution was a compromise document, giving national-democrats provisions that promoted the "national idea" (e.g., Ukrainian was made the sole state language) and the left promises of welfare provisions and emphasis on the "social character" of the state.[13]

The adoption of a constitution was hailed by many as progress, as Ukraine (unlike Russia in 1993) managed to avoid political violence. Some thought that Kuchma would use his powers to push through more radical economic and political reforms. These hopes, however, were dashed. Instead, Kuchma used his wide powers to appoint his allies to high office and thereby supervised development of crony capitalism, with political elites using their positions to acquire vast wealth. Examples included Pavlo Lazarenko, who served as prime minister from 1996–1997. A protégé of Kuchma from Dnipropetovsk, he acquired a fortune in energy and communication businesses. Kuchma eventually saw Lazarenko as a potential threat and dismissed him. Lazarenko fled to the United States, where he was convicted for money laundering. Other rich Ukrainians with political connections—commonly known as "oligarchs"—included Viktor Pinchuk, head of the Dnipropetrovsk "clan" who became a trusted confidant of Kuchma and even married Kuchma's daughter in 2002. Rinat Akhmetov, an ethnic Tatar, was the head of the rival Donestsk "clan" and made his fortune in metallurgy, machine-making, and communications. By 1996, at the age of 30, he was worth several billion dollars and was a major backer of various politicians and political parties. Although various oligarchs and clans were represented in Kuchma's "party of power," it is worth noting that rivalries among them occasionally turned violent, as when Yevchen Scherban, a member of parliament and prominent "oligarch" from Donetsk, was murdered in 1996, allegedly as a result of an order from Prime Minister Lazarenko, who was a leader in the Dnipropetrovsk clan.

Ukraine still had elections, but they became less and less free and competitive. Controls over the media, whether it was state-owned or privately (oligarch)–owned, hampered the democratic opposition, and rules regarding electoral spending were blatantly disregarded, much to the benefit of those parties who had richer benefactors. The Kuchma administration also used "administrative resources"—threats against local officials, criminal probes against opponents, pressure on state employees to vote for certain candidates, the doling out of money in an attempt to sway voters—to produce favorable electoral results. Kuchma also used his state-building credentials to win support among national-democrats, presenting himself as the only alternative to a return of unreformed communists.

Results from the 1998 parliamentary and 1999 presidential elections were not particularly encouraging, as seen in Table 9.2. The parliamentary elections were held under a new electoral law, with half the seats determined by proportional representation and half by single-member mandates defined by districts. Although there were complaints about the lead-up to the elections (particularly on media coverage of the candidates) and some irregularities on election day (e.g., vote-rigging), these elections were judged largely free and fair by international observers. The Communists, with strong bases of support in more populated eastern and southern Ukraine, emerged as the biggest winners, albeit short of a majority, whereas the national-democrats, such as *Rukh,* received only about 10% of the seats. The balance of power in the *Verkhovna Rada,* however, was held by independents (often wealthy businessmen) and small "centrist" parties, frequently the creations of the presidential administration or of oligarchic clans. For example, the Green Party was founded by big-business interests who thought the name might appeal to voters, *Hromada* was the creation of Pavlo Lazarenko, and Social Democratic Party (United) was run by Viktor Medvedchuk, head of the presidential administration.

Although many who yearned for democracy and positive political change were let down by the 1998 parliamentary elections, the 1999 presidential elections were more of a fiasco. The country's poor economic condition meant that many were unhappy with Kuchma. Given his low standing in public opinion,[14] it was hard to imagine how he could be reelected. Kuchma, however, benefited from various factors. First, Viacheslav Chornovil, the leader of *Rukh* and expected to be one of Kuchma's main challengers, was killed in a car

Table 9.2. 1998 and 1999 Elections in Ukraine

| 1998 Parliamentary Elections | | 1999 Presidential Elections | |
Party	Number of Seats	Candidate	% vote Rd.1/Rd. 2
Communists	121	Leonid Kuchma (Independent)	36.5/56.3
Rukh	46	Petro Symonenko (Communist)	22.2/36.8
Socialist/ Peasant Bloc	34	Oleksandr Moroz (Socialist)	11.3
Green Party	19	Natalia Vitrenko (Progressive Socialist)	11.0
People's Democratic Party	28	Yevhen Marchuk (Independent)	8.1
Hromada	24	Yuri Kostenko (Independent)	2.2
Social Democratic (United)	17	Hennady Udovwenko (Rukh)	1.2
Others	161	Others	3.5

accident in March, 1999, an event that many believed was no "accident."[15] Second, the presidential administration used a vast array of "administrative resources" to bolster Kuchma's vote, shut down opposition media outlets, and attack his most serious opponent, Oleksandr Moroz, leader of the Social- ist Party and a moderate leftist. Third, despite a public effort to unite behind a single candidate, the center-left opponents of Kuchma failed to do so. Mean- while, the authorities also discreetly supported fringe candidates (e.g., Natalia Vitrenko of the Progressive Socialists) to split the opposition vote. Ultimately, Kuchma was able to engineer a run-off against the uncharismatic and dog- matic Petro Symonenko of the Communist Party, a candidate who had little standing in most of the country and lacked the resources of Kuchma's political machine. Kuchma was duly reelected, although international observers noted numerous violations of democratic procedures, state control over the media, ballot-stuffing, voter harassment, and rigging of vote tally sheets.[16]

By the end of the 1990s, there was little positive to say about the state of democracy in Ukraine. Political opposition was weak and power was in the hands of the president and various oligarchic clans. When Ukrainians were asked in a survey in 1999 if they thought Ukraine was a democracy, only 17% said yes. Nearly 90% listed corruption as a serious problem. In another survey in the same year, respondents gave the political system under communism a higher rating than the one currently in place in Ukraine. Seventy-six percent of respondents indicated they were dissatisfied with how democracy was developing in Ukraine, and almost half (47.2%) said they would support having a strong leader who did not have to bother with parliaments and elections. Ukrainians expressed far more dissatisfaction with their political system than Poles, Czechs, Hungarians, or Romanians, although they were more supportive of democracy than Russians.[17] Overall, however, there was little positive to take away from public opinion surveys, which revealed high levels of disillusionment, disengagement, and frustration.

ECONOMIC COLLAPSE

Ukraine's economic problems in the 1990s were even more obvious than its problems in establishing a democratic government, and without doubt economic difficulties fed into some of the country's political problems. One could argue that Ukraine had at least a façade of democracy (e.g., elections with multiple parties), but there was no question that Ukraine had a severely dysfunctional economy that became so bad that the verb to "Ukrainianize" acquired in the Russian language the meaning "to bring to ruin."

Economic data capture part of the problem. As seen in Table 9.3, the Ukrainian economy experienced a range of problems including hyperinflation, declining growth, job loss, and minimal foreign investment. Many of the initial problems were related to an aging infrastructure inherited from Soviet mismanagement, the economic shock of the Soviet collapse, and the Kravchuk's administration's unwillingness to undertake economic reforms. Instead, the government printed money and continued to grant subsidies to ailing enterprises. Even so, many enterprises collapsed or were so indebted and short on capital that they were unable to pay their workers. Instead, workers were "paid in kind," meaning that in lieu of wages they received products (e.g., sausages, clothing, toilet paper) produced by their place of employment and then were expected to resell these products to generate cash or other necessities. Some Ukrainians were forced into "suitcase trading," taking basic wares to Poland, Russia, or Romania and trying to sell them there at a profit. Thousands of Ukrainian women, out of desperation, signed up for employment in Western Europe, only to be duped and forced into prostitution. More generally for those who remained in Ukraine, the collapse of production meant that many basic goods (e.g., sugar, cheese, milk) were in short supply, and hyperinflation meant that many Ukrainians could not afford to buy what was available.

Table 9.3. The Ukrainian Economy in the 1990s

Economic Variable	1991	1992	1993	1994	1995	1996	1997	1998	1999
Inflation Rate (%)	161	2730	10155	401	182	40	10	20	19
GDP* Decline	−11.6	−13.7	−14.2	−23.0	−12.2	−10.0	−3.0	−1.9	−0.4
Total Employment (1989 =100)	98.3	96.3	94.1	90.5	93.3	91.3	88.8	87.9	85.8
Private Sector as Share of GDP	10	10	15	40	45	50	55	55	55
Foreign Investment, per person	n/a	$3.40	$3.98	$3.18	$5.26	$10.42	$12.46	$14.86	$9.92

Source: Data from European Bank of Reconstruction and Development, reported in Anders Aslund, *Building Capitalism: Markets and Government in Russia and Transitional Economies* (Cambridge: Cambridge University Press, 2001).
*Gross Domestic Product, the total value of all goods and services in a given country.

In the fall of 1994, Kuchma adopted a "radical" reform package that envisioned cuts in state subsidies, privatization, and changes in laws to create a more business-friendly environment. As seen in the table, there was some improvement. Inflation markedly declined, allowing the government to introduce the *hryvnia* in 1996. The decline in production became less acute, although it would be 2000 before Ukraine experienced positive economic growth; and the overall decline in gross domestic product from the 1990s was calculated at 54%, worse than in Russia (40%)[18] and twice as severe as the general estimate for economic decline in the United States during the Great Depression. Under Kuchma, more and more of the Ukrainian economy became privately owned, but government programs to sell off economic enterprises (stores, factories, mines, farms) suffered from numerous problems, especially corruption. Those that had political connections were able to buy shares of companies at steep discounts and thereby become oligarchs. Often, new owners simply plundered their companies, selling off the enterprises' capital assets (e.g., industrial equipment), taking their profits, dismantling the enterprise, and ultimately putting workers out on the streets.

Although Kuchma advertised his programs as "radical reform," he failed to follow through on much of the agenda. Part of the problem was political resistance to the creation of a free market economy, particularly in eastern Ukraine, where aging state-owned industries required state support to stay afloat. Within the population, there was also no consensus on what to do. A survey in 1995 found that less than a third (31.4%) of Ukrainians thought they would benefit from private property, and fewer (23.8%) thought freeing prices was a good idea. Most (54%) thought the state should still bear the main responsibility for providing things necessary for a person's life.[19] Without a solid commitment to reform either from Kuchma or society at large, "particular clans looked after their particular interests and the reform project gradually lost impetus."[20] The result was confusion and bad policy. For example, tax rates as high as 90% on gross business income forced much of the economy onto the illegal or "black" market. Many of the promises of privatization, such as more efficiency and creation of a wide class of shareholders among the Ukrainian population, went unrealized. Plans to give workers preference in buying shares of their firms, with the goal of creating worker-owned enterprises, went nowhere, as managers used their financial resources and leverage over employees to fleece them of their shares.[21] Even so, private ownership in Ukraine lagged behind that of all East-Central European states (e.g., Poland, Slovakia, Hungary) and Russia, and the World Bank's structural reform index (a collection of various factors) showed that Ukraine lagged behind many post-Soviet states, including Georgia, Kazakhstan, and Moldova.[22] Foreign investment remained measly: compare the highest per capita figure in Ukraine ($14.86 in 1998) with $128 for Poland, $256 for the Czech Republic, and $397 for Estonia in the same year.[23]

The collapse of the Ukrainian economy had political as well as human costs. Ukrainians grew more and more disillusioned with their government, with "democracy," and even with independent statehood. Surveys from the early part of the 1990s showed that approximately 90% of the population thought that things in Ukraine were moving in the wrong direction.[24] Even with some economic improvement in the late 1990s, a survey in 1999 found that 94% of respondents were dissatisfied with the condition of the country, with economic reasons (poor living conditions, unemployment, lack of payment of wages, economic instability) as the chief causes of dissatisfaction. At the same time, however, there was still no consensus within the population on what the proper course of action should be, with 27% supporting a market economy, 30% backing a centrally planned economy, and 25% favoring some combination of the two.[25] Perhaps most disturbingly, some surveys in the 1990s found that Ukrainians were less and less enamored with the idea of an independent state. For example, one survey in 1996 found that 56% of respondents believed that Ukraine should unite with Russia in a single state.[26]

REGIONALISM IN POST-SOVIET UKRAINE

In addition to the need to secure a strong, well-functioning state and economy, Ukraine, as a new country, also needed a sense of national identity. As noted in this text, various regions of Ukraine had different historical experiences and arguably different interests and demands. When discussing the challenges of post-Soviet Ukraine, one writer understandably asked, "One Ukraine or Many?"[27] Forging a cohesive identity and overcoming regional divides was seen by many as necessary both to preserve independence and to move forward on political and economic reforms.

The broad contours of Ukrainian regionalism have been developed elsewhere in this text. To summarize, much of western Ukraine was formerly part of Poland and the Hapsburg Empire. This environment was more auspicious for the development of Ukrainian national consciousness, and the population in this region was overwhelmingly ethnic Ukrainian and Ukrainian-speaking. By contrast, eastern and southern Ukraine had been part of the Russian Empire. Residents in these areas were both more likely to be Russian speaking, and, in many cases, ethnically Russian as well. These regions were also far more industrialized and economically connected to Russia. Western Ukraine was added to the rest of Soviet Ukraine only as a result of World War II, and Crimea, which has an ethnic Russian majority, became a part of Ukraine in 1954. Although a majority of citizens in all regions of Ukraine voted for independence in 1991, western Ukrainians, together with elements of the intelligentsia in Kiev, were the drivers of the independence movement.

Despite its regional diversity, Ukraine experienced only one serious case of separatism: Crimea. Crimeans barely (54%) voted in favor of independence. Crimea was the only Ukrainian region with an ethnic Russian majority (67%), had no Ukrainian-language schools, and was part of Ukraine only because of an administrative transfer of territory made by Soviet leader Nikita Khrushchev. Crimea has a long association with the Russian Empire, dating back to Catherine the Great. Last of all, the Soviet Black Sea Fleet was headquartered there, and a large percentage of the population was active-duty or retired Soviet military.

Separatist mobilization began in Crimea as early as 1989, and Ukrainian authorities granted the region an autonomous status within the borders of Ukraine in February 1991. When Ukraine became independent, the calls for separatism or for rejoining Russia became far more pronounced. In May 1992, the Crimean parliament declared the region independent and proposed a referendum to vote on the matter. Many Russian political figures backed such moves. For example, then Vice-President Aleksandr Rutskoi argued that actions taken by Khrushchev in 1954 "under the influence of a hangover or sunstroke" did not "cancel out the history of Crimea."[28]

The government in Kiev, however, declared separatism illegal, while passing a law that gave Crimea a large measure of political, economic, and cultural autonomy. Kiev also pledged economic assistance to Crimea. These proved to be temporary solutions, however, for in 1994 a pro-Russian candidate, Yuri Meshkov, was elected to the new post of president of Crimea and began concentrating power in his hands.

Crimean separatism did not succeed. In March 1995, the Ukrainian parliament voted to suspend Crimea's constitution, abolish the post of the Crimean president, and place the Crimean government under the control of the national government. Crimea had no military forces of its own to resist, and Russia, despite rhetoric from some of its politicians, was unwilling to intervene militarily. Many in Crimea were tired of Meshkov, and public opinion in Crimea was, according to one study, ambivalent or vacillating, as most Crimeans wanted both Crimea to become part of Russia while at the same time not wishing to secede from Ukraine.[29] When it became apparent that Crimea simply was not going to rejoin Russia, Crimeans reconciled themselves to this fact and saw little utility to go out into the streets to protest. Notably, Crimean separatism received no support from elsewhere in Ukraine, as surveys showed that both ethnic Ukrainians and ethnic Russians in Ukraine favored maintaining the inherited borders of the Ukrainian state.[30]

The larger regional issue in Ukraine, however, was division between the western and eastern parts of the country, with the Dnieper River often serving as some sort of unofficial border between the "two" Ukraines. Of course, such a division was simplistic, as it was hard to put many Ukrainian regions in black/white categories. Nonetheless, one could capture a west/east divide on a number of issues.[31] Linguistic Ukrainianization, for example, was far more favored in western Ukraine than in eastern Ukraine, where, according to the 1989 census, a third of the population was ethnically Russian and Russian was the main language of public discourse. For historical, cultural, and economic reasons, those in eastern Ukraine were far more likely to favor maintaining closer ties with Russia. Those in the west, in contrast, saw Moscow as a threat or negative influence and wanted stronger ties with Europe and the United States. Because many of the old, Soviet-era industrial enterprises were located in eastern and southern Ukraine, residents in these areas were wary of movement to free markets and favored state control and support for the economy. Figures 9.1 and 9.2 shows the extent of regional division on questions of economic reform, which would, as noted, complicate efforts to initiate and sustain marketization.[32]

Figure 9.1. Do You Think Free Prices Are Necessary for Economic Recovery?

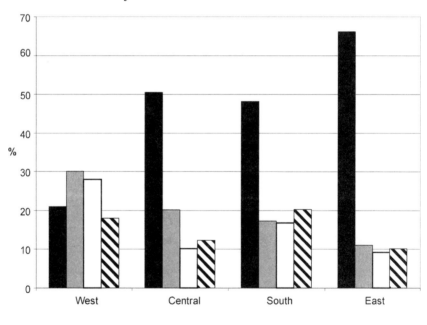

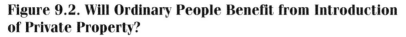

Figure 9.2. Will Ordinary People Benefit from Introduction of Private Property?

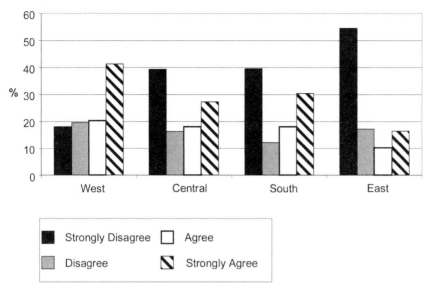

All of these factors manifested themselves in voting behavior, as those in western Ukraine voted for parties and candidates that tended to be pro-economic reform, pro-Western, and pro-Ukrainian statehood, whereas those in the east favored those parties, such as the communists, who endorsed closer ties with Russia and maintaining elements of the old Soviet economic system. The 1994 presidential election, for example, was highly polarized, with Kravchuk winning 70.3% of the vote on the Right [Western] Bank of the Dnieper and Kuchma winning 75.2% on the Left Bank. The margins were even more pronounced on the extremes, with Kravchuk winning more than 90% of the vote in Galicia, the base of the national-democrats, and Kuchma winning nearly 90% in the highly industrialized and Russified Donetsk region.[33] In the 1998 parliamentary elections, leftist parties won 44.6% of the vote in eastern regions, compared with only 9.6% in western Ukraine. Similarly, *Rukh* and other nationalist or nationalist-democratic parties received 65.5% of the vote in the west and only 9.2% in the east.[34]

As noted in the next chapter, these regional divisions have persisted into the 2000s, adding another dimension to the "Orange Revolution" and its aftermath. Nonetheless, the country has held together. Western Ukrainians have celebrated Ukrainian statehood and the gradual steps toward Ukrainianization (e.g., declaration of Ukrainian as the sole state language) and, probably to their own surprise, found themselves embracing, at various times, both Kravchuk and Kuchma as state-builders. As Andrew Wilson notes, the "Grand Bargain" national-democrats struck with both presidents meant that much of their state-building and cultural agenda was implemented by "centrist proxy."[35] Hard-line, radical nationalist groups, which took their inspiration from militant Ukrainian organizations such as the Organization of Ukrainian Nationalists, did form in western Ukraine, but they were politically marginalized. There was thus little prospect of Ukraine turning into a militantly nationalistic state (like Serbia) that would take actions against non-Ukrainians or non-Ukrainian speakers. Indeed, the opposite was true. The government never pursued forcible or radical Ukrainianization. The rights of Russian-speakers were upheld. Although the government eventually adopted economic reform, it did not abandon wholesale the smokestack industries of eastern Ukraine and consign eastern Ukraine to special misery. Indeed, on a per-capita income basis, Donetsk, for example, remains the richest region in the country, far richer than Galicia. The Ukrainian government, as noted later in the chapter, also tried to forge a good working relationship with Russia. Perhaps most important, political elites in eastern Ukraine became leaders of the country's most powerful economic "clans." Writing about the nonemergence of Donbass separatism, one writer noted:

> The Donbas local elites have, in general, comfortably integrated within those of the independent Ukrainian state. The Donbas elites understand that they have better opportunities within Ukraine than within a Russia which does not require another decaying industrial region with more troublesome coal miners. . . . Asked whether the Donbas would be better in Russia the Chairman of Donets'k oblast council, Vladimir Shcherban, replied: 'There are no "what ifs" in history. We have what we have. And we have to work from this reality instead of engaging in guesses. Donbas is an inalienable part of Ukraine.'[36]

UKRAINIAN FOREIGN POLICY BETWEEN EAST AND WEST

As suggested by the discussions on both state-building and regionalism in post-Soviet Ukraine, Ukraine's foreign policy orientation has been a major ongoing concern. Ukraine, of course, has a long history with Russia. For many Ukrainians, this history has been less than salutary, as Russia politically dominated over Ukraine, frustrating both the formation of an independent Ukrainian state and growth of Ukrainian culture. For others, however, ties with their fellow eastern Slavs were perfectly natural and even beneficial. Given Ukraine's history, its independence by definition meant separation from Russia, and Ukrainian state-builders had to establish institutions and an identity distinct from that of Russia. Some hoped that Ukraine would be assisted in that endeavor by creating stronger ties with Western states that would allow Ukraine to claim a "European," as opposed to a "Russian" or "Soviet" identity.

For much of the 1990s, however, Ukrainian foreign policy tried to strike a balance between West and East. Although Ukraine was not enthusiastic about the CIS, economic and cultural ties with Russia remained important. In simplest terms, Ukraine could not escape its history or geography. The problem, however, was that there was uncertainty about what course Russia would take. Russian President Boris Yeltsin recognized Ukrainian independence and spoke of creating strong and friendly relations between the two states. Other Russian officials, however, found it hard to reconcile themselves to Ukrainian independence, viewing Ukraine as part of Russia and Ukrainians as "Little Russians." Standing up to possible Russian threats and defending Ukrainian interests thus became a hallmark of defenders of Ukrainian statehood, including President Leonid Kravchuk.

Many Ukrainians thought that forging closer ties with Europe and the United States would offer Ukraine some protection against an unpredictable Russia. The problem, however, was that Ukraine was treated as a virtual pariah by the West in its first years of independence. Part of the problem was Kravchuk's reluctance to pursue economic and political reform. The larger issue, however, was the government's refusal to hand over its inherited nuclear missiles to Russia. Because Western governments put priority on cultivating good relations with Moscow, Ukrainian intransigence was seen as unnecessary and counterproductive.

This stalemate was broken under the presidency of Leonid Kuchma. Although one of his election slogans with respect to Russia was "Fewer Walls, More Bridges," upon election he shifted focus and tried to mend relations with the West. Ukraine agreed to give up its nuclear weapons, securing financial aid and security guarantees from Europe and the United States. Kuchma's economic reform plans also won him accolades from Western governments, and economic assistance began to flow into the country. Ukraine concluded a Partnership and Cooperation Agreement (PCA) with the European Union (EU) in 1994. It joined NATO's Partnership for Peace program and signed a Charter on Distinctive Partnership with NATO in 1997. Kuchma set EU membership as a long-term goal, and many in Ukraine endorsed NATO membership. Trade also expanded with European states, and over the course of the 1990s, the European Union provided more than €1 billion in economic and technical assistance. The United States also embraced Ukraine as a strategic partner, in part to serve as a buffer against Russia. By 1997, Ukraine was the third largest recipient of American foreign aid after Israel and Egypt. Through 2001, it had received $2.82 billion in American assistance.[37] Ukraine also took the lead in the so-called GUUAM (Georgia-Ukraine-Uzbekistan-Azerbaijan-Moldova) group, a coalition of states concerned with aggressive use of Russian power and interested in creating new energy markets.

Ukraine, however, did retain important ties with Russia. Although Kuchma often put priority on relations with Europe, he would note that Ukraine had a "multi-vector" foreign policy, which included a host of important ties with Russia. Chief among these was Russian provision of oil and gas, as Ukraine has few hydrocarbon resources of its own. Ukrainian dependence on Russian resources and the Russian-controlled pipeline network, however, gave Moscow room to play the energy card in other disputes (e.g., the Black Sea Fleet) with Kiev. Support from the West, however, strengthened Ukraine's hand, and in 1997 Ukraine and Russia agreed to divide the fleet and signed a treaty of friendship.

Ukraine's desire for closer ties with the West, however, mixed "like oil and water" as President Kuchma presided over an increasingly corrupt and non-democratic state.[38] There were many difficulties in implementing the PCA with the EU. Statements extolling the EU's and Ukraine's "common values" began to ring hollow, and the EU never indicated it would accept Ukraine as a full-fledged member. Western investment lagged because of concerns about corruption and the rule of law, and, especially after 1999, Western governments became more and more unspoken about the country's democratic shortcomings. For its part, the Ukrainian public was polarized by region on foreign policy issues, with those in the west favoring closer ties with Europe and those in the east and south putting greater priority on ties with Russia.

The result, in large measure, was confusion. The "multi-vector" foreign policy meant that there was no clear direction. As one observer noted:

> Ukraine's previous talk about integrating with the West was never matched by any real action. Kiev has been happy to take Western money, but it was equally happy to take free Russian gas. Beyond that, it has never had much of a foreign policy.[39]

After talking about Ukraine's "European Choice" in the 1990s, Kuchma, feeling spurned by Europe and the United States, began to turn to Russia in the 2000s. Ukraine joined with Russia and other CIS states in agreeing to create a Single Economic Space. Kuchma remarked that since European markets were increasingly closed to Ukraine, it was "better to have a real bird in hand than two in the bush."[40] Russia cut favorable energy deals with Ukraine in return for Russian ownership over refineries and other enterprises in Ukraine. Kuchma's embrace of Russia, however, had much to do with his own domestic troubles and the international fallout from a serious political crisis in Ukraine that shed new and disturbing light on Kuchma's abuse of power.

"KUCHMAGATE" AND POLITICAL CRISIS

Despite troubling aspects of the 1999 presidential election, there was some hope that Ukraine turned a corner with the new millennium. In December 1999, Kuchma appointed Viktor Yushchenko, former head of the National Bank, as prime minister. Yushchenko had a reputation for honesty and as a pro-Western reformer (he married a Ukrainian-American woman in 1998), and he began to implement economic reforms that had been neglected in previous years. Yushchenko helped renegotiate Ukraine's international debts and cracked down on illegal reexport of Russian oil and gas, one of the primary ways Ukrainian oligarchs had enriched themselves. Yushchenko pushed through tax reforms, which stimulated the growth of small enterprises that had been pushed underground by putative taxation. Meanwhile, tax breaks that benefited many of the oligarchs were lifted, "sweetheart" privatization deals were ended, and the Ukrainian treasury had sufficient increase in revenue to catch up on previous nonpayment of pensions and wages. After years of decline, in 2000 the Ukrainian economy grew 6%.[41]

These positive economic developments were overshadowed by a continued power grab by Kuchma and later revelations of abuse of power by President Kuchma and his clique that were caught on audiotape. In April 2000, at Kuchma's insistence, Ukraine held a referendum on political reforms designed to reduce the parliament's size and influence. The results of the referendum—more than 80% of Ukrainian voters approved the measures and turnout was an improbably high 81%—were seen by many in Ukraine and abroad as another example of a rigged election. Temporarily, however, it looked like Kuchma might have won a final battle with parliament and would further consolidate his authority. The tape scandal, also known as "Kuchmagate," intervened, however, preventing passage of Kuchma's political agenda. "Kuchmagate" began on November 28, 2000, when Oleksandr Moroz, one of Kuchma's most vociferous critics in parliament, accused Kuchma of ordering the death of Georgii Gongadze, an Internet journalist who wrote about the government's abuse of power and whose decapitated body was found in early November in woods outside of Kiev. Moroz's accusations were supported by audiotapes that were secretly recorded in the President's Office by Major Mykola Melnychenko, a security officer. On tape, Kuchma is heard asking the Security Service to "take care" of Gongadze, and at one point he suggests that he be deported to his native Georgia where he could be kidnapped by Chechen guerillas. Over the course of several months, more tapes were revealed. On these recordings, a foul-mouthed Kuchma is heard ordering electoral fraud, backing intimidation of judges and local officials, overseeing money laundering, bring complicit in the car "accident" that killed Chornovil in 1999, and even authorizing the sale of an advanced radar system to Iraq.

Although some disputed how Melnychenko was able to gain such access and whether or not he was a pawn for another politician or even a foreign government (he eventually won political asylum in the United States), the authenticity of the voices on the recording were repeatedly confirmed. Some of those heard on the tape confirmed that such conversations had occurred, although others, particularly those who were cast in an unfavorable light, such as Kuchma, denied them. In 2001, Kuchma finally acknowledged that the voice on tape was indeed his, but he alleged that the incriminating passages had been doctored on the digital recording. Few believed him. Polls in October 2001 revealed that the overwhelming majority of Ukrainians (86%) thought that the tapes were authentic.[42]

"Kuchmagate" had both international and domestic fallout. Internationally, the revelations only confirmed that Ukraine was making little progress toward democracy. The EU demanded that Ukraine investigate Gongadze's murder. The United States, particularly upset over alleged arms deals with Iraq, suspended its economic assistance.[43] As noted previously, Kuchma at the same time began to turn increasingly toward Russia. Within Ukraine, initial protests in late 2000 were forcibly broken up by the police, but in early 2001, various groups—students, independent trade unionists, some businessmen—came together as the "Ukraine without Kuchma" movement. Its street demonstrations were repeatedly broken up by the police and it gained no traction in a parliament that was decidedly pro-Kuchma. In 2001–2002, however, the anti-Kuchma opposition began to coalesce around two political leaders.

The first to go over to the opposition camp was Yulia Tymoshenko, a glamorous political figure who had served in the corrupt Lazarenko administration and more recently as deputy prime minister under Yushchenko. In January 2001, she was dismissed from her government post and taken to court for corruption charges dating back to the 1990s, when she was known as the "Gas Princess" for her close connections to the corrupt Ukrainian energy sector. Surprisingly, however, the charges against her were dismissed, and she emerged as a passionate (if somewhat compromised) figure of political opposition. Meanwhile, Yushchenko, whose reforms had upset many oligarchs, was dismissed from his post in April 2001. Before his dismissal, Yushchenko had signed a letter condemning the anti-Kuchma protests. Now out of the government, Yushchenko staked out a position as a competent, liberal reformer opposed to many elements of the "party of power." In late 2001, Yushchenko brought together several parties and movements to form "Our Ukraine" (*Nasha Ukraina*), a political coalition that would contest the 2002 parliamentary elections. Although many of Yushchenko's supporters were from *Rukh* and other national-democratic organizations, Yushchenko backed away from divisive issues such as linguistic Ukrainianization, thereby hoping to forge a national movement and transcend Ukraine's regional divisions.

Yushchenko and Tymoshenko would not be wholly successful. Although Our Ukraine won the most seats (70 of 225) decided by party-list voting, it did not do so well in single-mandate districts, where it was easier to buy votes and apply administrative resources to ensure the election of pro-Kuchma candidates. Thus despite winning less than 12% of the votes (half the percentage of Our Ukraine) from the party-list voting, the pro-Kuchma "For a United Ukraine" emerged as the largest bloc (119 seats) in parliament. Our Ukraine had 113 and Tymoshenko's bloc only 21, meaning that the balance was largely composed of Communists (with 66 seats) and various "independents" (95 seats), many of whom were local or regional oligarchs. Anti-Kuchma groups protested what they viewed as stolen elections, but the protesters were repressed and dissent soon died down. Politically, Ukraine remained highly polarized and from 2002–2004, its parliament would not function very well. Nonetheless, Kuchma had managed to hold onto power, even though it was increasingly obvious that he had done little to uphold his earlier promises to be a political and economic reformer. It would take 2004's Orange Revolution to break the grip of the "party of power."

NOTES

1. Taras Kuzio, *Ukraine: State and Nation Building* (London: Routledge, 1998), p. 1.

2. Alexander Motyl, *Dilemmas of Independence: Ukraine after Totalitarianism* (New York: Council of Foreign Relations, 1993), p. 150.

3. "Derzhava, natsiia, svoboda" (State, Nation, Freedom), *Samostijna Ukraina*, May 1992, p. 7.

4. Quoted in Mykola Ryabchuk, "Between Civil Society and the New Etatism: Democracy and State Building in Ukraine," in Michael Kennedy, ed. *Envisioning Eastern Europe* (Ann Arbor: University of Michigan Press, 1994), p. 50.

5. *Nezavisimost* (Kiev), June 23, 1993.

6. The Ukrainian Communist Party itself was banned in August 1991 and officially reformed only in June 1993.

7. Ryabchuk, 1994, p. 52.

8. *Slovo*, June 1992, p. 2.

9. *Post-Postup* (Lviv), June 15, 1993, p. 3.

10. According to the electoral law, turnout had to be at least 50% in an electoral district in order for the results to be valid.

11. *The Ukrainian Weekly*, April 3, 1994, p. 8.

12. Andrew Wilson, *The Ukrainians: Unexpected Nation* (New Haven, CT: Yale University Press, 2000), p. 173.

13. Wilson, 2000, p. 196.

14. A 1998 survey by International Foundation for Electoral Systems (IFES) found that only 13% of voters thought Kuchma deserved to be reelected.

Reports from numerous surveys in Ukraine can be found at http://www.
ifes.org.

15. In 2006, Ukraine's minister of internal affairs announced that on the
basis of evidence of which he is aware, he believes Chornovil's death was a
murder.

16. Paul Kubicek, "The Limits of Electoral Democracy in Ukraine," *Democratization* 8, no. 2 (Summer 2001): p. 124.

17. First survey was conducted by IFES in association with Gallup and
can be found at www.ifes.org. The other data come from on-line analysis of
the 1999 World Values Survey, administered in Ukraine and numerous other
countries. These surveys can be found at http: www.worldvaluessurvey.org.

18. Figures from Anders Aslund, *Building Capitalism: Markets and Government in Russian and Transitional Economies* (Cambridge: Cambridge University
Press, 2001), p. 118.

19. 1995 survey by Kiev International Institute of Sociology (KIIS), cited
in Kubicek, "Post-Soviet Ukraine: In Search of a Constituency for Reform,"
Journal of Communist Studies and Transition Politics 13, no. 3 (September 1997):
pp. 106–107.

20. Wilson, 2000, p. 196.

21. Paul Kubicek, *Organized Labor in Postcommunist States: From Solidarity to
Infirmity* (Pittsburgh: University of Pittsburgh Press, 2004), pp. 172–175.

22. Aslund, 2001, pp. 161, 279.

23. Aslund, 2001, p. 436.

24. Aslund, 2001, p. 384.

25. IFES 1999 Survey, at www.ifes.org.

26. Survey from KIIS, quoted in Sherman Garnett, "Like Oil and Water:
Ukraine's External Westernization and Internal Stagnation," in Taras Kuzio
et al., eds. *State and Institution Building in Ukraine* (New York: Macmillan,
1999), p. 124.

27. Wilson, 2000, p. 207.

28. Quoted in Roman Solchanyk, "The Politics of State Building: Centre-
Periphery Relations in Post-Soviet Ukraine," *Europe-Asia Studies* 46, no. 1
(1994): p. 54.

29. Paul Pirie, "National Identity and Politics in Southern and Eastern
Ukraine," *Europe-Asia Studies* 48, no. 7 (November 1996): p. 1097.

30. Kuzio, 1998, p. 80.

31. Much of this section is drawn from Paul Kubicek, "Regional Polarisation
in Ukraine: Public Opinion, Voting, and Legislative Behaviour," *Europe-Asia
Studies* 52, no. 2 (2000): pp. 273–294.

32. Results from KIIS Survey in 1995, reported in Kubicek, 1997, p. 110.

33. Kubicek, 2000, p. 284.

34. Data from Kubicek, 2001, p. 120.

35. Wilson, 2000, p. 174.

36. Kuzio, 1998, p. 83.

37. U.S. Secretary of State Colin Powell in *Zerkalo nedeli* (Kiev), July 7, 2001.

38. Garnett, 1999.

39. Jason Bush, "Whither Ukraine?" *Business Central Europe Magazine,* June 2001.

40. *Radio Free Europe/Radio Liberty Poland, Belarus and Ukraine Report*, September 23, 2003.

41. Serhy Yekelchyk, *Ukraine: Birth of a Modern Nation* (Oxford: Oxford University Press, 2007), p. 208.

42. Taras Kuzio, "Ukraine One Year after 'Kuchmagate'," *RFE/RL Newsline,* November 28, 2001.

43. Paul Kubicek, "U.S.-Ukrainian Relations: From Engagement to Estrangement," *Problems of Post-Communism* 50, no. 6 (November–December 2003): pp. 3–11.

10

The Orange Revolution and Beyond

The Orange Revolution, named after the campaign colors of Viktor Yush-chenko, was the most dramatic event in Ukraine since the country achieved independence in 1991. After more than a decade of political and economic stagnation during which Ukraine fell further and further behind its Western neighbors such as Poland and Hungary in terms of political and economic development and developing good relations with the West, millions of Ukrainians came out into the streets to demand democracy and political change. The immediate cause behind the Orange Revolution was efforts by the Ukrainian authorities to falsify the country's presidential elections and deny victory to Viktor Yushchenko, who endorsed a more free-market, democratic, and pro-Western program.

The Orange Revolution, however, was about more than just Yushchenko's candidacy. It was a rejection of years of misrule by President Leonid Kuchma and his circle and an affirmation by Ukrainians that they wanted a freer, more prosperous country that could legitimately aspire to join the European Union. Many observers compared it to other popular upheavals, such as the Velvet Revolution in Czechoslovakia, that helped bring down communism in Eastern Europe in 1989 and put those countries on a democratic, Western-oriented path. Ukraine did not have the equivalent of such a revolution in 1991, when it gained independence, as former communists prevailed in elections, denying power to national-democratic forces such as *Rukh* and becoming increasingly authoritarian over time. The Orange Revolution thus represented a second chance for Ukraine, an opportunity to put Ukraine back on a clear path toward democracy.

Without question, the Orange Revolution produced real changes in Ukraine. Nonetheless, it has not been able to sweep all elements of the old system away. "Orange" forces accused each other of corruption, producing an "Orange Divorce" in 2005. Viktor Yanukovych, the man Yushchenko ultimately defeated during the Orange Revolution, returned to power as prime minister. Ukraine's bid to join the European Union stalled. It is safe to say that Ukraine is not on the same path as Russia, which, under President Vladimir Putin (2000–2008) has slid deeper and deeper into authoritarianism; however, expectations that it would easily establish an effective democratic government, as in East-Central Europe, have not yet been realized.

THE CAMPAIGN TO UNSEAT THE "PARTY OF POWER"

The background to the Orange Revolution lies in Kuchmagate, the unsuccessful "Ukraine without Kuchma" movement, and the 2002 parliamentary elections. As noted in Chapter 9, President Kuchma, although touted by many as a reformer in the mid-1990s, acted as the head of an increasingly corrupt "party of power," which had relied on a variety of tactics including, based on digital audiotape evidence, murder of opposition journalists. Popular mobilization in the wake of the "Kuchmagate" revelations failed to produce change at the top, but political opposition to Kuchma began to coalesce in two political parties. The first was Our Ukraine, a coalition block established by Viktor Yushchenko, who had served under Kuchma as prime minster from December 1999 to April 2001. Yushchenko was credited with reforms that had helped to turn Ukraine's decrepit economy around, and, despite previous connections to Kuchma, was not part of the corrupt "party of power" and had a reputation for both competence and honesty. The other source of opposition was the Bloc of Yulia Tymoshenko (BYuT), named for Yulia Tymoshenko, a former deputy prime minister who was charged with corruption under Kuchma but who insisted on her innocence (even as she donned designer outfits that she could not have afforded on her official government salary) and rallied the various forces of the "Ukraine without Kuchma" movement. Unlike *Rukh*, which never represented a serious threat to the governing authorities, Our Ukraine and the BYuT looked to be formidable opponents, with Our Ukraine winning more votes than any other party in the proportional or party-list component of the 2002 parliamentary elections. Despite this "victory," however, Kuchma and his allies managed to cobble together a bare majority in the parliament, denying the anti-Kuchma forces the prospect of gaining control over the parliament.

The real prize, however, was the Ukrainian presidency, which controlled most of the reigns of political power. In April 2004, the Ukrainian Parliament rejected Kuchma's bid to change the constitution to allow him to run for a third term. Seeking to preserve his political power—or at least avoid prosecution for corruption should one of his opponents win—Kuchma sought a loyal political successor that his political machine, relying on various nefarious practices, could help win the presidency. That man would be Viktor Yanukovych, who was the prime minister and hailed from Donetsk in eastern Ukraine. Yanukovych was far from the ideal candidate—he had served in prison on two occasions as a youth for assault and came across in the campaign as thuggish and uncouth (he often used prison slang and derided his opponents as *kozly* [goats or bastards]). He had a reputation for criminality, brutality, and heavy-handed business tactics, and on his way to the top he had alienated some of the moderates within the "party of power." Nonetheless, the office of prime minister was the best launching pad for the presidency, both for political organization and because he could try to take credit for Ukraine's relatively strong economic performance in 2003 and 2004.

The stakes, on both sides, were high. Taras Kuzio, an acute observer of Ukrainian politics, noted that:

> Kuchma and his oligarchic allies saw the election as an opportunity to consolidate autocratic rule and thereby safeguard their personal and clan interests. From their standpoint, the ascent of any non-centrist candidate, whether from the left or the right, would be a disaster because it might lead to a redistribution or confiscation of the assets they had accumulated under Kuchma and even to imprisonment or exile. In addition to the Gongadze murder, Kuchma himself was implicated in a host of other illegal acts, such as ordering violence against journalists and politicians, election fraud, corruption, and arms trafficking.[1]

The opposition's calculation was the reverse, as many speculated this would be their best and last opportunity to prevent Ukraine from becoming an authoritarian state. The opposition placed its bets on Yushchenko, who was thought to be a stronger candidate. Our Ukraine's performance in 2002, coupled with Yanukovych's shortcomings and Kuchma's low public standing, convinced members of the opposition that they could win the 2004 presidential elections.

All sides expected an ugly campaign. Kuchma himself, who had used an array of administrative resources and condoned outright falsification of the vote in 2002, ironically predicted that the 2004 elections would be Ukraine's dirtiest. The opposition, however, was ready: exit polls would be used as a check against falsification; international observers would be in Ukraine to minimize electoral day shenanigans; independent media—vital given the fact that most of the television stations were in the hands of the state or owned by Kuchma loyalists—did all it could to spread Yushchenko's message and counter negative allegations about him made in state-owned media; and people would be ready to take to the streets in case the election was stolen. Crucial on the last front was *Pora!* (translated as "It's Time!" or "Enough"), a prodemocratic student organization that had been organizing for more than a year and was assisted by students from Serbia and Georgia who had led efforts to overthrow corrupt governments. Given setbacks in the late Kuchma years, as well as unfair elections conducted in Russia and Belarus, the opposition knew it had to be ready for a government willing to play dirty. Polls in April 2004 indicated that only 16% of Ukrainians believed a free election was possible, with 70% believing the opposite.[2]

Few, however, could have predicted the strangest twist of all of the campaign. In the first week of September, Viktor Yushchenko checked into a clinic in Vienna, Austria with what appeared to be a serious case of food poisoning. Yushchenko's condition was extremely serious, and it took doctors a couple of weeks to stabilize and treat him. Although he recovered, his face and body were scarred by lesions. The largest question, of course, was who was behind this poisoning? He had recently dined with the head of Kuchma's security service. Other theories suggested that underworld figures from the Ukrainian mafia or even Russian intelligence forces might be the perpetrators. Some in the opposition even alleged that Yushchenko made the whole thing up, suffered from a failed Botox injection, ate some bad sushi, or simply poisoned himself to elicit sympathy. Pro-government forces even sent a fabricated fax to media outlets indicating that there had been no poisoning. In December, after the first two rounds of voting, tests in Austria confirmed that Yushchenko had a blood-dioxin level 6,000 times higher than normal. How and by whom Yushchenko was poisoned has yet to be established.

Comically, as it turned out, Yanukovych tried to have his own "Yushchenko" moment, when he campaigned in western Ukraine in front of a largely hostile crowd. Yanukovych had placed provocateurs in the crowd, who were supposed to throw a rock at him. The plan was that this attack would win him sympathy and allow him to characterize Yushchenko supporters as thugs. Instead, a Yushchenko supporter threw an egg at Yanukovych. When it hit him, Yanukovych was expecting a heavier rock and dramatically fell to the ground. The sight of a man weighing well over 200 pounds being felled by an egg was used with great effect by his detractors.[3]

Public opinion polls in the months before the election gave Yushchenko the edge over Yanukovych. Yanukovych, however, did the best he could to rally voters to his cause. He endorsed laws to allow dual citizenship with

Russia and making Russian a second state language in order to win votes from ethnic Russians and Russian speakers. He promised to double state pensions. He tried to portray Yushchenko as a radical Ukrainian nationalist. Some asserted that Yushchenko's American-born wife was a CIA agent.[4] One anti-Yushchenko campaign poster showed the faces of Yushchenko and U.S. President George W. Bush—unpopular in Ukraine—merging into "Bushchenko." Russian President Vladimir Putin, who was popular in Ukraine, campaigned on his behalf. Russian sources allegedly invested $300 million to Yanukovych's campaign coffers.[5] Yushchenko, however, had his own wealthy backers—both in Ukraine and among the Ukrainian diaspora—and ran a professional campaign that made extensive use of the Internet. His campaign slogan, *"Tak!"* (Yes!) projected optimism and explicitly drew on the popular campaigns to topple authoritarian and corrupt leaders in Serbia and Georgia. Most observers predicted a close contest in the initial round of presidential voting, with Yushchenko and Yanukovych advancing to a run-off to decide the presidency.

ELECTION SHENANIGANS, POPULAR MOBILIZATION, AND THE ORANGISTS' VICTORY

The first round of the presidential elections was held on October 31, 2004. Twenty-four candidates ran, but it had been clear for months that the "two Viktors" were the primary contenders. Reports from election day noted numerous instances of fraud, and the Central Election Commission, which was dominated by supporters of Yanukovych, waited 10 days to release the official results. Surveys indicated a majority of Ukrainians thought the results were falsified.[6] Nonetheless, as seen in Table 10.1, Yushchenko won more votes than any other candidate, and he was the overwhelming choice of voters in western and central Ukraine. Under Ukrainian law, however, a presidential candidate must win a majority of the votes. Lacking a majority, Yushchenko was forced into a run-off with Yanukovych, who came in second and dominated in Russian-speaking areas of southern and eastern Ukraine.

The run-off election, held on November 21, would be the decisive event. Oleksandr Moroz, the third-place finisher, had thrown his support to Yushchenko; Symonenko, the Communist Party leader who had come in second in the 1999 presidential ballot, endorsed Yanukovych. Again, a tight race was anticipated, but most observers thought that Yushchenko would prevail in a one-on-one contest. Indeed, independent exit polls on election day showed Yushchenko with an eight-point lead. Election observers, however, reported numerous problems of election fraud: ballot stuffing, abuse of absentee ballots, large numbers of "at home" voting, and inflated turnout rates so that in some districts—notably in Donetsk—more than 100% of registered voters turned out to vote. Yushchenko's campaign produced even more damning

Table 10.1. Results of the 2004 Ukrainian Presidential Elections

Candidate/Party	Round One	Round Two	Round Three
Viktor Yushchenko Our Ukraine	39.9%	46.7%	52%
Viktor Yanukovych Party of Regions	39.3%	49.4%	44.2%
Oleksandr Moroz Socialist Party	5.8%		
Petro Symonenko Communist Party	5%		
Result	Yushchenko and Yanukovych advance to run-off	Elections declared fraudulent; additional round is scheduled	Yushchenko is declared the winner

evidence: phone calls from the Yanukovych campaign revealing that the Central Election Commission was "correcting" electoral data as it came in from electoral districts.[7] On November 22, Putin congratulated Yanukovych on his "victory," even though the official results, which indeed did show Yanukovych with a three-point margin of victory (which had been ordered by his campaign) were not released until November 24.

The protests and controversy, however, had already begun. As noted, *Pora!* was prepared for mass political protests. Hundreds of thousands of orange-clad protesters, mainly students but also housewives, professionals, blue-collar workers, and pensioners braved the cold and assembled on Kiev's *Maidan Nezalezhnosti* (Independence Square) to protest the results. Viktor Yushchenko and Yulia Tymoshenko appealed to the crowd to remain in the square and not to give up the fight. They heeded these words, setting up camp on the square, lest they abandon it and the police cordon it off to prevent further protests. Similar protests and sit-ins occurred in other Ukrainian cities, mainly to the west of Kiev where Yushchenko was widely supported. On November 23, Yushchenko, noting the irregularities reported by numerous Ukrainian and international observers, claimed victory and was symbolically sworn in as president at a half-empty session of the Ukrainian parliament. On November 25, he appealed to the Ukrainian Supreme Court to address the allegations of fraud and not certify the validity of the elections. To support these claims, Yushchenko's campaign submitted audiotapes, which had been recorded by the government's own Security Service, that implicated Yanukovych's campaign and Kuchma's administration in ordering false reporting of the vote.

For more than a week, Ukraine teetered on the brink of mass violence. Yanukovych accused the "Orangists" of launching an illegal coup d'état. Police and military units tried to prevent people from arriving on the *Maidan,* and efforts were made to stop trains from western Ukraine (Yushchenko's strongest area of support) from coming into the capital. Meanwhile, trains and buses loaded with Yanukovych backers, many of whom were allegedly paid and given free vodka, were brought in from eastern Ukraine. In eastern Ukraine itself, some local leaders threatened to hold a referendum on separatism if Yanukovych's victory was overturned. Local police and interior ministry troops guarded government buildings, and many feared they would, as they had in 2000, use violence to disperse the crowd. The eyes of the world, however, were turned to Kiev, and officials from the European Union and the United States voiced support for the protesters and that the election results be nullified.

Although the standoff between the protesters and the government was tense, the *Maidan*, festooned in orange, assumed a sort of carnival atmosphere. Student leaders instructed the crowds in methods of nonviolence. Internet connections allowed the protesters to stay in touch with the outside world. Representatives of *Pora,* Our Ukraine, and other groups held press conferences on the square. Makeshift kitchens were set up. Poets and singers entertained the crowd. *Hrinzholy* (Sleigh), a band from Transcarpathia, sang *Razom nas bohato* ("Together We Are Many"), which became the theme song for the Orange Revolution.

Falsifications, No!
Machinations, No!
Understandings, Yes!
No to lies!
Yushchenko, Yushchenko
Is our president
Yes! Yes! Yes!
Together we are many! We cannot be defeated!
We aren't scum!
We aren't goats (*kozly*)!
We are Ukraine's sons and daughters!
It's now or never!
Enough waiting!
Together we are many! We cannot be defeated![8]

The authorities were faced with a difficult choice. It was clear that the crowd, which at times approached 1 million people, was not going to dissolve. The evidence of election fraud was solid. Officials in western Ukraine refused to recognize the election results. The world was also watching Ukraine, and Yushchenko had appealed to the EU and individual European political leaders

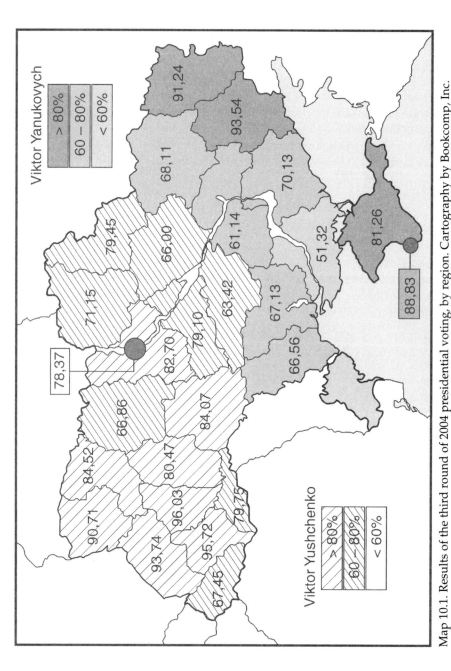

Map 10.1. Results of the third round of 2004 presidential voting, by region. Cartography by Bookcomp, Inc.

for support. It was unclear if the army or security forces would obey orders to use force against the protesters. Elites within the "party of power," including the head of the security forces, began to back away from Yanukovych.[9] On November 29, Kuchma accepted the need for new elections, and on the next day he proposed keeping the presidency as a temporary solution and making Yushchenko his prime minister. Yushchenko rejected this offer. Meanwhile, on December 1, the Ukrainian parliament voted to fire Yanukovych's government (he was still prime minister), a clear indication that the tide had turned. On December 3, the Supreme Court declared the elections null and void and ordered a new round of voting. Yushchenko did agree with Kuchma on constitutional changes that would henceforth weaken the powers of the Ukrainian president, and most believe Yushchenko also agreed to give Kuchma immunity from any future criminal prosecution. Changes in the electoral law, including oversight by the Central Election Commission, were rapidly pushed through parliament to ensure a fairer vote. That the vote was so swift and so overwhelming—402 of the 450 members voted in favor of new elections—indicates just how quickly much of the old "party of power" abandoned Yanukovych. On December 11, doctors in Austria confirmed that Yushchenko had been poisoned by dioxin, offering a reminder that Yushchenko's opponents had done more than just try to steal the vote.

The crowds, encouraged by the actions of the court and pep talks by Yushchenko and Tymoshenko—whose tough talk against the criminality of the Kuchma regime made her the real firebrand of the Orange Revolution—stayed on the *Maidan* until the final round of voting, held on December 26. These were the most monitored elections in history, with 300,000 Ukrainians and 12,000 foreign observers present to ensure a fair count.[10] The results, which gave Yushchenko a majority of 52% of the vote, confirmed what had been reported in exit polls. As seen in Map 10.1, in addition to winning overwhelmingly in western Ukraine, Yushchenko also won in most of central Ukraine and did reasonably well in parts of southern and eastern Ukraine. In contrast, Yanukovych's base was confined to the heavily Russified regions of Donetsk and Luhansk in eastern Ukraine. Yanukovych challenged these elections in court, but his suit was dismissed. The Central Electoral Commission certified Yushchenko's victory on January 10, 2005, and he was sworn in as Ukraine's president on January 23.

THE PROBLEMS OF GOVERNING AND THE ORANGE DIVORCE

The Orange Revolution brought high hopes to many Ukrainians. The grip of the "party of power" had been broken. Yushchenko was president. Tymoshenko, the favorite of the crowds on the *Maidan*, was installed as the new prime minister. Many hoped that the new government, in addition to upholding a commitment to civil rights and democratic principles, would bring Kuchma, Yanukovych, and other corrupt members of previous governments to justice. Others hoped that Ukraine would now be better positioned to join the European Union, which had just expanded in 2004 to former communist countries such as Poland, Hungary, and Slovakia. Yushchenko declared that the world would now see a "genuinely different Ukraine . . . a noble European nation, one that embraces genuine democratic values."[11] Ukraine, was now, according to the new foreign minister, a "prodigy," a "moral leader," a place in which the heart of Europe was beating.[12]

Many of the expectations of the revolution, however, would be dashed. In short, although Yushchenko and Tymoshenko, aided of course by millions of orange-clad protesters, proved that they could bring down a government, they were less able to govern effectively. Even though the two joined forces against Kuchma, they had different priorities and inclinations. Tymoshenko, who talked about redoing thousands of corrupt privatization deals of the 1990s and increasing government spending, was more of a populist and a social democrat. Yushchenko, who had once been head of Ukraine's National Bank, endorsed a more free-market approach and was less inclined to move against the "oligarchs" who had amassed a fortune in the 1990s. In his words, "It's time to bury the war hatchet and forget where it lies."[13]

In 2005, these differences of opinion, suppressed during the Orange Revolution, boiled over. Yushchenko balked at Tymoshenko's plans to revisit privatizations. He was against her efforts to impose controls on energy prices. He argued that the government could not afford massive increases in pensions and social spending. He appointed his long-time ally (and godfather to his daughter) Petro Poroshenko as head of the National Security and Defense Council and gave him additional powers, including the power to issue orders to government ministries, thereby bypassing Prime Minister Tymoshenko. Tymoshenko, naturally, saw Poroshenko as a threat to her own position, creating a schism within the government. Yushchenko complained that he was forced to act as a "nanny" among governmental actors.[14]

In addition, the government was beset with numerous scandals and allegations of corruption. These included use of a luxurious apartment and a $40,000 cell phone by Yushchenko's son; falsification of academic credentials by Yushchenko's nominee to be minister of justice; abuse of power, including acceptance of bribes and interference with the judicial process by Poroshenko; and widespread claims of financial improprieties by Tymoshenko, Poroshenko, and officials in the presidential administration. With the government virtually paralyzed, Poroshenko resigned and Yushchenko dismissed Tymoshenko in September 2005, bringing in Yurii Yekhanurov to act as the new prime minister. Yekhanurov oversaw Ukraine's privatization process in the late 1990s, and his praising of the "oligarchs" as the "national bourgeoisie" elicited disappointment among those who thought the Orange Revolution would result in action against the oligarchs. Significantly, Yushchenko cut a deal with Yanukovych's Party of Regions faction in the Ukrainian parliament, whereby the Party of Regions agreed to support Yekhanurov's nomination in return for amnesty against prosecution for electoral fraud, parliamentary immunity for officials on local councils (many of which had collaborated with vote rigging in 2004), and legislation to guarantee existing property rights, de facto preventing reprivatization of ill-gotten gains in the 1990s.[15] Analyzing this arrangement, one foreign correspondent suggested, "Kuchma must be laughing up his sleeve. His successor is endorsing out of weakness, the corrupt political and economic system that he created—after all that was what Viktor Yanukovych was supposed to do."[16] A Ukrainian writer acknowledged that there had been an "oligarchization of power" throughout 2005. More charitably, an American observer noted that thousands of Ukrainians—civil servants, politicians, journalists, business people—had "deep financial and personal interest in maintaining the corrupt status quo," making the Orange Revolution the "easy part" compared with the battle against entrenched corruption.[17]

Despite Yushchenko's efforts to stabilize the government, the damage had already been done. The economy, which grew at a robust 12% in 2004, expanded by less than 3% in 2005. His technocratic, gradualist approaches ran up against the myth, held by many, of the Orange Revolution as a catalyst for radical change and social justice. Public confidence in the authorities plummeted, with one survey in November 2005 finding that 59.7% of respondents believed the country was headed in the wrong direction—more than had expressed such a view in April 2004. Even a plurality (44%) of those who had voted for Yushchenko agreed that the country was on the wrong track. In a reflection of widespread disillusionment with the results of the Orange Revolution, only 23% of respondents believed that elections led to a more democratic society and only 14% believed they helped produce less corruption.[18] Meanwhile, Ukraine's bid to join the European Union (EU) stalled, as the EU was preoccupied with difficult expansion negotiations with Turkey, and rejection of a proposed EU Constitution by French and Dutch voters in 2005 created an internal crisis for the EU.[19] Relations with Russia also deteriorated as Russia and Ukraine argued over a proposed Russian price increase on natural gas delivered to Ukraine. Russia temporarily cut off gas supplies that went through Ukraine onward to Western Europe and eventually doubled the price of gas for Ukraine. Many suggested that this crisis was provoked in part to punish Yushchenko for his pro-Western orientation and to promote pro-Russian forces in Ukraine's March 2006 parliamentary elections.[20]

THE RETURN OF YANUKOVYCH

On top of all of the problems of managing the Orange Coalition, one additional specter haunted President Yushchenko: Viktor Yanukovych. Although defeated in the 2004 presidential elections, he had not been tried for any criminal misconduct—although there were plenty of grounds on which to do so—and he and the Party of Regions had a significant number of seats in the Ukrainian parliament. As noted previously, Yushchenko even made deals with him to ensure the appointment of Yurii Yekhanurov as prime minister. Yanukovych, however, wanted more. As seen in 2004, he could count on a solid bloc of voters from populous regions in eastern Ukraine. With the economy experiencing a downturn in 2005 and the squabbling among the Orangists creating disillusion among many of Yushchenko's former backers, he could plausibly make a bid to become prime minister himself.

The March 2006 parliamentary elections would give him this opportunity. They were the first parliamentary elections held under a full proportional representation system, under which voters would vote for a party and the party would receive a number of seats roughly proportional to its total vote. With the split between Yushchenko and Tymoshenko, the Party of Regions was likely to become the largest single party in the Ukrainian parliament. With the support of the Communists and other parties, the Party of Regions might be able to form a coalition government and thus give back to Yanukovych his previous job as prime minister. In 2006, however, the added bonus was that thanks to constitutional changes agreed on by Yushchenko during the Orange Revolution, the prime minister's office was more powerful than before, gaining the authority to nominate most of the government ministers and control the country's legislative agenda. Recognizing that the Party of Regions could return to power and potentially undo many of the gains of the Orange Revolution, the "Orange" parties, Our Ukraine, the BYuT, and the Socialist Party headed by Oleksandr Moroz, agreed to cooperate to preserve an "Orange" government.

The results of the elections are displayed in Table 10.2. These elections, which were also monitored by domestic and international observers, were judged free and fair, marking significant progress for Ukraine from previous years. The Party of Regions, as many expected, did win a plurality of votes, thanks again to its strong base of support in the more industrial, Russified regions of eastern and southern Ukraine. Yushchenko, however, suffered a double blow, as Our Ukraine was also bested by the BYuT. Two other parties, the Socialists and the Communists, crossed the 3% threshold, which enabled them to claim seats, but for the Communists in particular these results were disappointing because, in the 1990s, they were the largest party in Ukraine. No party had a majority, so the key consideration was what grouping or coalition of parties would be able to command a majority (226 out of 450) of the parliamentary seats. Looking at the breakdown in seats, one saw that the three "Orange" parties, provided they could agree on a coalition, would be able to form a government.

Alas, they could not do so. Talks among the parties dragged on for more than three months. Tymoshenko, as the leader of the now largest "Orange" party, insisted that she be named prime minister. Many in Our Ukraine, recalling problems when Tymoshenko had been prime minister the previous year, balked, and some publicly entertained the notion that Yushchenko would make a deal with the Party of Regions instead. Petro Poroshenko of Our Ukraine also insisted that he become speaker of parliament, a position that Oleksandr Moroz had held in the past (1994–1998) and wanted to hold again. Given the feuding between Poroshenko and Tymoshenko, it is not surprising that she was also against Poroshenko serving in any prominent post. Finally, a tentative deal among the parties was reached, but members from the Party of Regions and the Communists blockaded parliament to prevent Tymoshenko from being sworn in as prime minister. Then, in a surprise move, Moroz, who had made public the "Kuchmagate" tapes in 2000 and had been a solid member of the anti-Kuchma opposition, defected to join with the Party of Regions and the Communists in what was called the "anti-crisis" coalition. This move was partially motivated by personal ambition—Yanukovych agreed to Moroz's request to become speaker—but there were also real policy differences in the Orange camp, with Moroz, a former communist, against measures to privatize land and to have Ukraine join NATO. In July 2006, amid physical skirmishes and calls of "Moroz is Judas" in the parliamentary chamber, Moroz became speaker of parliament and Yanukovych, head of the Party of Regions, was nominated to be prime minister. Although some Yushchenko allies argued that this event was a coup d'état and that the president should call for another round of elections, Yushchenko, uncertain what result additional elections would bring, approved Yanukovych's appointment as prime minister.

Not surprisingly, cohabitation between President Yushchenko and Prime Minister Yanukovych was difficult to manage. They had, of course, been bitter rivals, and the division of powers between the president and prime minister was unclear. Yanukovych appointed his own people, many of whom were

Table 10.2. Results of the 2006 Parliamentary Elections

Party	% vote	Seats
Party of Regions	32	186
Tymoshenko Bloc	22.3	129
Our Ukraine	14	81
Socialists	5.7	33
Communists	3.7	21

implicated in the 2004 vote-rigging, to posts in government, whereas Yush-chenko retained powers to name the foreign minister and defense minister. The two leaders disagreed on a host of issues, ranging from foreign policy to economic reforms to constitutional powers of the different branches of government. Yanukovych maintained that he was now a committed democrat and that, by virtue of his election victory in 2006, he was entitled to rule in the name of the Ukrainian people. Critics of Yanukovych were unconvinced of his conversion to democratic principles, maintaining that the Party of Regions was "unreconstructed and unrepentant" and that it was committed to a "vertical of authority modeled on Putin and remorseless employment of its financial resources to penetrate administrative structures and buy up those who can be bought."[21] They argued that his government oversaw corrupt privatization deals that benefited members of the "Donetsk clan" such as the billionaire Rinat Akhmetov, the main financier behind the Party of Regions. The parliament delayed legislation to advance Ukraine's bid to join the World Trade Organization. Yanukovych also worked to improve relations with Russia and stated his opposition to Ukrainian NATO membership.

For nearly a year, Ukraine stumbled along without a clear direction, with members of the opposition frequently boycotting or disrupting the work of parliament. Many in the Orange camp were concerned with several actions of Yanukovych's government, including parliamentary investigations of its opponents, the closing of political debate programs on state television, pressure on regional media, and politically motivated raids on small businesses.[22] Brushing aside criticism, Yanukovych attempted to solidify his position by enticing members of Our Ukraine and BYuT to join the "anti-crisis coalition." Eleven members of parliament changed sides, and, by the spring of 2007, it looked like Yanukovych's coalition might garner 300 seats in parliament, enough to override presidential vetoes and amend the constitution. Noting that deputies were prohibited from changing parliamentary factions and that financial incentives (e.g., bribes) lay behind the movement to Yanukovych, Yushchenko intervened, calling in April 2007 for the disbanding of parliament and new elections. This move was dubbed an unconstitutional coup by his opponents, and parliament refused to disband. The result was a standoff, similar to the one that ended in bloodshed in Moscow in 1993. Ukraine looked as if it was on the brink of violence, especially when Yushchenko asserted control over interior ministry troops. In late May 2007, the two sides reached a compromise, agreeing on new elections for September 2007.

THE ORANGISTS' SECOND CHANCE?: 2007 PARLIAMENTARY ELECTIONS

Given the polarization in Ukrainian society, few expected the 2007 elections to produce a radical change in the relative power of the country's political forces. The Orange forces did believe, however, that these elections offered them a chance to make up for their mistakes in 2005 and 2006. Yanukovych, aided by American campaign consultants, tried to portray himself as a good democrat and a good manager of the economy (which had rebounded from low growth in 2005), but some actions by his government, such as an attempted ban on candidates from BYuT because of a previously unenforced technicality in the electoral law (the government's policy was overturned by the courts), led many to worry. The Orangists, desperate to unseat Yanukovych, campaigned to recapture the glory of the Orange Revolution. This time, however, blue-clad protesters (from the Party of Regions) occupied prominent places on the *Maidan*, pledging that they would not be defeated.

In late September 2007, election observers descended yet again on Ukraine. The September 30, 2007 elections, despite a few irregularities (again, mainly in eastern Ukraine), were judged free and fair, affirming again the progress the country had made since 2004. The results of these elections are displayed in Table 10.3. The Party of Regions commanded roughly the same number of votes, and their voters, as before, were located overwhelmingly in eastern and southern Ukraine. BYuT, however, gained significantly since 2006, winning the most votes of any party in most of central and western Ukraine and placing second in large parts of the east and south. BYuT could therefore claim to be the closest thing Ukraine had to a genuinely national party. Yushchenko's Our Ukraine, which had joined with a host of smaller parties, fared about the same as it had in 2006, but Tymoshenko's "victory" revealed that she was the most popular figure among the Orangists. The Communists remained bit players, but the Socialists, hurt from Moroz's defection to Yanukovych in 2006, did not even gain enough votes to cross the 3% threshold and enter parliament. Instead, the party of Volodymyr Lytvyn, who had been a leading figure in the Kuchma figure and had been accused of hindering the investigation into the Gongadze murder case, entered into parliament as a "centrist" faction.

Table 10.3. Results of the 2007 Parliamentary Elections

Party	% vote	Seats	+/−from 2006
Party of Regions	34.4	175	−11
Tymoshenko's Bloc	30.7	156	+27
Our Ukraine	14.2	72	−9
Communist Party	5.4	27	+6
Lytvyn Bloc	4.0	20	+20
Socialist Party	2.9	0	−33

As expected, the elections did not produce a radical shift in power, but it did produce just enough for the combined Orange forces of BYuT and Our Ukraine to possess a slim (228 of 450) majority in parliament. Yushchenko suggested that it might be better to create a National Unity Government composed of all major political parties. Tymoshenko, however, rejected any cooperation with Yanukovych. Despite concerns among some in Our Ukraine about Tymoshenko returning to become prime minister, the two Orange parties agreed to form a coalition government. It should be pointed out, however, that given their bare majority in parliament and acrimony between Tymoshenko and Our Ukraine—and Tymoshenko clearly has her eye toward 2009 presidential elections—governance may be difficult.

In sum, Ukraine's Orange Revolution, despite some superficial similarities to the Velvet Revolution in Czechoslovakia or the Solidarity movement in Poland at the end of the 1980s, did not produce similar results. There have been, without question, real changes for the better. Civic freedoms are more respected than before. Recent elections have been free and fair. After a slowdown in 2005, the economy has rebounded, resulting in nearly double-digit growth in 2006 and 2007. The forces of the "party of power," however, have not been completely vanquished. Corruption remains a major problem. Cynicism about the nation's political leadership is acute. Regional divisions are pronounced and, in some eyes, threaten the viability of the country. Ukraine's aspirations to join the European Union will not be realized in the near future. Relations with Russia, which is turning back to authoritarianism, remain problematic. Much work remains to be done to create a better environment for investment and business growth.

These difficulties need not be intractable. Young democracies in Eastern Europe and elsewhere have overcome similar problems. Ukrainians survived a decade of stagnation under Kuchma, and, at minimum, the Orange Revolution demonstrated in a most dramatic way that Ukrainians need not be passive and that they have an ability to act and produce positive change. Although some may have soured on the results of the Orange Revolution, few can forget the feelings of hope and empowerment that it created. Young Ukrainians, in particular, appear to be more supportive of democracy and Ukraine's turn toward the West and are more optimistic about their future. For a country that has been through so many difficulties—indeed, as documented in this text, Ukraine has had more than its share of tragedies—it is refreshing that many Ukrainians can, at least, envision a better future for themselves in which they can enjoy two important victories all denied to previous generations: national independence and the advent of democratic government. In contrast to most of Ukrainian history, Ukraine's future lies in the hands of Ukrainians themselves.

NOTES

1. Taras Kuzio, "From Kuchma to Yushchenko: Ukraine's Presidential Elections and the Orange Revolution," *Problems of Post-Communism* 52, no. 2 (March/April 2005): p. 4.

2. Poll by Democratic Initiatives reported in *Ukrainska pravda*, April 26, 2004.

3. Those interested can find the footage at http://www.youtube.com/watch?v=qFAt-43woGQ, accessed November 9, 2007.

4. Olena Yatsunska, "Mythmaking and Its Discontents in the 2004 Ukrainian Presidential Campaign," *Demokratizatsiya* 14, no. 4 (2006): pp. 519–533.

5. Serhy Yekelchyk, *Ukraine: Birth of a Modern Nation* (Oxford: Oxford University Press, 2007), p. 215.

6. Kuzio, 2005, p. 14.

7. Yekelchyk, 2007, pp. 216–217.

8. Translation by the author.

9. Lucan Way, "Kuchma's Failed Authoritarianism," *Journal of Democracy* 16, no. 2 (April 2005): pp. 131–145.

10. Yekelchyk, 2007, p. 218.

11. Viktor Yushchenko, "Our Ukraine," *Wall Street Journal,* December 3, 2004.

12. Borys Tarasyuk, Speech at International Republican Institute, Washington, DC, March 10, 2005.

13. *Washington Post,* September 23, 2005.

14. *Ukrainska pravda,* September 8, 2005.

15. *Ukrainska pravda,* "Memorandum of Understanding between the Government and the Opposition," September 22, 2005.

16. Peter Lavelle, "Ukraine's Post-Orange Order," *RIA Novosti* (Moscow), September 12, 2005.

17. Valentyna Hoshovsurka, "How to Stop the Oligarchization of Power?" *The Day Weekly Digest* (Kiev), January 31, 2006, and Anne Applebaum, "Poison and Power in Ukraine," *Washington Post,* April 12, 2006.

18. Freedom House, "Public Views on Ukraine's Development, Election Law Changes, and Voter Education Needs," January 10, 2006, available from www.freedomhouse.org, accessed September 12, 2006.

19. Taras Kuzio, "Is Ukraine Part of Europe's Future?" *Washington Quarterly* 29, no. 3 (Summer 2006): pp. 89–108.

20. Yekelchyk, 2007, p. 223.

21. James Sherr, "The School of Defeat," *Zerkalo Nedeli Weekly* (Kiev), July 22–28, 2006.

22. Tammy Lynch, "The Edge of Anarchy in Ukraine," Distributed on Ukraine List, #416, May 26, 2007, available at http://www.ukrainianstudies.uottawa.ca/pdf/UKL416.pdf, accessed October 16, 2007.

Notable People in
the History of Ukraine

Bandera, Stepan (1909–1959). A nationalist leader from western Ukraine who served as head of the Organization of Ukrainian Nationalists (OUN) and the Ukranian Insurgent Army (UPA), which fought Soviet forces during World War II and into the 1950s. He was murdered in Munich Germany by an agent of the Soviet secret police. An enemy of the Soviet state, he is considered a national hero by many Ukrainians.

Chornovil, Vyacheslav (1937–1999). A long-time anti-Soviet Ukrainian journalist and political figure, arrested several times in the 1960s and 1970s for his political views. He was an advocate of Ukrainian independence and a founder of the pro-independence People's Movement of Ukraine (*Rukh*) in 1989. He ran unsuccessfully for the Ukrainian presidency in 1991. A major figure in political opposition throughout the 1990s, he died under suspicious circumstances in a car accident in 1999.

Danylo of Galicia (1201–1264). A notable early ruler over Ukrainian lands, serving as king of Galicia (in western Ukraine) from 1237 to 1264. In 1240, he battled against the Mongols when they conquered Kiev. Afterwards, he continued to fight them while cultivating ties with European states. His assault on the Mogols in 1249, however, failed, and by 1259 he was forced to surrender.

Drahomanov, Mykhaylo (1841–1895). A Ukrainian writer, historian, and political thinker. He was an advocate of socialism and a federal eastern Slavic state. A leading member of the Ukrainian *hromada* (community) in Kiev, he was exiled from the Russian Empire in 1876. His ideas were influential among nationalists in Austrian-ruled Galicia and contributed to the emergence of the first Ukrainian political party, the Radical Party, formed in Galicia in 1890.

Dziuba, Ivan (1931–). A Ukrainian writer and literary critic who was a major figure among Ukrainian dissidents in the 1960s and 1970s. His manuscript, *Internationalism or Russification?* (1965) critiqued Soviet policies because, in his view, they destroyed the Ukrainian language and culture. He was arrested in 1972 and released only after he repudiated his critique. In the late 1980s, he emerged as an important spokesperson for Ukrainian interests then became a major cultural official in the postindependence period.

Franko, Ivan (1856–1916). An important Ukrainian writer, literary critic, journalist, and social and political activist. He was a leader of the socialist movement in western Ukraine and helped found the Ukrainian Radical Party in 1890. Later, however, he wrote critically of Marxism, and in 1904 he co-founded the National Democratic Party. His literary and political work are considered important for the development of Ukrainian nationalism.

Gorbachev, Mikhail (1931–). The last leader of the Soviet Union (1985–1991). His policies of *glasnost, perestroika,* and democratization unwittingly helped spawn nationalist dissent throughout the Soviet Union and the eventual collapse of both communism and the Soviet state. The accident at the Chernobyl nuclear power plant in Ukraine in 1986 is said by many to have bolstered his calls for reforming the Soviet system, particularly media freedoms.

Hrushevsky, Mykhaylo (1866–1934) An important Ukrainian writer, historian, and political figure. His *History of Ukraine-Rus* (1898) argued for a distinct history of Ukraine, separate from that of Russia. Although chair of Ukrainian history at Lviv University, he spent most of his time in Russian-ruled Ukraine. In 1917, he returned from Russia to Kiev, where he joined the Ukrainian Party of Socialist Revolutionaries and was elected chairman of the Central Rada (Council). In 1918, he was elected president of the short-lived Ukrainian People's Republic. When the Soviets took control of Ukraine, Hrushevsky immigrated to Western Europe. In 1924, because of his sympathy for socialist ideas, the Soviets allowed him to return to Kiev as a member of the Ukrainian Academy of Sciences. In 1931, he was forced to live in Moscow because Soviet authorities took a dim view of his promotion of Ukrainian nationalism. His writings were not promoted when Ukraine was under Soviet rule, but in post-Soviet Ukraine his advocacy of a separate Ukrainian history has become the new orthodoxy.

Khmelnytsky, Bohdan (c. 1595–1657). Hetman (leader) of the Zaporozhian Cossacks in southern Ukraine from 1648 to 1657. He led an uprising in 1648 against Polish-Lithuanian rule and established the Ukrainian Hetman (Cossack) state (1648–1782). He was forced to turn to the Russian tsar during his war with the Poles, however, and the Treaty of Pereiaslav in 1654 between the Russians and Ukrainian Cossacks made most of Ukraine a protectorate of Russia.

Kravchuk, Leonid (1934–). Ukraine's first president after the country gained independence from the Soviet Union. Under Soviet rule, he had been a high-ranking official in the Communist Party, becoming head of the Ukrainian *Verkhovna Rada* in 1990. In 1991, after the Communist coup failed in Moscow, he openly advocated Ukrainian independence and was elected president of Ukraine on December 1, 1991. Although he helped secure Ukrainian independence, his rule was associated with corruption and economic decline, and he lost his bid for reelection to Leonid Kuchma in 1994. Afterwards, Kravchuk served in the *Verkhovna Rada* and was a leading figure in the Ukrainian Social Democratic Party (United), a party associated with big business interests.

Kuchma, Leonid (1938–). Ukraine's second president from 1994 to 2005. Before Ukrainian independence, Kuchma was the director of the Yushmash missile and rocket factory in Dnipropetrovsk. In 1992, he became prime minister of Ukraine, and in 1994 was elected president. Early in his presidency, he acquired a reputation as a pro-Western economic reformer, but by the end of the 1990s, his administration was plagued with allegations of corruption, which culminated in the "tapegate" scandals that connected Kuchma to the murder of an opposition journalist. Barred from running for a third term in 2004, he tried to ensure the election of his prime minister, Viktor Yanukovych, but, after widespread protests, this failed. Kuchma has yet to be prosecuted for any crime or corruption while in office.

Mazepa, Ivan (1639–1709). Hetman (leader) of the Ukrainian Cossack state (Hetmanate) from 1687 to 1709. He sought to unite all Ukrainian territories into a single state. Making an alliance with Poland and Sweden, he fought Russian rule but was defeated at the Battle of Poltava in 1709. Today he is celebrated as a patriot and hero by many Ukrainians.

Mohyla, Petro (1597–1647). Head (Metropolitan) of the Orthodox Church in Polish-ruled Ukraine from 1632 to 1647. He was considered a reformer, bringing in European ideas, updating the liturgy, and emphasizing religious education. He is considered by many to be a defender of Ruthenian/Ukrainian culture. He founded the Mohyla Academy in 1632, which was re-organized in 1991 and is now one of Ukraine's leading universities.

Moroz, Oleksandr (1944–). A major political figure in post-Soviet Ukraine. As leader of the Socialist Party, he ran for president in 1994, 1999, and 2004, coming in third each time. He opposed the rule of President Leonid Kuchma and, in 2000, made public the audiotapes that implicated Kuchma in several political scandals. He stood with Viktor Yushchenko during the 2004 "Orange Revolution," but in 2006 made a deal with Yushchenko's opponents in order to become speaker of the Ukrainian parliament.

Petliura, Symon (1879–1926). A journalist and writer who became a leader in Ukraine's unsuccessful effort to gain independence after the 1917 Bolshevik Revolution in Russia. He organized Ukrainian military forces against the Bolsheviks in 1917, participated in the 1918 coup that overthrew the pro-German Hetmanate government and, in February 1919, became leader of the Directorate, an independent Ukrainian government. The Directorate was ultimately defeated by the Bolsheviks, and Petliura fled to Poland and later went into exile in Paris. In 1926, he was assassinated by a Ukrainian-born Jew for his alleged sanctioning of massacres against Jews.

Shcherbytsky, Volodymyr (1918–1990). A leader of the Communist Party of Ukraine from 1972 to 1989 and a close ally to Soviet leader Leonid Brezhnev (1964–1982). His rule of Ukraine was characterized by the expanded policies of Russification and fierce suppression of dissent. He opposed many of the more liberal reforms of Soviet leader Mikhail Gorbachev and is held responsible for helping to conceal the impact of the Chernobyl nuclear power plant explosion. He was removed from power in 1989.

Shelest, Petro (1908–1996). Leader of the Communist Party of the Ukrainian Soviet Socialist Republic from 1963 to 1973. During his tenure, there was a brief flowering of Ukrainian culture. He was forced into retirement by the Soviet leadership, which allegedly saw him as too independent and sympathetic to Ukrainian nationalism.

Shevchenko, Taras (1814–1861). A Ukrainian artist and poet whose works are often considered to provide the basis for the modern Ukrainian language. Born a serf, his first collection of poems appeared in 1840. He was arrested and exiled between 1847 and 1857 for his critique of tsarist and imperial rule. His writings are credited with fostering the Ukrainian national consciousness, and in post-Soviet Ukraine he is widely celebrated as a heroic figure.

Skoropadsky, Pavlo (1873–1945). Ruler (Hetman) of an independent Ukrainian state from April-November 1918. A former tsarist general, he was supported by Germany, but was overthrown by a popular uprising after German forces retreated from Ukraine at the end of World War I. He fled to

Germany, where he died in 1945 as a result of an injury sustained during Allied bombing.

Stalin, Joseph (1879–1953). The leader of the Soviet Union from 1929 to 1953. His rule is most associated with industrialization, collectivization, Soviet victory over Nazi Germany, and political repression and terror. His decisions helped produce the "Great Famine" in Ukraine in 1932–1933, in which millions of people perished. One of the targets of political repression under his rule were Ukrainian nationalists, many of whom were killed, imprisoned, or sent to labor camps, both before and after World War II.

Tymoshenko, Yulia (1960–). A Ukrainian politician and one of the leaders of the 2004 Orange Revolution. In the 1990s, she was the president of a Ukrainian energy company and served as deputy prime minister for energy from 1999 to 2001. She was accused of corruption, briefly jailed by the government, and in 2002 became a leading figure in the "Ukraine without Kuchma" opposition movement. In 2005, she served as prime minister and returned to that post in December 2007. She is the head of the political party Yulia Tymoshenko Bloc, generally considered pro-Western and in favor of democratic reforms.

Volodymyr I (Vladimir I in Russian) (c. 958–1015). Known as Volodymyr the Great, he was Grand Prince of Kievan Rus. He converted to Christianity and baptized all of his subjects as Christians in 988. He also expanded the borders of Kievan Rus, uniting various Slavic tribes and making an alliance with the Byzantine Empire, thereby making Rus the most powerful state in Eastern Europe.

Yanukovych, Viktor (1950–). A Ukrainian politician from Donetsk in eastern Ukraine. He twice (2002–2004 and 2006–2007) served as prime minister. In 2004, despite efforts on his behalf to rig the election, he lost the presidential elections to Viktor Yushchenko, who prevailed in the "Orange Revolution." As head of Ukraine's largest party, the Party of Regions, Yanukovych, remained an important figure after 2004, serving briefly as prime minister and after 2007 as leader of the opposition. He generally favors closer ties with Russia.

Yaroslav I (c.978–1054). Known as Yaroslav the Wise, he was a son of Volodymyr the Great and one of Kievan Rus's greatest rulers. He united the major principalities of Novgorod and Kiev, and under his reign (1019–1054) Kievan Rus reached the pinnacle of its cultural and military power. Among his achievements are the construction of hundreds of churches, including Saint Sophia Cathedral in Kiev, establishment of schools and monasteries, promulgation of a basic legal code (*Ruska pravda*), and building of the Golden Gate of Kiev.

Yushchenko, Viktor (1959–). Elected president of Ukraine in 2004 as a result of the Orange Revolution. Previously, he served as head of the Ukrainian National Bank (1993–1999) and as prime minister (1999–2001). Considered a political and economic reformer, he was dismissed as prime minister by President Kuchma in 2001 and founded an opposition political party, Our Ukraine. He was elected president despite being poisoned by unknown actors and vote-rigging by the government. The popular protests of the Orange Revolution forced a revote in December 2004, which he won.

Bibliographical Essay

Ukraine has, in some respects, been rediscovered since gaining independence in 1991, as a host of works have been written on the country's history, politics, economics, and social and cultural makeup. Many of these are written by academics and are intended primarily for a scholarly audience, but several are accessible to a more general reader interested in Ukraine. Not surprisingly, given the fact that Ukraine for much of its history was ruled by foreign powers, many earlier accounts of "Ukrainian" history can be found in volumes on Russian, Lithuanian, and Polish history. Specialized works specific to Ukraine tended to be published in North America by institutes, such as those at Harvard University and the University of Alberta, which are dedicated to Ukrainian studies.

There are several good general reference works on Ukraine. Two very comprehensive histories are Orest Subtelny, *Ukraine: A History*, 3rd edition (Toronto: University of Toronto Press, 2000), and Paul Robert Magosci, *A History of Ukraine* (Toronto: University of Toronto Press, 1996). Magosci's *Ukraine: An Illustrated History* (Seattle: University of Washington Press, 2007) is far shorter and is both extremely pleasing visually and very informative about political and cultural aspects of Ukraine's history. Andrew Wilson's *The Ukrainians: Unexpected Nation* (New Haven, CT: Yale University Press, 2000) is more analytical in approach and takes a more skeptical view of what he views as myths surrounding the Ukrainian nation. A more journalistic treatment, yet still informative and highly readable, can be found in Anna Reid, *Borderland: A Journey through the History of Ukraine* (Boulder, CO: Westview Press, 1997). A condensed rendering of the work of the great Ukrainian historian Mikhaylo Hrushevsky can be found in Michael Hrushevsky, *A History of Ukraine*, ed. by O. J. Frederiksen (New Haven, CT: Archon Books, 1970). The Canadian Institute of Ukrainian Studies is also compiling the *Internet Encyclopedia of Ukraine*. While it is still a work-in-progress, parts of it can be accessed at http://www.encyclopediaofukraine.com.

For the history of Kievan Rus, the *Russian Primary Chronicle* is an indispensable, if flawed, source. An accessible edition is that of Samuel Cross and Olgerd Sherbowitz-Wetzor, eds. and trans., *The Russian Primary Chronicle: Laurentian Text* (Cambridge: The Mediaeval Academy of America, 1953). Simon Franklin and Jonathan Shepard's *The Emergence of Rus, 750–1200* (New York: Longman, 1996) is extremely detailed. James Billington's *The Icon and the Axe* (New York: Knopf, 1996) is a classic treatment of this period, and Janet Martin's *Medieval Russia, 980–1584* (Cambridge: Cambridge University Press, 1995) is a good reference, although both of these works implicitly accept that Russia is the successor state to Kievan Rus. For more on the controversies surrounding the legacy of Rus, see Jaroslaw Pelenski, *The Contest for the Legacy of Kievan Rus* (Boulder, CO: East European Monographs, 1998).

There are fewer works on Polish and Lithuanian rule in Ukraine. The best book-length source on Lithuania that covers its rule over Ukrainian lands remains Albertas Gerutis, ed., *Lithuania: 700 Years* (New York: Manyland Books, 1969). Recommended works of Polish history, which discuss events on Ukrainian lands, are Jerzy Lukowski and Hubert Zawadzki, *A Concise History of Poland* (Cambridge: Cambridge University Press, 2001), and Norman Davies, *God's Playground: A History of Poland*, 2 vols. (New York: Columbia University Press, 1982). On the Cossacks, see Linda Gordon, *Cossack Rebellions: Social Turmoil in the Sixteenth-century Ukraine* (Albany: SUNY Press, 1983) and Serhii Plokhy, *The Cossacks and Religion in Early Modern Ukraine* (Oxford: Oxford University Press, 2001).

Many books are dedicated to Ukraine's complicated relationship with Russia. Peter Potichnyj et al., eds., *Ukraine and Russia in their Historical Encounter* (Edmonton: Canadian Institute of Ukrainian Studies, 1992) is a series of essays that covers Russian-Ukrainian relations from Kievan Rus to Soviet times. Dominic Lieven, *Empires and Russia* (London: John Murray, 2000) and Goffrey Hosking, *Russia: People and Empire, 1552–1917* (London: HarperCollins, 1997) both cover developments in Ukraine as part of a larger work on the multinational Russian Empire. A work that is more focused on Ukraine within the Russian Empire is Alexei Miller, *The Ukrainian Question: Russian Nationalism in the 19th Century* (Budapest: Central European University Press, 2003). The most complete work on the rebellion of Ivan Mazepa is Orest Subtelny, *The Mazepists: Ukrainian Separatism in the Early Eighteenth Century* (Boulder: East European Monographs, 1981). For more on Taras Shevchenko, the leading Ukrainian literary figure, see Pavlo Zaitsev, *Taras Shevchenko: A Life*, trans. and ed. by George Luckyj (Toronto: University of Toronto Press, 1988).

Most works that cover Ukraine's experience under the Habsburgs are dedicated to the development of Ukrainian nationalism. Examples include Paul R. Magocsi, *The Roots of Ukrainian Nationalism: Galicia As Ukraine's Piedmont*, (Toronto: University of Toronto Press, 2002), Andrei Markovits and Frank Sysyn, eds. *Nationbuilding and the Politics of Nationalism: Essays on Austria Galicia* (Cambridge: Harvard Ukrainian Research Center, 1984) and John Paul Himka, *Religion and Nationality in Western Ukraine: The Greek Catholic Church and the Ruthenian National Movement in Galicia* (Montreal: McGill University Press, 1999).

There are comparatively more publications on Ukraine under Soviet rule, with many works devoted to Ukraine during the Russian Revolutions and civil war, the famine under Stalin, and the region's experience during World War II. The definitive text on the revolutionary period of 1917–1920 is John Reshetar, *The Ukrainian Revolution, 1917–1920: A Study in Nationalism* (Princeton: Princeton University Press, 1952). John Armstrong's *Ukrainian Nationalism* (New York: Columbia University Press, 1955) examines the rise of Ukrainian nationalist movements in interwar Poland and their subsequent role during World War II. The classic work on the Ukrainian famine is Robert Conquest, *The Harvest of Sorrow* (Oxford: Oxford University Press, 1986). Bohdan Krawchenko's *Social Change and National Consciousness in Twentieth-Century Ukraine* (London: MacMillan, 1985) covers the entire Soviet period and offers insights and the development and emergence of a Ukrainian national identity. Roman Szporluk's *Russia, Ukraine, and the Breakup of the Soviet Union* (Stanford, CA: Hoover Institution Press, 2000) is a collection of essays that covers Ukraine both during and after the communist period.

Two books describe events leading to Ukrainian independence exceptionally well. The first is Taras Kuzio and Andrew Wilson, *Ukraine: Perestroika to Independence* (New York: St. Martin's, 1994), written by two leading scholars on Ukrainian politics. Bohdan Nahaylo, who worked with Radio Free Europe/ Radio Liberty, provides a highly detailed account in *The Ukrainian Resurgence* (London: Hurst, 1999).

There are numerous books on post-Soviet Ukraine. One of the first to appear was Alexander Motyl, *Dilemmas of Independence: Ukraine after Totalitarianism* (New York: Council on Foreign Relations Press, 1993), which presents a good overview of the issues facing Ukraine in its first years of independence. Taras Kuzio ranks among the leading experts on post-Soviet Ukraine. His many publications include *Ukraine Under Kuchma* (New York: St. Martin's,

1997), *Ukraine: State and Nation Building* (London: Routledge, 1998), and (edited with Robert Kravchuk and Paul D'Anieri) *State and Institution Building in Ukraine* (New York: St. Martin's 1999). Andrew Wilson's *Ukrainian Nationalism in the 1990s: A Minority Faith* (Cambridge: Cambridge University Press, 1997) takes a somewhat skeptical view of the power of Ukrainian nationalism. Paul D'Anieri's *Understanding Ukrainian Politics: Power, Politics, and Institutional Design* (Armonk, NY: M. E. Sharpe, 2006) engages the political science literature to explain Ukrainian politics and is the closest thing to a textbook on contemporary Ukraine. For foreign policy issues, see Sherman Garnett, *Keystone in the Arch: Ukraine in the Emerging Security Environment of Central and Eastern Europe* (Washington: Carnegie Endowment, 1997). Works on Ukraine's Orange Revolution include Andrew Wilson, *Ukraine's Orange Revolution* (New Haven, CT: Yale University Press, 2005), Anders Aslund and Michael McFaul eds., *Revolution in Orange. The Origins of Ukraine's Democratic Breakthrough* (Washington, DC: Carnegie Endowment, 2006), and Taras Kuzio, *Democratic Revolution in Ukraine: From Kuchmagate to the Orange Revolution* (London: Routledge, 2008).

Index

About the Author

PAUL KUBICEK is Professor of Political Science at Oakland University.

Other Titles in the Greenwood Histories of the Modern Nations
Frank W. Thackeray and John E. Findling, Series Editors